Gone Wild

Gone Wild

STORIES FROM A LIFETIME OF WILDLIFE TRAVEL

MALCOLM SMITH

Whittles Publishing

Published by
Whittles Publishing Ltd.,
Dunbeath,
Caithness, KW6 6EG,
Scotland, UK
www.whittlespublishing.com

ISBN 978-184995-177-7

Printed by: Production Managed By Jellyfish Solutions Ltd.

Contents

Dedication

For my best mate who was with me on several of these excursions and who has put up with much inconvenience with hardly a grumble.

Introduction

I dislike travel. Considering the 30 stories in this book, that probably seems a very strange statement. Let me explain. The bit I do like is that more exciting aspect of the often tiring drudge of getting somewhere: arriving. And I particularly like arriving in the dark. There is something especially exciting about opening the curtains on a window that first morning – or gazing out from the door flap of a tent – and looking in awe at the vista that unfolds before your eyes. Providing there's a vista to be admired.

My most memorable experience of 'morning after arrival awe' was in Saudi Arabia. We had reached the Uruq Bani Ma'arid campsite on the western edge of the fabled Empty Quarter of the Saudi desert late in the evening. It was pitch black all around; it was a cloudy evening so even the usual, myriad points of starlight in the sky weren't illuminating the sands. There was no moon so it was impossible to visualise my surroundings. In the early morning when I stepped outside in the dazzling sunshine, I gasped in astonishment. The camp was virtually surrounded by huge orange-pink sand dunes, each one folded into the next and all of them wind-smoothed into voluptuous curves. It was one of the most stunning first morning sights I have ever witnessed.

I admit it's rather different if all you can see is high rise buildings. Surprisingly perhaps, even then there can be wildlife nearby. I recall waking up in a somewhat downmarket Mumbai hotel, the windows so dirty – on the outside – that I couldn't see the House Crows squawking incessantly in the street below. In Cape Town, my view of Table Mountain from the hotel window was almost completely obscured by office blocks; even so, Speckled Pigeons – their red eye patches like large blood stains – still visited the window ledges nearby.

My travelling experiences are far from worldwide; the places I have been to, the people I've met and the wildlife I've gone to see have often been dictated by commissions to write a feature for magazines, newspapers or for a book. But these have also been the trips producing the most interesting and unusual – sometimes even dangerous – experiences. Many of the people I've met, often experts on a particular species – the Arabian Oryx, the Mediterranean's Monk Seal or the Florida Manatee for instance – have been as central to these stories as experiencing the animal itself. Without those experts and other contacts I've met over the years, there would be far, far fewer stories for me to tell. People such as: Wade Harrell of the US Fish and Wildlife Service with whom I spent a morning watching a family of Whooping Cranes feeding in marshes on the Texas coast and discussing his hopes for this very rare bird's future; my good friend Gabriel Sierra on the Spanish plains getting a close-up view of several male Great Bustards' fantastic courtship display as they contorted themselves into shimmering white bundles, one of the most extravagant bits of pre-mating wooing to be found in nature; Thorvaldur Björnsson and his friends collecting eiderdown from the nests of the Eider duck on islands off the coast of Iceland; Miro Uljan, a local hunter and forester, with whom I hunkered down for a long evening in a hide in a Slovenian spruce forest to watch Brown Bears; or Wayne Hartley from the Florida-based Save the Manatee Club with whom I canoed along a spring-fed, warm water river while over a hundred of these gentle lumbering giants lolled on the riverbed below us.

Without such people, I could not have written many of the stories in this collection at all: a Kenyan Dorobo tribesman, Robert Lentaaya, who uses an incredible working partnership with small wild birds called honeyguides to lead him through forest and scrub to a wild bee nest so they can share the honeycomb the bird implores him to harvest; the Parsis in Mumbai, helping explain to me the rituals of their ancient faith and who invited me to a funeral where the bodies of their dead are laid for birds to consume on the so-called 'towers of silence'; Stein Erik in Norway whose buoyant optimism at the start of an evening's Elk search turned to dismay after four hours of finding nothing but a glimpse of a rapidly disappearing Elk bum; or Phil Newman, then with the Countryside Council for Wales, who led me swimming into coal-black sea caves among the cliffs of the impressive Pembrokeshire coast as he tried to complete an autumn count of the numbers of Grey Seal pups reared there.

All of them, and others, have been unfailingly helpful in giving me local information and explaining what they were attempting to achieve. François Arcangeli, then mayor of the little French Pyrenean commune of Arbas, dedicated to the reintroduction of Brown Bears in spite of enduring and numerous death threats, and having blood thrown at him for his troubles. Many others went the extra mile to give as much help as they possibly could: Dimitris Skianis, our 'Mr Fixit' – and sometime translator – on the Greek Island of Alonissos who arranged meetings with a variety of people who had rather strongly opposed views on the need to try and conserve rare Monk Seals in the Aegean waters.

Over the years, searching out some of the places and animals I needed to find to justify my trip hasn't always been straightforward. Just occasionally, my excuse being over-enthusiasm, it has got me into what might be described as some tight corners. Nevertheless, it has made the years of wildlife travel much more fun, at least in hindsight. The most disconcerting moment was being confronted in Oman by armed policemen kitted out in military fatigues, one of them the spit of Saddam Hussein in his forties; I was convinced I was going to be arrested. Another anxious few minutes involved getting behind a (really quite small) tree as a tonne of previously sedated Black Rhino, blundering to his feet having been given an antidote, had escape on his mind. And bluffing my way past one set of bureaucratic officials after another and signing forms I had no hope of understanding before being accompanied by a guard on to Southeast Asia's largest open refuse tip. Waking up in my tent in the black African night to the sound of small trees crashing near our campsite as a family of elephant came uncomfortably close. Being convinced of an impending crash into jagged rock outcrops as my gung-ho 4WD driver took a shortcut, hurtling us down a dangerously steep sand slope in the Saudi desert, so steep we were hanging forward in our seat belts. Or feeling a little vulnerable having been left (albeit temporarily) by my guide in Rajasthan, Satto Singh, amongst some thorny acacia scrub with python burrows and tracks in the sandy ground all around, not knowing whether one of these huge constrictors was likely to peep out near my feet.

There have been several odd and amusing encounters too: the Tuareg tribesman in the middle of the Sahara, traditionally clad bar his rather ill-fitting and incongruous spectacles; the young Bedouin girl in Jordan, whose age I couldn't fathom, who broke off from singing as she herded her goats in the mountains above the archaeological wonders of Petra to sit next to me in amazement because I was watching some birds with my binoculars; or the young Moroccan lad who came running barefoot a kilometre or more through prickly scrub desert to accompany me watching yet another bird, then pick up a stone and hurl it with such accuracy it all but hit the subject I had been hoping to identify.

Some of these stories are about unusual locations and events, adventures in out-of-the-way places, and also the tribulations of trying to get even a brief glimpse of the very animal I had travelled to find: a chance meeting while completely lost in a canoe on a myriad of little waterways in Holland's Biesbosch National Park resulted in one of the closest views I've ever had of a European Beaver; or the couple of hours spent crouched in swirling damp clouds and cold drizzle on a knife-edge ridge in the rugged Madeiran mountains in complete darkness to hear just two ghostly – and rather faint – wailing calls from one of the rarest birds in the world as it flew in to its nesting burrow somewhere below us.

Several stories are about some of the most impressive landscapes and places I have ever seen: the dehesa of Spain's far west – Extremadura – those extensive, oak-dotted pasturelands that can stretch as far as the eye can see and which nurture a cornucopia of wildlife from night-prowling Genets and Wild Cats to avuncular Black Storks and sail-pasts of huge Griffon and Black Vultures riding the sun-warmed thermals above; the alpine pastures of Schynige Platte, sitting amongst some regal, snow-white St Bruno's Lilies, listening to marmots whistling, and looking out to the ice and snow-carpeted Monch, Jungfrau and Eiger alpine peaks; or the Niger River through western Mali, spotting the occasional hippo basking in its warm waters, and watching a Bozo fisherman hand-throwing his net from a pirogue while Golden Bishops were rising and falling like giant bumblebees above the riverside marsh grass.

So here are some stories from a fair chunk of a lifetime of wildlife travel. I hope you enjoy them.

Arresting Moments

It seemed best not to make any sudden moves. And not to make a hurried attempt to try and hide my binoculars either. As the Omani police Jeep approached and I could see clearly its two occupants kitted out in their military-style fatigues, some pretty negative thoughts raced through my mind.

I didn't have my passport. Or any other identification. What if they didn't believe I had binoculars to look for birds? Did it sound a likely story anyway? What more sinister use could I have binoculars for? And, yet more pessimistically, what were conditions like in Omani prisons? Possibly not exactly luxurious, I thought. What's more, my wife in our hotel a little way along the coastal frontage of Muscat, Oman's capital, didn't know where I was. I had mentioned going to look for some birds but not where. And her previous concerns about my habit of getting up too close and personal with military installations, and insisting on going into places where entry was forbidden, suddenly seemed rather prophetic. My anxiety levels were rising.

I suppose most people assume that wildlife watching, watching birds in particular perhaps, is a pretty leisurely business. Hours spent whiling away the time in a hide overlooking a shallow lake liberally endowed with various herons, egrets and other wading birds. Or going for fair weather walks in forests, stopping frequently to listen to some twittering high up in the canopy (and swearing when you can't even see their origin). And any serious wildlife watcher these days carries so much magnification equipment in the form of telescopes and binoculars, it's no longer necessary to employ SAS-like skills of blending in with your surroundings in order to get close to your subject.

Unfortunately, it's not always quite so leisurely. And finding locations where you are likely to spot certain animals can involve venturing into some tricky spots. So it is that military bases and training areas can be something of an occupational attraction if you are interested in wildlife. Why? Because land used for military training, or sealed off for some other purpose, is at least not ploughed up every year and used intensively for growing farm crops or rearing livestock. In the developed parts of the world most land is in some kind of agricultural use. Farmed crops are the last place you would want to look to see much wildlife. A field of peas, for instance, is good for Wood Pigeons (though less so for the farmer) but little else. A field of wheat liberally dosed with pesticides is good for nothing but wheat or barley. So, even though military training areas might in places be pockmarked by the end result of explosions or disturbed by soldiers running about firing guns, they're going to have more wildlife than modern intensive agriculture ever nurtures. If you want to look for wildlife, you most certainly wouldn't start in a field full of barley.

One incident where I got a little too close for comfort to armed soldiers was on the Aegean island of Lesbos where, at the time, the Greeks were using gunboats to patrol ostentatiously up and down the sea between it and the nearby Turkish coast a few kilometres to the east. Greek/Turkish relations were going through one of their more tense phases. In fact, things were distinctly tense. In 1987, the Turkish survey ship, *Sismik* was about to enter Greek waters and conduct a survey for oil reserves. The Greek Government gave orders to sink it if it did so. The Turks drew back but the incident nearly started a war between the two countries.

Come the following summer and our family holiday on Lesbos, I was occasionally on the lookout for birds. The Greek military, though, were on the lookout for Turks. Our two interests met where there was some very nice looking scrubby habitat. Nice for birds anyway. But it happened to be at what turned out to be a Greek military base.

Undeterred and ignoring the 'no entry' signs (I think they were only in Greek) and the helicopter landing pad we passed, I drove along a military road until stopped by a soldier with something like an AK47. He was coming towards our hire car. And the AK47 was aimed our way. Having spotted my binoculars – a dubious piece of equipment to hold at a military base in times of tension – as I scanned through the open car window for birds, the gun barrel was getting closer by the second and the soldier was now shouting, really quite loudly. In my limited experience, guns and shouting soldiers are never a good mix.

Recalling the last AK47 I had pointed at me – in the Saudi desert by an Arab companion who pretended to fire it assuming it wasn't loaded (it was though, happily, the safety switch was engaged) – a retreat seemed the best approach. '*Signomi, signomi!*' we shouted in poor Greek at the gun barrel and its soldier through the open window, hoping he understood that we were attempting to say 'sorry'. I turned the car around and drove away … slowly. Why slowly? Because I assumed racing off would arouse his further suspicions that we were up to no good. And I feared a burst of AK47 fire from behind.

Getting into an argument doesn't usually help in these circumstances, as I learnt some years later in southern Spain. I had parked my hired car outside the high fence of a military base; there was a large expanse of flower-rich pasture on the other side of the road but nowhere else to pull in. Almost immediately, armed soldiers arrived on the scene. Not AK47s this time but more traditional rifles. I was told to move; parking there was 'not possible'. I tried to persuade them that this was a good place to see birds. And that it 'was possible' to park there because I had already done so. Surprisingly, they weren't too interested in such semantics. So I showed them pictures in my bird identification book, especially pictures of Great Bustards, the world's heaviest flying birds to try and impress them. I said they might be in these very pastures on the roadside opposite their base. Not impressed in the slightest. Then I made precisely the wrong move. I stayed put and scanned the said open areas with binoculars. Looking for Great Bustards. An officer appeared and, in broken English, made it extremely clear that I would be arrested if I didn't drive away ... immediately. Bustards or no bustards, it wasn't the time to argue.

Arguing doesn't help either when confronted by police who are very obviously likely to fine you ... or worse. Even if they weren't intending to dream up some rather harsh penalty, they certainly will be if you start to argue with them. So I have learnt to do the opposite – I ingratiate myself. Usually it gets me away with a mere rebuke. In southern Morocco it wasn't quite so straightforward.

It was on a beautifully sunny, late autumn afternoon that I was driving back to a small town just south of Agadir where I was staying. I had spent the day on the south side of the Atlas Mountains. I knew it would be getting dark soon so I was hurrying along. If you have ever driven in Morocco you might understand why. Driving there in urban areas in daylight – when no one follows any traffic rules and you have to dodge donkey carts and mopeds travelling the wrong way – is bad enough. Doing the same in darkness with poor street lighting is more anxiety-provoking still.

So it was that I entered a speed-restricted stretch of road at maybe 10 km/h over the limit. Flagged down by uniformed traffic police with radar guns, I pulled in at the side. Mohammed was a young Moroccan policeman with excellent English. Complimenting him on his language skill, we got into a conversation about the university he had attended (the University of Fez apparently) and police college. It was all very amicable. 'But,' said Mohammed eventually with a look of feigned regret, 'I am sorry but I have to fine you for driving too fast.' 'Do you really? How much?' I asked. '300 Dirham [£20],' said Mohammed. So I counted out three 100 Dirham notes and passed them to him. 'Thank you,' said Mohammed very politely. Oddly, the notes didn't go into his pocket. 'Now I will return to you 200 Dirham,' he said in distinctly measured tones as he passed me two of the notes back, one at a time, 'So please, you have good meal tonight, a tagine maybe. And please no speeding.' With that I was on my way ... a little slower. And Mohammed had pocketed 100 Dirham. It was a better deal than 300.

All these events – military firmness, guns pointed in my direction and fines – passed rather rapidly through my mind as the Omani police Jeep drew closer.

I should not have been where I was. A couple of days earlier, I'd spotted a boarded-off area of land near the sea. It said 'no entry' but I'd peeped through a crack in the boards and there were trees and bushes in there. Trees and bushes usually mean birds. And trees and bushes are not abundant commodities in an arid country such as Oman. In there, I thought, I might find attractive little sunbirds with the fine, down-curved beaks they use to probe inside flowers to extract their nectar.

So, one day out for a walk on my own, I managed to move one of the large boards a little and squeezed inside the no-go zone. It turned out to be the site of former buildings and a garden being readied for redevelopment. There were scattered trees and bushes and I'd started to take a careful look at them. But no birds.

When the Jeep first appeared about 100 m away, I thought – rather over-optimistically – that if I just carried on looking up into the trees with binoculars, they might drive past and ignore me. No chance.

Instead, they continued to drive in my direction and stopped 20 m away. The policeman in the passenger seat got out first and walked towards me, arms akimbo, one hand on his (thankfully) holstered revolver. Tall and well built, dressed in camouflage fatigues, beret at a jaunty angle and sporting a large black moustache, he looked just like Saddam Hussein in his forties. Now I don't know about you, but an armed Saddam lookalike in military fatigues walking purposefully towards you when it's obvious you're somewhere you're not supposed to be – and carrying a pair of binoculars into the bargain – isn't likely to give you a feeling of calmness and serenity. It didn't.

A few seconds later, the police driver got out. A younger man (no moustache), he came my way too and, I thought, a tad more purposefully. Perhaps he needed to chalk up some arrests I thought. What should I do? Take the initiative and speak first or wait until I was spoken to, presumably, I assumed, rather harshly? I did the former and blurted out one of the few Arabic phrases I know.

'As-salamu alaikum,' I stuttered (the traditional Arab greeting meaning 'peace be with you'); it shows I can still be an optimist even at such times. Just. Immediately, the Saddam lookalike's grave and ominous appearance vanished. A smile broke out across his face. 'Wa alaikum as salaam,' he replied ('And upon you be peace'). We shook hands. He introduced me to his driver. We shook hands too. He beamed as well. We all beamed big smiles. Smiles. Handshakes. I could have kissed them I was so relieved. Quickly I thought that a kiss probably wouldn't be the best idea I'd had for a while. The policeman who once looked like Saddam (even his moustache seemed less threatening and more friendly now) offered me a cigarette. I refused politely – which I instantly thought to be a bad move – but they both lit up and it didn't seem to matter a jot that I didn't smoke. We laughed, though at what or why I'm not sure. For my part it was pure relief.

Then they broke into English. 'How do you like Oman? Are you staying long? Muscat is a fine city, yes? Where do you come from?' and maybe other touristy questions too. I lauded praises on everything I could think of. Everything and everywhere was wonderful I said (actually it was very good!). And it was most certainly very much better now!

I showed them my binoculars and pointed up in the trees, mumbled about birds (I still hadn't seen any) and they looked interested. In truth they either didn't understand what I was talking about or they were simply being polite. No mention was made of what I was doing in this fenced-off site or how I'd got in there in the first place. I was probably marked down as that well known foreign oddity – a Brit.

Oman has a history of good relations with the UK and here it was in spade-loads. I wish I'd remembered that when I first spotted the police Jeep. And then they were off. Friendly goodbyes. Another handshake all round. And yet more smiles. They waved from the Jeep as they turned and drove away. I stood there for a while breathing some very big sighs of relief. And looked again for a few birds.

I didn't find any.

A Tip Too Far

Animals aren't capable of considering aesthetics. For all wild creatures, obtaining sufficient food trumps any other consideration. In what sort of location the food might be found is of zero consequence. Getting it is all that is important.

So refuse tips are very often attractive places for birds. Indeed, what could be better; a mix of human throwaway detritus that includes waste food and a plethora of insects that feed off it into the bargain. Not only do those birds that delight in eating dead meat – the carrion-eaters such as kites, eagles or crows – get a feed, but also so do some much smaller representatives of the avian world that make a meal of insects. Pretty little wagtails for instance. A scruffy refuse tip can be bird nirvana.

In Mali, I once watched flocks of huge Marabou Storks – as tall as a small person – gorging on some of the distinctly putrid contents of refuse dumps. The bird guidebooks show these storks as rather svelte; tall, grey-backed birds with red heads although they do possess a less than svelte, fleshy-red throat pouch that hangs down in front of their chests. In reality they look pretty ugly, dirty with dust and a few feathers missing courtesy of fights between birds to get the best refuse pickings. And that pouch looks rather like a lop-sided and grossly distended pair of testicles swinging from side to side as they move. I can't say that Marabous are the most attractive birds I've ever seen.

British refuse tips, a once familiar feature of our countryside and suburbs, are now rapidly, and thankfully, disappearing as we recycle more and more of our refuse or use it in other ways. But they were once a haven for gulls and other birds too. You could spot such a refuse tip from several kilometres away. There was always a characteristic white cloud of gulls in the air above it. And those gulls were clearly finding it easier to grab some rotting, tipped-out food than search under the seashore shingle for a few tough cockles and mussels that have to be tugged out of their shells before they can be consumed.

The problem for bird fanatics is that, except in much of Africa and the Middle East, most refuse tips are not open to the public or were long ago closed down. Those still in use are often fenced off to keep people out and prying eyes at a distance. Not the safest of places to explore courtesy of disease-carrying rats or rabies-carrying feral dogs. Who would want to visit them? Who indeed?

And so it was that I found myself in Mumbai, the business and entertainment capital of India. I was there to research a feature for *The Telegraph Magazine* about the enormous and rapid decline of vultures in India (and its neighbouring countries) and how that was impacting on the Parsis who traditionally encouraged vultures to eat their dead. With its 14 million or so inhabitants and a reputed 5 million street dwellers who have no more than the clothes they stand up in – and sometimes pitifully few of those – this teeming city is in the top ten of the most populous in the world. If it's the street-food kiosks along Chowpatty Beach, the brassware at Chor Bazaar, or the history of the famous Taj hotel you're interested in, Mumbai has tour guides happy to help you negotiate this sardine can of a city. Even tours of Dharavi, one of the city's larger slums – the one made famous by Danny Boyle's 2008 film, *Slumdog Millionaire* – are increasingly popular. But there is one place in Mumbai that no tour company or guide will take you, one that is sealed off from prying foreign eyes – that is the putrid Deonar refuse tip, the city's main refuse dumping ground.

Mumbai's Deonar tip covers over 140 ha of land and is piled with stinking, decomposing garbage as high as a seven storey building. Each and every day it receives 5,500 tonnes of refuse, 600 tonnes of silt from the city's drains and 25 tonnes of medical waste. Between March and June the daily amount of silt dumped there rises to more than 9,000 tonnes because of drain cleaning in advance of the annual monsoon. Come the monsoon, horrendous pollution runs off it into streams that appear out of its rotting bowels. That water pours down the Thane Creek and out into the Arabian Sea, polluting its inshore waters. The largest open refuse tip in Asia, it has been in operation since 1927 when the British started dumping here on land that was then on the city's outskirts. But Mumbai has grown. Today, urban slums crowd up against the southern and western edges of this monstrous pile. Health problems blight the shanty communities around it.

I'd been talking to experts at the Bombay Natural History Society (BHNS), the RSPB's equivalent in India, and I had mentioned the Deonar tip. I knew that it once had thousands of vultures circling over it and pouncing down on to its scraps of food. But they had all died out. Or so the BHNS people believed. I thought I should check it out, and at least find out what birds had taken over from the once omnipresent vultures. The society gave me a driver and a vehicle for the morning to get there. They were not very optimistic about my chances of getting on to the tip itself but at least, they suggested, I could see where it was and have a squint at whatever birds might be in the air above it.

We – my young Hindu driver and I – set off through Mumbai's honking traffic. Everyone honks their car horn incessantly here. And that is irrespective of whether there is anything in the way. My driver did the same even when, on rare occasions, a short stretch of road was empty. Needing something to honk at is clearly unnecessary.

On the rather flimsy pretext of studying the birds feeding on the tip (it was hardly a study), I managed to blag and bluff my way past three sets of bureaucrats in track-side shanty offices, each of them trying to prevent me from getting any further. It all made my driver distinctly uncomfortable. He wriggled incessantly. He looked nervous and harassed. He frequently suggested turning back (using rudimentary sign language because we couldn't otherwise communicate). And he looked generally much paler than when we had set out.

Bureaucracy is an advanced art form in India. It could win the Turner Prize hands down. Supposedly an inheritance from the days of the Raj when English civil servants showed the locals the skills of endless form-filling, the bureaucrats of India have raised it to another level of time-consuming complexity and expertise.

Speeding it up usually requires a little money to oil the snail-like flow of any action that might eventually result. I had forgotten about this when our vehicle was flagged down at each of the three sets of scruffy track-side shanties. At each I jumped out and signed papers put in front of me oblivious as to their content. Presumably I was absolving the authorities of any responsibility for my safety and wellbeing. I argued incessantly as the tip officials tried to tell me that further progress towards the gross smelling object of my desire was definitely not possible. But persistence paid off. Or it does at the Deonar tip anyway. Trying to seem as official as I possibly could, I insisted that it was of vital importance for me to see the birds living there and that I had come all the way from the UK to do so.

Maybe the unfailingly polite but very discouraging tip bureaucrats asked me for some cash to oil the bureaucratic structures but I have no idea if they did. I couldn't understand a word of Marathi or Hindi (or any other of the plethora of languages in the country) and they spoke no English. So our communication was almost zero and no bribe changed hands. Perhaps my journey would have been easier if it had.

Eventually I had evidently cleared every hurdle except the last. It was essential, I gathered, that I was accompanied on to the tip by a uniformed guard complete with his menacing *lathi*, the long wooden stick so beloved of the Indian police for 'crowd control'. His function? As far as I could gather he was there to protect me if rabid dogs came our way or some of the refuse pickers inhabiting the tip gave up picking refuse and robbed us instead. It seemed a sensible precaution in the circumstances.

My driver's increasingly worried looks, his pallor and his wriggling didn't improve with the uniformed guard sitting between us. He obviously thought I was completely nuts.

So here we were, driving on to the biggest refuse tip in Asia, a tower block of society's discards, the sickly, putrid smell cloying and stomach-churning in the sun-heated air. The wood and corrugated iron-roofed slum dwellings suddenly seemed a long way below. I jumped out of the vehicle, followed quickly by the guard who looked somewhat poleaxed. He clearly wasn't expecting me to walk about up there. Needless to say, my driver stayed put. He looked even more nervous and pale than before. Walking about with guard in tow, our driver kept edging the vehicle up to us wherever we went. It wasn't exactly relaxing but who can relax in a place like this?

Processions of refuse lorries drove past us on to the tip plateau to deposit the waste in a thick cloud of dust. And every time one disgorged its fly-ridden contents, stick-thin families of garbage pickers descended immediately on the stinking mass, combing it for anything of value: bits of plastic, metal, paper, even perhaps some discarded food worth eating. Down the side of the tip away from the slums, women were busily washing clothes in the disease-ridden waters ambling alongside this monstrous muck-pile. Scruffy, emaciated dogs kept their distance. Whether any – or all – of them carried rabies I had no idea. I was just thankful that they didn't come close.

Birds there were a-plenty. Hundreds of Black Kites hung in the hot, dust-laden air above, diving on to the refuse when they spotted something organic – anything organic – to eat. There were no vultures amongst them. Flocks of pretty grey and yellow-tinted wagtails, incongruous in this foul, smelly landscape, flitted from pile to pile, picking off insects which were in copious supply. Back in Britain Yellow Wagtails are birds of wet meadows, farmyards and streams. Not here. For an insect-eating wagtail, Deonar was heaven on earth. But my most surreal experience of the morning was to spot, amid all this squalor, rabid dogs, refuse pickers and stench, a phalanx of hundreds of egrets standing bolt still on top of one part of the tip. All incongruously clean and pure white in this dirty environment, they looked like rows of choirboys spruced-up in line for an important church service on a saint's day. In a strange way, it made perfect, if perverted, sense. Here was a cathedral to squalor, an environmental eyesore the governing authorities of this huge, sprawling city seem incapable of addressing. And maybe the neat, well-turned out choirboys were a surreal vision of a cleaner future. If there is one. The trouble is, that dream never seems to become reality. Plans to close the squalid Deonar tip and replace it with a modern refuse disposal, energy production and recycling facility have been under discussion for decades. And they keep failing.

After an hour or so of tip walking, my driver was looking so agitated I thought he might faint. My guard started to tap his *lathi* rhythmically against his leg in a not-very-subtle display of impatience. It was time to leave. I can't say I was sorry.

Later that day I talked to a few people who lived in a nearby area of tin shacks, poor people with a hovel not a home, but who still managed to send their kids to school, and in uniform. 'If I'm lucky I can earn maybe 10,000 rupees [£100] a month, enough to support my family, that's me, my wife and five children,' said Arnav Mehta, a shanty dweller who regularly picks over the Deonar tip. 'Yes, we do go ill, sometimes it is fevers or diarrhoea and sometimes a rash on the skin, but that's the way it is here.'

So closing Deonar has huge implications. Shutting off the supply of refuse available to the pickers will have dire consequences for the thousands of families that depend on it. They would no longer be able to obtain thrown-away paper, rags, metal and plastics and sell them on for recycling if they don't have a tip to scavenge on.

Mumbai's refuse pickers and slum dwellers don't trust the city authorities. What jobs will they ever have if they can't pick refuse? What would become of their little repair shops and the hovels that somehow convert bits of discarded metal into something useful if they are moved away compulsorily and find themselves living ten storeys up in a high-rise block? And what are the chances of Mumbai's slum dwellers all getting improved homes and better living standards in a city riven with corruption? Will they be moved on instead to some other slum?

Finding a place for the city's refuse-reliant birds to get a feed is the least of the problems. There are plenty of other refuse tips in a myriad of other towns and cities across this vast subcontinent. They can simply fly off to another.

Dawn in the Dehesa

It is early morning in spring and the cool, rather languid air is flavoured with the heady aroma of Rosemary and Marjoram. The rising sun, as yet a golden-red globe on the horizon, will soon start to suffuse its warmth. Mist rises between the olive-coloured oaks as the dew of the cold night slowly evaporates and the trees begin to cast long shadows like rows of medieval soldiers preparing for battle.

I'm in Spain, not far from the ancient conquistador town of Trujillo, and I'm standing at the side of a narrow track surrounded on all sides by a scatter of these stately oaks.

I could be almost anywhere in Extremadura the far west of Spain and the country's least populated region, because I'm in the midst of the Spanish dehesa – called *montados* in neighbouring Portugal – and it stretches as far as I can see in every direction, clothing virtually all of the land.

Of all the incredibly beautiful places in the world, to me this part of Spain is one of the most attractive and evocative. A patchwork of dappled sun and shade, the dehesa is a landscape of scattered Holm and Cork Oaks growing on flower-specked grassland grazed by sheep or cattle. In more open spots where the oaks are few, there's a little cereal cultivation too.

But this dehesa landscape is far from being natural. And I think that is part of the reason I find it so attractive. Man-made, it remains even today a living landscape worked by farmers. The antithesis of a modern-day, intensive farming operation, dehesa farming is a gentle and eminently sustainable exploitation of the land that has changed hardly at all for centuries. As a result, it has become one of the richest wildlife habitats in Europe.

As I stand here on the trackside, and the last puffs of dampening mist evaporate off the dew-wetted grasses and flowers, a chorus of birds is tuning up for a day of song. Greenfinches with their mellow cadenzas and little yellow Serins with their jingling tunes like tiny splinters of falling glass compete for attention with the roller-coaster pitches of Woodlarks. But I can't see any one of them; they are all hidden from view in the olive-leaved trees.

A flash of blue and cinnamon, coupled with some harsh shrieks, gives away a posse of Azure-winged Magpies as they zoom in follow-my-leader flight from the low branches of one oak to the next, never staying visible for too long. Another chorus begins. Gathering metronome-like pace, cicadas – large, brown-winged insects – begin their incessant chatter in one tree and then in another as the warming shafts of the sun illuminate the oaks in succession in its morning's heat-giving voyage across this bewitching landscape. Once the cicadas get going, they will not stop until the cool of the spring evening returns and they slow to a halt, one at a time, finding it not warm enough to give them the energy to keep the tiny membranes on the sides of their abdomen clicking rhythmically. All day long in summer, theirs is the background beat to everything else that makes any sound out here, like an old steam train puffing in the distance from dawn to dusk or an elderly grandfather clock ticking steadfastly in a cottage.

As I walk between the sentinel oaks absorbing these sounds, ground beetles in lustrous greens, coffee and anthracite make their first forays of the day, and shrew-sized, brown-furred spiders go scuttle-about from their trap burrows. Some vivid blue Grape Hyacinths and rose-pink Gladioli are in early flower, contrasting with the brown and yellow, bluebell-shaped Dipcadi to give the green tablemat of turf under the trees a pointillist speckle of colours. Elsewhere on the warming ground, a scatter of dead oak branches is pockmarked with the burrowing of a myriad of wood-dwelling insects. This place is alive with creatures great and small.

As the temperature rises, a couple of huge, pale chocolate-coloured Griffon Vultures drift in the heating air above, their enormous wings held out like a pair of ragged curtains to catch every puff of updraft. They are setting off on yet another day's high-level patrol across the blue skies, their all-spotting eyes fixed on the dehesa below to spy any animal that might have breathed its last during the night.

But some of the wonders of the dehesa are much more difficult to spot than the very obvious vultures. Wildcats and the more widespread Common Genet, a small, spotted, long-tailed, cat-like mammal sacred to the Ancient Egyptians, patrol between these trees at night on the lookout for small mammals and birds to pounce on. A few packs of forest-breeding wolves, today undergoing a steady increase here after years of persecution, and an occasional Eagle Owl do the same.

For a wildlife enthusiast, it is difficult to convey the riches of the dehesa without talking in superlatives. For amongst the threatened bird species here that depend on this habitat are the ultra-rare Spanish Imperial Eagle, about 300 pairs of which survive; the massive Black Vulture, Europe's largest bird of prey; and the magnificent Black Stork, all of which use the dehesa for hunting, but breed on distant cliffs or in more dense forested country. The little paper-swallow-like Black-shouldered Kite, a gorgeous, pale grey and black bird of prey more characteristic of the African savannah, does the opposite. It nests in dehesa trees but hunts mainly on the open plains, searching for small rodents, lizards and large insects to hover over in silence, then drop on to kill.

A few weeks before, at the end of February or early March, the distant throaty honking of a flock of elegant Common Cranes wheeling somewhere high in the cool air would have been the signal that they were shouting goodbye to their winter home. This year I am too late to see them. Fuelled by energy-rich dehesa acorns for their long haul flight back to their Scandinavian and Russian breeding grounds, they would have been starting out on their first leg northeast up to northern Spain. All winter, umpteen small groups of Europe's 60,000 cranes – 4-feet-tall birds with tails reminiscent of an Edwardian lady's bustle – would have strutted through these dehesas. Even though I've seen them many times, I can't help but find these supremely elegant birds a thrilling sight. Now they are gone for another year.

It is so easy, on a spring morning such as this, to get carried away with the entrancing beauty of the dehesa. And just as easy to forget that it is, without doubt, an arid and a harsh landscape too. Bread-oven hot in midsummer, ice-cold in winter, this man-made habitat covers over 30,000 km^2 of rolling land in western Spain and eastern Portugal. That's an area of land larger than Belgium and Luxembourg put together.

But how was it created? One theory is that in the turbulent 16th century when the conquistadors – Francisco Pizarro, Hernán Cortés, Francisco de Orellana and others – were destroying the ancient Inca and Aztec civilisations of Southern America with Spanish swords, equally sharp steel was being used by a much larger army of peasants to cut down the primeval forests of Extremadura, Spain's westernmost region. But the Extremeños were seemingly more selective than their brother conquistadors in what they felled. Creating land for sheep grazing from the forest, they understood the importance of leaving some trees for summer shade and to harvest the products the oaks yielded.

There are alternative explanations; one is that the dehesa could have been created by setting forests alight – an easy task in the blistering summer heat when every scrap of vegetation here is tinder dry – and the burnt ground planted with Holm and Cork Oaks. The scattered Cork Oaks with their naturally thick, fire-protecting bark might have been the only trees to survive such a conflagration because Holm Oaks, the other major dehesa tree, don't possess thick, corky bark to protect them in a fire.

However it came into being, the dehesa remains a living landscape supporting one of the most sustainable farming systems I know of. The farms, known here as *fincas*, average perhaps 600 ha apiece but with some much larger; they support a little cereal growing in more open areas – usually oats or barley varieties suited to dry conditions – and use little or no fertiliser or pesticides. Elsewhere under the dehesa oaks, livestock grazing is the main land use.

Sheep are the usual graziers, goats only occasionally. Deer, necessitating high fences to keep them contained, less so. Cattle are common too; red-brown or black, fighting bulls are frequently raised in the dehesa to become the toro bravos of the corrida where a heady mix of death, bravery, costume drama and sensual performance all intermingle. It is a controversial spectacle, much criticised outside Spain. But it's still popular here, particularly in Extremadura and Southern Spain, and its continuation plays a role in supporting the dehesa economy.

Then there are the pigs. Delightful, small, dark pigs. Near-black Wild Boar descendants, they roam in small herds and feast on the copious quantities of acorns that fall in autumn, often competing with the cranes that do the same. The ham produced from these pigs – *jamón de bellota* – is flavoured with the taste of acorns and commands high prices, both in Spain and abroad. I'm not a meat eater but am told it's a delicacy. Any bar worth its olives in every village here in Extremadura will have *jamón de bellota* available. Invariably, the hams will be hanging from the ceiling on large hooks, a new one taken down for slicing whenever the previous one has given up every scrap of its delicately-fragranced meat. They are hard to miss.

Dehesa trees are never left to grow old naturally. They are regularly pruned, the cut branches left on the ground for livestock to graze their leaves. Larger branches are often sold to make charcoal. Pruning is done to encourage the trees to branch outwards rather than upwards, increasing their shade-bearing area, a necessity for livestock in the blistering sunshine of an Extremaduran summer.

But the most economically productive component of dehesa farming comes from the Cork Oak trees themselves. Their naturally thick, corky bark – built-in fire protection – gradually loosens from the trees and can be harvested about every decade without causing the tree any harm. It is a skilled job, carried out using a special curved axe – a *machado* – wielded with extraordinary precision when you see the task being done. Where Cork Oaks abound in the dehesa, the dark orange-red stems of recently harvested trees are a striking and characteristic sight. These trees can live for 200–300 years and be harvested for their cork many times over. Although much of the lower quality cork is used to make products such as wall tiles and sports equipment, the best quality goes to make wine bottle corks. Since Dom Pérignon first introduced cork to seal his now famous champagne bottles, the wine industry worldwide has always used them to bung a good proportion of the 20 billion or so bottles sold each year. And Spain and Portugal produce 80% of the world's cork.

If, like me, you're an avid wine drinker, you will be more than aware that many of the corks that once stoppered every bottle you purchased have been replaced. Some at the cheaper end of the market contain a plastic bung; many others – especially everyday drinking whites – simply have a plastic-lined screw cap. And the prevalence of these screw caps is why I'm bothered about the future survival of the dehesa. Today, cork stoppers only fill the necks of maybe 60% of wine bottles, mostly those at the more expensive end, more so for red wines and for any wines that need to mature in the bottle. Why has this happened? The answer is cork taint. Some wines, when you open them, have a musty smell, usually described as a 'corked' wine. The mustiness is apparently due to a chemical called TCA produced by moulds growing within the pores of the cork combined with traces of the bleach used to sanitise the bung. So much is generally agreed.

A lot more is not. Wine experts and wine industry insiders quote a wide array of figures about how commonplace – or not – cork taint actually is, from a low of less than one bottle in a hundred to as many as one in twelve. Much of the variation might be explained at least partly by whoever is doing the tasting, how well they recognise the taint and how bad that taint really is. A severely corked bottle is obvious; it has a foul, wet carpet odour. But very slight taint is often a product of a wine taster's nose; after all, discerning wine quality is an art not a science. Anyone who reads a wine column with its flamboyant references to a 'plum palate; hints of ripe and sour cherry' or a 'sexy bouquet' will know what I mean.

Even though the cork producers have been fighting back by sterilising their corks more thoroughly and by promoting alternative cork products, a major slump in the quality cork market wouldn't only jeopardise the jobs of around 40,000 cork harvesters and processors. Production of the plastic or aluminium (for the caps) alternatives consumes large amounts of chemicals and energy – replacing a natural and biodegradable product. If sustainability is ever to be translated into practical reality, cork would win every time.

So if significant price drops hit the cork industry, it could cause dehesa farmers to go out of business or to consider alternative crops. Luckily for the dehesa wildlife, there isn't much that you can grow here and make a profit from. The soils are notoriously thin and poor while the climate – cold winters and arid bakehouse-heat summers – make that extremely difficult.

But there is one crop that can prosper: eucalyptus trees (mostly Australian natives) grow well in the climate of the western Iberian Peninsula. But, because of their volatile oil content, they are an extreme fire hazard. And as a wildlife habitat, eucalyptus is a disaster; it supports virtually no animals – vertebrate or invertebrate – and few plants grow on the forest floor under the trees. Although it attracts much lower government subsidies than planting the native dehesa trees, the attraction is that eucalyptus can be harvested within a decade. Quality cork cannot be harvested until an oak is nearly half a century old.

Finding out what is happening to the dehesa as a result of the drop in the use of cork stoppers is fraught with problems. There appear to be no reliable statistics and measuring the extent of dehesa is problematic: it is hard to know when the trees become so widely spaced that the dehesa has transformed into open plain, or so much more densely spaced that they merge into what is more aptly described as forest.

National and regional laws in Spain and Portugal forbid the felling or digging out of dehesa/montados trees. Authorisation to do so is rarely given, except when the trees are dead or diseased. While rumours abound that trees are sometimes removed or felled under dubious circumstances to make way for more productive crops or for real estate, travel large parts of this vast area and there is not much evidence of dehesa tree felling. It would, though, be quite difficult to know whether treeless plains were, until recently, dehesa. Planting young trees to produce the dehesa sentinels of the future isn't commonplace either though.

More important, perhaps, is the protection that the two countries, as Member States of the European Union, are giving to large areas of dehesa under the EU's Habitats and Wild Birds Directives. That protection is not intended to cover all of the dehesa but a representative proportion of the best parts.

The protection of this fabulous wildlife habitat and its sustainable form of farming depends on its farmers being able to make a living out of it. So, get at it! Try to drink wine from bottles with real corks. Use only natural cork if you bottle your own wine. Buy cork products. And eat *jamón de bellota*; as much as you can afford! Surely that's not too difficult is it?

Thank Goodness for William the Conqueror

The barked command woke us both with a start.

'Don't move suddenly! Stay where you are!' We – my walking companion John Cubbin and I – were dozing contentedly, lying flat out on short-cropped grass amongst the crispy brown hues of bracken above the rather oddly named Rakes Brakes Bottom. The autumn sun was warm, we were sheltered from the breeze by some robust heather and we had downed a pint or so of beer with our pub lunch after a morning spent walking across a mix of heathland, grassy pasture and damp woodland. So we were having a very pleasant nap. Until then.

The command came as a shock. We struggled to wake, unsure as we blinked into the hazy brightness of the sky of what might be trained unerringly in our direction. Reality slowly dawned. Ten metres away, an imperious lady on horseback, all done up in classy riding gear, was warning us to keep still or risk frightening her tall, bronze-brown charge. We obeyed instructions. Neither of us fancied a horseshoe coming too close. Especially one fixed to a rather large horse's foot.

The New Forest, shoe-horned – if you will forgive the metaphor –between the conurbations of Southampton to the east and Bournemouth to the west, is a bounty of rolling heaths, cottongrass-resplendent mires, impressive woodland, grazed grasslands and crowfoot-tangled streams. Grazing with ponies and cattle by commoners, whose rights go back 1,000 years, keeps the heathland and grassy slopes from naturally reverting to forest. In highly populated southern England, it is a haven of beauty and tranquillity. Perhaps it's not surprising that it is one of my favourite places.

This particular day John and I had planned a route that would take us into its veritable bowels. Avoiding most paths and tracks, we wanted to be striding across its darkly purple heaths, pushing through the knee-high toughness of its bracken-carpeted slopes and ambling in the shade of its towering broadleaved woodlands. There were hunting birds to look out for, diminutive Hobbies – much like small versions of Peregrines – that perform aerial tumbles while hunting for insects. And Green Woodpeckers to spot – ground hunters searching grazed grassy areas for ants. But instead, and completely unpredictably, what entranced us were the New Forest's bogs. We looked in admiration at their palette of autumnal colours: their red, yellow and leafy-green Sphagnum mosses; their fluffy-white bunches of cottongrass swaying in the soft breeze; while their sticky, red ochre, insect-eating sundews became a passion.

Another interesting aspect of the New Forest is its place names. The origin of some is pretty obvious to anyone. But others are perhaps lost in the mists of time. We set off from Deadman Hill (near the town of Fordingbridge), originally perhaps the site of a gruesome murder or a former gallows on which to hang local sheep stealers or suchlike villains. Downslope at first, we tramped across Little Cockley Plain (what does 'Cockley' refer to?) with its rank heather and pale coffee sedges hiding the brown remains of the delicate Heath Spotted Orchids. Needle-thin, vibrant blue damselflies were flitting around the squishy flushes and rusty-bottomed streams as we walked by.

A little further on we had our first close encounter with one of the New Forest's ninety-something (according to Natural England's experts who seem to have counted them) valley mires: the bogs which fill up the lowest-lying parts of shallow, waterlogged valleys, are known here as 'bottoms'.

Recognising that discretion was the better part of valour, John Cubbin walked gingerly behind as I strode all too confidently across Ashley Bottom until the volume of peaty-black water around me made it essential to hop from one bleached-yellow tussock of Purple Moor Grass to the next. Our tussock-hopping built up a wave tempo across the mire as its thin carpet of floating vegetation behaved rather like a suspension bridge in a high wind. Just as John said something about breaking step, I missed a tussock and plunged a leg to thigh-depth in a viscous slurp of cold, peaty water. Not far away, three dainty Fallow Deer hinds were grazing on a bracken and birch tree slope that reached down in finger-folds to the wetter sedges and cottongrass below. They must have seen our antics, looked up momentarily…and carried on grazing as if in despair. It was a story I recounted in the Travel pages of *The Independent* though I think I omitted the bit about Fallow Deer.

Most people that visit the place – now a national park – don't stray further than a couple of hundred metres from a carpark, of which there are an incredible 150 throughout the Forest. Dog walkers go further, though most stick to the numerous footpaths. Only avid walkers get in to the quieter spots. And amazingly quiet they can be. Around Ashley Bottom (I just had to mention it again) there were no people in sight. The only sound was the breeze rustling in the short-cropped heather and the haunting, wailing call of a Redshank – an attractive wading bird with scarlet legs and beak – distracting us, perhaps, from chicks it had secreted nearby. It was hard to believe that we were less than 16 km from the edge of bustling Southampton, one of the largest conurbations in southern England with a quarter of a million residents. Sometimes I've spent a whole morning around here without seeing anyone at all, not even a dog walker.

From Ashley Bottom we headed a few kilometres east through the cool shade of the high beeches, pines and oaks of Amberwood Inclosure where the woodland understorey is liberally peppered with hollies, crabapples bearing their small acidic fruits, and rowans. The New Forest woods, the broadleaved parts and not the commercial conifer or mixed conifer/broadleaved plantations (which are known here as 'inclosures' because they are fenced to keep browsing deer out), are one of the best places in Britain for wood-boring insects and a plethora of fungi growing on the living trees or on deadwood littering the forest floor. Sensitive forest management here by the Forestry Commission leaves deadwood where it falls, thereby allowing natural decomposition, helped by the wood-boring insects and fungi. We turned over one or two decaying logs and there were plenty to be found on the damp wood which was rapidly becoming more like cardboard.

All this rot always reminds me of some not terrifically profound words attributed to Jimi Hendrix: 'Once you're dead, you're made for life,' he had said at some point in his short existence. And he was dead right, if you'll forgive the pun. Highly improbable though it is that he was referring to forest timber, his aphorism goes to the very heart of the cyclical process of life, death, decomposition and new life that characterises all plants and animals, rock heroes included.

Somewhere on our day's walk we had passed a small pond or two. But we didn't spend much time at them nor did we really appreciate their wildlife importance as we walked past. Reading about them more recently I discovered that many of the New Forest's ponds are seasonal, drying up in most summers, but that many are awash with wildlife. Frogs and toads abound. Some have Great Crested Newts, miniature dragon-like amphibians. Kingfishers visit them with an eye on snapping up a stickleback when there's enough water to go fishing in. And the numbers and colours of dragonflies and damselflies can defy the imagination. Twenty-seven different species breed in the ponds and mires of the New Forest, the largest concentration in Britain.

And so it was that we ended up (well-planned from our trusty OS map rather than the electronic voice-over of a mobile navigator) at the cottage-like Royal Oak Inn on the edge of Fritham village, one of the oldest pubs – maybe the oldest – in the New Forest. After all this walking we needed what we thought was a well-earned stop. As we got close, we had something of a short-term culture shock. It was as if we had returned from a long trek in the Australian Outback or somewhere else equally distant from human civilisation. Suddenly we were amongst the throng, thrown into the bustling, tourist picture-book New Forest. Here were people taking their dogs for an afternoon stroll. There were families throwing frisbees and picnickers sitting near roadsides feeding the ponies below signs telling them not to feed the ponies. And all semblance of the silence we had experienced for a few hours became a distant memory.

We ordered a so-called 'ploughman's lunch' and (too much) beer at the Royal Oak, something very few 'ploughmen' probably consume these days but a symbol of some long-gone bucolic countryside idyll that probably never existed. Still, it's something those of us Brits, who have tilled nothing more than the occasional garden border with a trowel, like to eat in a pub to give us a sense of continuity with our Medieval farm serf ancestors. Checking up on the origin of these things – as I am all too frequently tempted to do – I find that *Pierce the Ploughman's Crede* (*c.*1394) first mentions the traditional ploughman's meal of bread, cheese and beer. The *Oxford English Dictionary*, though, notes the first recorded use of the phrase 'ploughman's lunch' as 1837. Perhaps the OED was simply a bit slow catching on; there was plenty of ploughing before that. Who knows.

Refreshed – and slightly wobbly – we wandered from Fritham village between the veteran trees of Queen North Wood and turned east, soporific now, to overlook Rakes Brakes Bottom replete with its woody, dwarf bushes of aromatic Sweet Gale, scimitar-shaped leaves of yellow-flowered Bog Asphodel, and a plethora of insect-eating sundews with their sticky, gobby-wet leaves. Jet-black dragonflies zoomed like dogfighting Spitfires around the whippy willows and white-barked birches at the side of the mire where the ground was still waterlogged but not awash. There the dragonflies were more sheltered from the cooling autumn breeze.

Nearby, on a dry slope overlooking said Rakes Brakes Bottom, is where being soporific got the better of us both and we had settled down for a snooze on the ground. The gentle wafts of sleep would have lasted much longer if the imperious horsewoman had not turned up and made her presence felt. The moral of that story is that if you have had too much beer at lunchtime and you need to sleep off its effects, choose a bit of grass distant from a bridleway.

After our sudden awakening we decided to stroll on. We set off across Rakes Brakes Bottom and, as if to prove that we were actually walking on water – albeit water with a covering of vegetation – John pierced the vegetation mat with his stick and promptly nearly lost it as it plunged down over its hilt. We moved on, stepping very cautiously. We skirted Ragged Boys Hill, another enigmatic New Forest name whose origins we hoped were still understood by someone somewhere. Maybe it has some link to the so-called ragged schools, charitable organisations dedicated to the free education of destitute children in 19th century Britain, though there were no obvious remains of a building out here. Then it was a shortcut through Broomy Inclosure, and up a final, energy-sapping, grassy slope to High Corner Inn at Linwood and the end of one of the most varied 13 km it must be possible to tramp anywhere in southern England.

For the very existence of the New Forest we have William the Conqueror to thank. Not that he gets thanks for much else. But, without the protection he decreed in the 11th century, a few small wooded areas might be all that remained today.

A scene I kept thinking about on one of my walks through the New Forest was the one in the 1979 film, *Monty Python's Life of Brian*, in which Reg harangues a group of masked activists and asks them what the Romans had ever given 'us', expecting no suggestions. Instead, he gets increasingly irritated as a list of benefits – from roads and sanitation to education and public order – get shouted out by the activists at the meeting and completely undermine his argument. William the Conqueror's Norman legacy is seemingly very much more mixed than that of the Romans, and controversial too. Some historians view him as one of the creators of England's greatness; others as inflicting one of the worst defeats in English history and of obliterating Anglo-Saxon culture. He most certainly brought about huge changes in the Church, aristocracy, culture and language of Britain. But he did protect the New Forest, in his time just a part of the extensive woodland that still covered much of lowland Britain.

Sometime around 1079 he made it a royal forest, though conserving its wildlife was not top of his personal agenda. He wanted it for hunting, mainly deer, but maybe some Wild Boar too. The deer are still here; the boar long gone. But protecting the Forest for the King had its downside. A horrendous amount of what we might euphemistically refer to nowadays as 'collateral damage' resulted from his decree. More than 20 small hamlets and isolated farms were demolished. What happened to their inhabitants isn't recorded.

King William got his comeuppance though. Two of his sons died in the Forest: Prince Richard sometime between 1069 and 1075 as a result of a hunting accident (some years before his father's death in 1087) and King William Rufus, William II – named, apparently after his ruddy-faced appearance – was killed by an arrow, more likely murder than accident, in 1100. One of Rufus' claims to notoriety was that he introduced mutilation for anyone flouting the Forest Laws. Local folklore asserted that his death was punishment for the crimes committed by his father when he created it as his 'new forest'.

According to Florence of Worcester, not as you might imagine a female but actually a well-educated male monk who died in 1118, the forest was known before the Conquest as *Ytene*, its early Anglo Saxon name. It was first recorded as 'Nova Foresta' in the Domesday Book in 1086 where a section devoted to it also mentions the town of Southampton, today the largest conurbation near its edge. It is the only forest that the book describes in detail.

About 90% of the New Forest is still owned by the Crown and, since 2005, the bulk of it is a national park. The Forest – in reality a mix of heaths, bogs, what are locally called 'lawns' (grazed grasslands), broadleaved woodland and plantations of conifers – probably has more protective designations than any other place in Britain.

But what makes the New Forest equally special for me is its cultural inheritance and the long history of its traditions of land use dating back to the Conqueror's times. Without those traditions the Forest wouldn't be what it is: albeit a managed landscape but much of it uncompromisingly wild, a place out of time in the modern world, a contrast with the hubbub of modern urban Britain on its doorstep but strangely distant from it.

The most important element of that is the long established right of common grazing, a right which is attached to certain properties in the forest. Anyone holding such rights can graze 'ponies, cattle, donkeys and mules' on the open areas of grassland and heath. About 5,000 animals graze the forest, more ponies than cattle. Without controlled levels of grazing, the heaths and grasslands would slowly develop into scrub – gorse, bracken, bramble and small trees – eventually changing these habitats back into forest. It is the long established mix of habitats, rather than any one of them singly, that make it such a special place for wildlife and which conveys its enormous scenic attraction.

There is also a right of 'common of mast', the right to turn out pigs in autumn to devour acorns and beechmast that falls from the woodland trees. Pigs devour both and also provide a useful service because acorns are poisonous to cattle and ponies. In the past, large numbers of pigs were put out in autumn but today that has declined to maybe a few hundred. Some property owners have other common right too; estovers refers to the collection of defined amounts of firewood while rights to dig lime-rich clay as a soil fertilizer and to dig turves of peat for heating are apparently not used these days.

All of this commoning is overseen by the New Forest Verderers, originally part of the ancient judicial and administrative hierarchy of the vast areas of Royal Forests set aside by William the Conqueror. The title 'Verderer' comes from the Norman word *vert* meaning green and referring to woodland. The Verderers met regularly as a Court to adjudicate over disputes – they still do today – and their powers are widely drawn. The Official Verderer is appointed by the Queen; the others are a mix of appointed and locally elected Members. In effect, the Verderers are the guardians of the commoners, of their common rights and of the Forest landscape.

Much of the day-to-day management of the livestock grazing in the Forest is the responsibility of five Agisters who are employed by the Verderers, each one allocated a defined part of the Forest. Their role is ancient and their title derives from 'taking cattle to graze in exchange for payment'. Most are commoners themselves, they are expert horsemen and they have an intimate knowledge of the Forest. They ensure that the commoners keep their stock in good condition and they enforce byelaws made by the Verderers, they organise the annual autumn roundup and marking of the Forest ponies, and they get called out to road accidents involving livestock (which many people claim are too commonplace) or to incidents such as ponies getting stuck in a bog, which – if our experience is typical – could also be quite frequent.

Neil McCulloch, the landlord of the Royal Oak at Fritham, is one of the 400 or so New Forest commoners with grazing rights over its open land. He's fairly typical; most have a job in addition to their commoning. But putting out livestock to graze and checking their condition isn't the same as it was before tourists began to visit the New Forest. Today it can be a frustrating business. 'Calling it a national park is good for tourism. Most hotels, cafes and B&Bs say the same. It attracts more people,' said McCulloch when I interviewed him a few years ago for a feature I wrote about the Forest for *The Guardian*.

'We're a traditional freehouse catering mainly for walkers, cyclists and people from nearby campsites. Without a good trade, we couldn't survive as a pub,' he said to me. 'But I'm torn. As a commoner I don't want to see more traffic on the roads. I graze cattle and pigs out in the Forest. In summer you can't get around to move or check livestock because there's so much congestion on all the roads. It's already a big problem here, and it's getting worse,' he added.

The New Forest gets more visitors than any other national park in the UK: around 13 million day visits a year. Tourism is by far the biggest money spinner, providing a third of the local jobs and generating at least £70 million per annum. While many visitors don't stray far from its picturesque villages, picnic sites and roadside carparks, increasing numbers of horseriders, cyclists, ardent walkers and naturalists get off the beaten track to experience the magic of the place. Cars and cyclist numbers are increasing, clogging up many of the roads in summer when it's sometimes all but impossible to make any progress through a small town such as Lyndhurst in the centre of the Forest. And that brings with it more pressure for more carparks which few local people want.

The New Forest is without doubt a place of superlatives. Over half of Britain's 2,500 species of moths and butterflies are found here. Its most ancient gnarled trees are home to more lichens growing on their bark than anywhere in the lowlands of Europe. And it is the only place in Britain where vibrant pink Wild Gladiolus grows alongside Bluebells under swathes of knee-high bracken.

In spite of growing numbers of tourists, much of the New Forest is a place of surprising peace and solitude. I've stood on the peat-stained hummocks of Yew Tree Heath in its northeast and watched a group of hessian-coloured Fallow Deer merge imperceptibly into the rust-tipped bracken. I've been in spots silent enough to hear the wailing of a distant curlew and the nearby hum of bees searching the violet-hued heather. And, more recently, I've wandered over its heathland at dusk to enjoy a long, dry purring, so-called 'song' – the least musical song you might ever hear – reverberating in the enveloping evening gloom. Nightjars.

The first Nightjar starts up his monotonous purring, from a distant tree perhaps. Then another starts churring from a different direction, a play on two pitches of sound and almost impossible, sometimes, to be sure from where it is being sung. But there's better still. In late spring on a warm evening the males display; it's a heartening sight in the early dusk: the bird claps his wings together, then flies with slow wing beats interspersed with long glides, holding his wings in a slightly raised posture. He shows off the white wing patch near the extremity of each wing, visible in the fading light. And all to impress the females. It most certainly impresses me.

Nightjars scything through the darkening sky, hawking for insects as they turn this way and that, calling quietly all the while, is a common sight at dusk in summer in William's New Forest. And it is one of the most magical experiences of the natural world.

That Warming Feeling

It's late evening on Hvallatur Island off the west coast of Iceland and I'm watching dainty Black Guillemots swim amongst the tangled olive-green seaweed in the shallows around its rocky shore. Haunting calls from wading birds drift this way and that on the wind while snipe zip overhead, climbing and diving in the still-lit sky, their tail feathers humming to advertise their island breeding spots below. It is mid-June and it will soon be midnight but it won't be getting any darker and in a couple of hours the light will be gaining once again. Hvallatur is around 50 km south of the Arctic Circle so it's not quite 24-hour daylight. Instead, the few small hours assume a dim, blue-grey half-light, enough to be able to see what's around but not clearly.

An icy breeze blows while the still snow-capped mountains visible on the Icelandic mainland add to my summer feel of chill. Ironic, then, that I've come here to take part in the annual collection of one of the most insulating natural materials known, a rural industry established for over 1,000 years. Eiderdown collecting. It was an experience I later recounted in the *CNN Traveller* and *The Telegraph* magazine.

To get here I had driven from Iceland's capital, Reykjavik, north to the pretty little port town of Stykkishólmur to get the late afternoon ferry which crosses to Brjanslaekur on the Snæfellsnes peninsula much further north. The ferry calls at Flatey Island en route, a little over halfway across the wide (and cold) expanses of Breidafjördur Bay. On Flatey I met my contact, Thorvaldur Björnsson, a taxidermist at Reykjavik's Museum of Natural History, a part-time eiderdown collector and – as I was later to notice – an inveterate user of snuff (I mention it only because I have met no other snuff users).

From Flatey it was more than half an hour northeast in a RIB to Hvallatur island. Thorvaldur and his wife, along with six other families, own Hvallatur island and its only habitation, which they use as their summer base. Hvallatur is the main island, but altogether they own 200–300 uninhabited tiny islands and islets out here in Breidafjördur Bay. At low tide it is possible to walk between some of them; others necessitate the RIB to get access by sea. I'm here to spend a few days with them to see first-hand how eiderdown is gathered.

Why go to Iceland to collect eiderdown? Because Iceland is home to a quarter of a million breeding pairs of Common Eider ducks – out of maybe two million pairs in the world – all inhabiting northern climes from Alaska and Greenland to northern Europe and northern Russia.

Male Common Eiders are stunners; black and white with green markings on the head, they are large sea ducks and a little larger than Mallards. Female eiders are much less colourful, basically mottled brown all over, although close-up the dark and light brown intricacies of their feathering gives them an attractively mottled appearance. Every summer, these females pluck a myriad of tiny, mud-coloured down feathers off their breasts to insulate their eggs in grassy nests on the ground hidden on islands like Hvallatur and on headlands on the Icelandic mainland. Collected by hand, eiderdown remains an important and traditional cottage industry for this island nation. The down is used to fill the warmest, lightest and most luxurious duvets money can buy. They certainly don't come cheap.

Every year, around three to four tonnes of incredibly lightweight, brown-coloured and highly insulating feather down is taken from eider nests without harming the birds or affecting the hatching of their eggs. Over 400 Icelanders, mainly landowners, are registered as eiderdown collectors, some with just a few nests to pluck the insulation from and others with more than 2,000 nests to get around. Even Iceland's President, Ólafur Ragnar Grímsson has a colony at his farm home on a headland on the west coast near Reykjavik.

It's an industry that has been active since Iceland was first settled in the ninth century. And it is a rare example of sustainable exploitation from which the collectors gain financially, the birds are protected and might even be increasing in number, and those highly affluent consumers who can afford the incredibly expensive but highly insulating duvets that are the end product of this cottage industry keep very much warmer at night.

Before the Russian Revolution in 1917, Imperial Russia was the main eiderdown supplier in the world. The Russian Orthodox Church owned some eider colonies near the White Sea and had monks gather and process the down to make comforters for the high clergy. In the 20th century, the USSR even used eiderdown inside astronauts' suits. Today, though, Iceland provides at least 70% of eiderdown worldwide.

Down is warmer than feather-filled duvets because the much smaller feathers trap more insulating air. Most down-filled duvets use down from domesticated birds, mostly geese and ducks killed for meat. Far cheaper because it is available in huge quantities, none of the common – but far, far cheaper – alternatives are as insulating as the real McCoy of course. But any feathers are much better than no feathers.

'It takes the down from about 65 nests to produce a kilo of finally cleaned and sterilised down,' Thorvaldur tells me. 'We've been collecting down since 1992, the year after we bought the islands. We're here for about three weeks in June to do the collecting and the previous owners probably did the same every summer, right back to the 1700s or before. We have five inflatable boats so we can split into small groups to get to the different islands,' he says. Our conversation is occasionally interrupted by Thorvaldur's need to tip out a little brown tobacco snuff on to the back of his hand and then sniff it up each nostril in turn. Then we pause for the impending sneeze caused by said snuff and a couple of wipes with a handkerchief before we can continue our conversation. Some might regard it as a bad habit. There certainly are far worse.

Small, fine down feathers form a layer underneath the visible outer feathers and insulate a bird's body. But on a female eider's chest, the down feathers become loose at breeding time, which enables them to pluck them off in their thousands and line their nests, shallow depressions in small grassy hollows.

Being PC has clearly not entered the thinking of a male eider. They are, instead, notorious for their lack of contribution to the whole nest building, egg incubation and chick rearing process. They simply chill out, relaxing in the shallow waters around the edges of the islands. Once they have copulated with their chosen female, that's it; job done for another year. No responsibilities and no further work. But what these work-shy drakes are good at is making a far-carrying, crooning call to their plainer looking females, just to keep in touch and, maybe, to reassure their nest-confined mate that all is well around and about. It's a haunting sound that carries on the breeze through the day and, now in midsummer when there is no darkness, through the night too.

The first day of my eiderdown collecting is sunny with only a gentle breeze, though I hesitate to claim that it's warm. Suffice it to say that it is about average for a June day on Iceland's coast. Three of us – Thorvaldur, 16-year-old Fannar Mar Andresson, the son of one of Thorvaldur's friends, and me – set off from Hvallatur at low tide. We paddle through the shallow seawater across barnacle-encrusted black rocks to nearby Trésey, a much smaller mound of an island, its slopes grassy and well grown enough to hide more eider nests than I would ever have guessed could be hidden there. Mottled brown and sitting tight on her four greenish eggs, the first female eider we encounter suddenly flies off with a clatter of her wings when we are no more than a couple of metres from her nest, a grassy scrape between some rocks lined with a large bunch of minute and incredibly soft brown feathers. It's my first look at eiderdown in the nest.

I pick some up; it's so incredibly soft and warm. And more than that, it is virtually weightless. A small handful of this precious commodity seems to weigh nothing. Squeeze it into a ball and it springs back immediately after I release my hand pressure.

That is why, Thorvaldur assures me, an eider duvet is so insulating and retains its shape.

'We remove the eggs carefully, take out all the down, then replace the eggs after filling the nest with dry hay. We cut and dry the hay ourselves on the island. Studies done here have shown that the hay insulates the eggs just as well and the eggs hatch normally,' says Thorvaldur as he deposits our first handful of dry, brown down inside the hessian bag he carries.

Each nest we find, the female eider comes zooming off at the last minute, glides down to the sea below to meet up with others, maybe her mate included, does a lot of dipping in the cool water – presumably to wash – then waddles back to the nest just a few minutes after we have left it. She even looks rather pleased to have the short break from the many hours of egg incubating. The eggs are left without incubation for only a few minutes and, set in a very shallow depression on the ground and often sheltered by some small boulders, they are unlikely to get cooled by the wind at all rapidly. Even in the chilly Icelandic air, the eggs barely have time to cool a little before she is incubating them again.

Eiders start nesting in late April or early May on Iceland and their four, five or even six eggs hatch after 28 days in June. Some of the eggs we moved on Trésey had tiny holes being chipped from the inside of their shells as a ready-to-emerge chick started its journey into the world. Within 24 hours of hatching, the tiny grey down-covered chicks follow mother down to the sea where she (again, not the drake) teaches them to feed in the shallows and to find mussels, crabs and other crustaceans. The nest is deserted. With more females bringing chicks on to the water, crèches develop with flotillas of chicks and adults, probably a precaution to protect their charges against attacks from hungry gulls on the lookout for a nutritious chick. They are safer out on the water than they would be on land.

In two hours of searching Trésey we take a bunch of down from each of 97 eider nests. In total that's just over a kilo of the precious duvet filler. Back on Hvallatur with our harvest, Thorvaldur takes me to a small, stone-built hut. Inside, a diesel generator circulates warm air through wire mesh shelves piled with masses of earthy brown eiderdown. After drying slowly in the warm air flow, a small shaking machine separates out any strands of grass from the down, which is then sterilised. The down is then sold for about €670 to dealers on the Icelandic mainland. After further cleaning and sterilising it is sold on to the duvet-makers. On the islets owned by Thorvaldur and his group, there are about 3,800 pairs of these attractive ducks yielding 50–60 kg of down worth up to €40,000 each season.

With an estimated quarter of a million pairs of eiders breeding in the whole of Iceland – one of the largest populations in the world – and maybe thousands of people collecting the valuable down, including many farmers on their own land, Iceland produces up to 4,000 kg a year. That's around € 2.7 million at 'wholesale' prices; by the time the dealers sell it to the duvet makers, it is worth far more.

I interviewed Fuglavernd, the Icelandic Society for the Protection of Birds, to see if they had any concerns about down collecting. 'Harvesting eider duck down is not harmful for the ducks at all,' Björk Thorleifsdóttir of the Society told me. 'It is very beneficial for them as the people take care of the colonies and try to create new ones and thus give the ducks all kinds of protection, especially against predators'.

And it is predators that are a huge concern to the down collectors, though I get the impression that it is more because their down collection might reduce rather than out of real concern for the ducks. On the islets we collected down from, Thorvaldur and Fannar were constantly on the lookout for signs that ravens or gulls had taken eggs from an eider nest. We found several nests they said had been destroyed by one or the other of their bête noires.

On the Icelandic mainland, escaped mink (once reared for their fur) now living wild are a major problem for many ground-nesting birds, not just eiders. The Icelandic Government supports mink trapping and shooting. Arctic foxes – common and natural predators on Iceland – take eggs and, sometimes, the adult birds; more controversially, landowners often shoot them too, especially if the eiderdown cash crop is threatened.

So eiderdown collecting is not quite as benign as its proponents claim; its impact on the eiders is either neutral or even beneficial but other native animals on Iceland such as ravens and Arctic Foxes (the only land mammal native here) get short shrift. Fuglavernd has its concerns about predator control when I ask them about it. 'Most of the control of predators benefits the huge numbers of breeding birds we have in Iceland – all of which nest on the ground and are vulnerable – but we need to make sure that rare predators, such as the White-tailed Eagle, remain fully protected and no one starts to kill them. In any case, the eagles sometimes take mink so they are working with the eider farmers,' Thorleifsdóttir told me.

Thankfully the islands out here off the west coast are free of mink. There are no foxes here either. And that's the way Thorvaldur Björnsson and his fellow down collectors want it to stay. 'Mink are under control in the northeast part of Iceland but not elsewhere,' Helga Jóhannesdóttir of the Icelandic Farmers Association tells me. 'Eider farmers can shoot foxes at any time if they threaten breeding birds or livestock. Some use electric fences to protect colonies on the mainland and others use sticks fixed in the ground to protect the nests from predatory birds [this apparently makes it harder for them to land at a nest]. Incredibly, other eiderdown collectors broadcast radio music 24/7 because the foxes don't like the noise but the eiders don't seem to mind.'

'A farmer tries to attract eiders to his area, makes comfortable places for nesting and protects the area 24 hours a day. The eiders are clever and even though they come to the same nesting area every year, they move to the next area if the farmer there offers them better protection,' Jóhannesdóttir claims. Whatever else, Iceland's eiders seem to be doing very well out of this deal.

Back in Reykjavik a few days later, I called at Dün & Fidur, a shop specialising in making and selling eiderdown duvets and pillows on the Icelandic capital's oldest shopping street, Laugavegur. I had arranged to meet its owner, Oli Ben, who has been running his business here since 1959. The eider duck down is the top of his extensive duvet range; eiderdown duvets and pillows are made to order only. I hesitate to ask about prices. 'A single size duvet filled with eiderdown costs € 2,690 and a double, € 4,036,' Oli tells me as I take a rather obvious sharp intake of breath. 'I know it is expensive, but they are the top quality of course. We mostly sell to Japanese, German or American tourists, but some Icelanders buy them too. They are incredibly lightweight and warm. They really are the best that money can buy,' he tells me.

I didn't need any convincing about how warm they are, but you have to be able to afford one. Especially when a top quality goose down duvet costs a fraction of these prices. I brought a few eiderdown feathers home with me from Trésey … but no duvet.

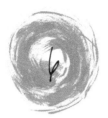

A Cruise With a Difference

From a distance they looked like giant bumblebees. And in this part of Africa, I thought perhaps they could be. But as our boat moved closer to the bank of the muddy River Niger, it became obvious that they were something very different.

Bishops. Golden yellow and black, they were a striking sight along the riverbanks. But these were not the colourfully-clad priests of an Eastern Orthodox Church. These were birds. To give them their full name, these were Yellow-crowned Bishops (also known as Golden Bishops) and there were lots of them. They are birds of much of Africa south of the Sahara. No one knows how many there are but, happily, they are a common sight.

Hardly a metre of the reed-palisaded riverbank passed by without a bishop showing off his finery. And the vibrantly coloured males were displaying to their rather dull coloured, brown females somewhere in the reedbeds where they will eventually build their little nests. I say 'little' because Golden Bishops are very small birds. At just 10 cm long, they are smaller than Europe's Blue Tit. But when the males are displaying they make themselves appear larger. With their golden yellow back and rump feathers fluffed right out, they launch themselves vertically with rapid wing-beats a metre or two into the air. They look like woolly spheres and make insect-like buzzing noises at the same time. Then they flutter back down into the reeds. No wonder it's not impossible, albeit from a distance, to think you might be looking at a giant bumblebee. Along the banks of the sluggish Niger they were both abundant and endlessly entertaining.

At 4,200 km, the Niger River is the third longest in Africa after the Nile and the Congo. Rising in Guinea not much more than 200 km from the West African coast, it flows northeast inland into Mali. East of Timbuktu on the southern edge of the Sahara, it bends to the southeast as if trying to move away from the desert it confronts, flowing across western Niger, into Nigeria and then south, finally entering the Atlantic Ocean through an extensive delta of marshes, reclaimed farmland and forest where controversy has raged for years about the environmental and social impact of oil extraction.

I was travelling by *pinasse* – a long, canoe-shaped boat with a woven roof, open sides and an outboard motor – from Mopti in central Mali to the once fabled Timbuktu. Powered by a small engine, it would take all 15 of us along the river. We were a group of members of the 153 Club (named after the old Michelin map of Northwest Africa) who had arranged an off-the-beaten-track trip in Mali with guides supplied by the travel company EXPLORE. And part of that trip was along the Niger. It was three (long) days of great adventure, camping out on the riverbanks for two nights en route and early, post-dawn starts to stand a chance of travelling 400 km, propelled by a small outboard motor, in that time.

Olive-brown water gave way to marsh grass, which stretched as far as we could see on either side of the *pinasse* though our boat's pilot kept us to the river channel and away from the muddy shallows. An occasional, elegant, white-headed African Sea Eagle gazed down imperiously from a riverside tree as we glided past. And globes of weaverbird nests dangled precariously from shrubs leaning over the water like lanterns to be lit come nightfall.

Now and again, hovering above the water ready to plunge in to grab a small fish was a black and white chequer-boarded Pied Kingfisher. Chestnut-coloured African Jacanas, long-legged wading birds, walked delicately over the plate-sized leaves and creamy white flowers of water lilies burgeoning in the shallows. And all the while there were nearby flypasts of dragonflies and a more distant plethora of egrets, herons and geese making their way from one area of wetland to another, disturbed perhaps by fishermen or rice farmers.

It all seemed a tad surreal. After all, Mali is one of the most arid countries in the world, at least the northern half of it sanded over by the Sahara. But the Niger River is its lifeblood. And here we were after the rainy season with the river bursting its banks and bringing much needed water to extensive areas of rice fields and marshes further downstream. Good for wildlife and local people. Apart from having an adventure holiday, I was writing a travel feature for *The Guardian*, a feature about the issues faced by people and wildlife along the Niger, for *CNN Traveller* magazine, and a briefing piece about WaterAid's work in Bamako to improve clean water supplies and hygiene standards to lower disease.

Our Malian adventure had started in Bamako, Mali's bustling, sometimes steamy capital, from where we travelled by road in a minibus to Segou. On the way we passed women pounding pestles into giant mortars on the roadside, adding water and mixing the resultant brown slurry by hand. This didn't look much like the skincare centre of Mali but the resulting unpleasant smelling 'butter' – made from the nuts of huge Shea trees – is very effective for treating skin problems. At about 1,000 Malian francs (£1.30) a litre, it is used in a huge range of western skin cosmetics that cost many times more.

Pressing on next day to Djenne after our overnight stop in Segou, we settled in for well over 300 km of tree-scattered savannah, frustratingly viewed only through a bus window. There was no time to stop and savour what we were seeing and spot what wildlife might have been about. Here, the African savannah long ago lost its lions and herds of wildebeest. The French colonialists did for most large animals in Mali and the locals long since finished them off. But I did spot intriguingly colourful birds among the trees. And if you're into 'I Spy' on journeys, 't' for termite mound – orange-brown pinnacles of what appear to be rock – and 'b' for baobab – that sumo wrestler of the tree world with its curiously obese trunk – are dead certs here.

Famed for its huge mosque – the largest banco structure (a mix of mud, cereal crop chaff and water) in the world, smoothed and svelte in its outer finish – Djenne, built on an island between the Niger and Bani rivers, is ruined by the open sewers that meander their way along the rough sandy streets. A gorgeous mosque but a smelly town, we were careful to hop over each runnel we came across. And there were many. A variety of flies and other sundry invertebrates appeared to be hatching from the putrid liquids while scrawny chickens wandered about, picking up bits of I'm-not-sure-what from the sewers. I was just hoping that local chicken wasn't our meal later that evening.

Djenne's mosque, a World Heritage Site, is impressive alright, softly contoured, Saharan-sand coloured and topped off with a few ostrich eggshells, the whole thing reminiscent of some early collaboration between Dali and Gaudi if that's not stretching belief too far. It has to be repaired by the townsfolk with fresh mud every time there's a sizeable downpour of rain.

Nearby, we visited our local guide's home village. Senossa, like every village in Mali, was awash with children smiling, excited, covered in dust and disarmingly eager to hold our hands, tag along … and persist for cadeaux. These were Fulani people, cattle herders that were formerly nomadic but who have settled here in villages. Vieux, our guide, introduced us to his uncle, the village head, and gave us unnecessarily graphic descriptions of the hammer and (hopefully clean and sharp) chisel-like blade used for circumcising boys aged seven. We were taken to see the village's honeymoon suite, a room with a larger than average mattress on the floor, a mosquito net and vibrant pink taffeta curtains, not quite Laura Ashley.

Moving on to Mopti the following morning, we piled into our *pinasse* moored on the riverbank; rucksacks and small suitcases at the back, us on wooden seats in rows at the front. Once we had left the town behind, there were few people to see apart from an occasional farmer tending a crop, usually rice, near the river. By early evening on that first day, the river, already wide, burgeoned for tens of kilometres with extensive marshes either side. We had reached the so-called Inner Niger Delta crossing Lake Débo, one of the few year-round areas of water in this biblical floodland which, when there's been a good rainy season, covers maybe 45,000 km^2 of marsh and farmland.

The delta has an average width of nearly 90 km, making it one of the largest seasonal wetlands in the world, a watery wonderland and a maze of seasonal waterways, lakes and marshes in which the precise track of the Niger is impossible to define. In the distant haze, an occasional agglomeration of farmers' huts sat in the water, small waves lapping into their open entrances. Shimmers of colourfully dressed women were doubled-up planting rows of rice in some faraway shallows. And a scatter of trees rose from the water, the remains of forests that once clothed much of this great wetland.

Little wonder that skeins of duck and egrets glided across the sky. For wintering duck from Northern Europe, this delta is paradise. Around half a million Garganey, perhaps a quarter of a million Pintail plus a host of terns and wading birds such as Ruff and Black-tailed Godwit winter here. Depending on the quantity of floodwater – the huge variations in which can make the difference between starvation and plenty for the million people that rely on the delta – the birds might be spread about or concentrated on much smaller areas of marsh. When we were there, the big flood had spread them out enormously, there was so much waterlogged land.

Many of Britain's breeding swifts and maybe some of our swallows pass over this floodplain en route to and from southern Africa too. After all, when it is flooded it must be a good place for migrants to pick up lots of aerial insects having almost starved themselves flying over the vast arid stretches of the Sahara just to the north. The Inner Delta is the first stretch of verdant ground many migrant birds will have seen for 2,000 km. For many, it's a life-saver.

There are African duck and wading birds here too of course; birds such as black-and-white African Wattled Lapwings, tiny Kittlitz's Plovers on shallow sandbanks, and flocks of aptly named White-faced Ducks. Gliding slowly along I managed to spot one bird I was particularly keen to see and assumed – wrongly as it turned out – that I would see more of. It was a Black Heron, half the size of our European Grey Heron and all black with yellow feet (though they were well out of sight in the brown water). It was motionless behind a scatter of reeds in the shallows. This is the heron with a clever habit of arching its wings into an umbrella shape over its head, seemingly shading the water from the bright sun, presumably so that it can see its prey better. Interestingly, no other heron has evolved this strategy. Unfortunately I didn't see the Black Heron's umbrella trick. Maybe it wasn't sunny enough. At least I had seen the bird.

Other birds that breed here include a range of herons and egrets plus African Spoonbills and Long-tailed Cormorants. Trouble is that these birds nest in forest treetops although they feed out in the marshes. Most of the forests that were once widespread have been felled for fuel, and only scattered trees remain. Which is why this place is not as idyllic as it appears and why so many of these breeding birds are declining.

Travelling on a *pinasse* is comfortable enough. The woven roof provides sun protection. But visiting the toilet at the very rear of the canoe is a dodgy affair. With the boat moving on sometimes choppy water, I inched my way on a narrow board along the side of the vessel, at the same time leaning inwards and holding on to what bits of the woven roof I could grab. Then it was a case of opening a little wooden door outwards, moving out of its way to let it open, and then entering the tiny 'cabin' in the very rear of the boat. Perched above the water, the cabin had a hole in the floor. A *pinasse* is not the best place to be if bowel problems strike.

But for me the highlight of this river voyage was to camp on the riverbank two nights in succession. Our guides chose gloriously isolated sandy spots, thankfully – and surprisingly – unperturbed by mosquitoes though one night we did encounter clouds of far more acceptable and very attractive, pale green lacewings fluttering on to our food and almost everything else. Unfamiliar raucous bird calls, the sun's globe setting over the water, a rustle of warm breeze, and the gentle 'clut ' of the river water tapping against its banks as the coal-black African night descended. It might be a cliché but it was simply magical.

One of those evenings as dusk approached, I walked well away from the tents into some scattered scrub. I had been attracted by a persistent harsh call from a bird I couldn't see. Evidently skulking by nature, it took some time to make its appearance. This one was clearly a skulking maestro. But it turned out to be a bird with a fine name, a Yellow-crowned Gonolek, a bird the size of a thrush but, boy, what colours! Dark brown on the back with striking crimson underneath combined with a yellow crown; these were surely the sort of colours to be flaunted. Not for this bird they weren't – it retreated into a bush and out of sight again.

It was soon after dawn on one of these camping mornings with few of my fellow travellers up and out that the nearby sandbanks fingering out into the river had attracted some early birds. They were a mix of elegant, blue-grey and black Egyptian Plovers and some equally compact-looking Grey Pratincoles, pale grey and white but with scarlet beaks and legs, African birds both.

The plover is a very unusual bird. While its supposed trick of walking into the open mouths of crocodiles and retrieving bits of meat from between the predator's teeth might be make-believe, it does have other unusual habits. Its two or three eggs are not incubated by the parents but are buried in sun-warmed sand, temperature control being achieved by the adult sitting on the sand with a water-soaked belly to cool them. If the adult leaves the 'nest', it smooths more sand over the eggs. The chicks can run as soon as they hatch and are able to feed themselves shortly afterwards. The adults cool the chicks in the same way as with the eggs and the chicks might also drink water from the adult's belly feathers. If danger threatens, the adults bury the chicks in the sand from which they extricate themselves, Houdini-like, when the danger has passed.

Most, probably all, of the Niger's crocs have been killed years ago so we were very unlikely to see an Egyptian Plover doing a bit of cleaning in one of the most dangerous jaws in the living world. We didn't see one crocodile on our three-day river journey. But twice we spotted a large, lumbering, grey-brown animal near the river's surface in shallower water. As we approached in the *pinasse*, it dived and disappeared down into its depths. These were African Manatees – a species of sea cow with no close relatives and descended, a very long time ago, from primitive elephants that took to water and eventually became aquatic.

Supposedly protected (although laws are hardly ever enforced out here), experts think that very few manatees survive in this river; they are invariably trapped and killed to eat. One manatee can provide an awful lot of meat. Others are caught by chance in fishing nets though their fate is the same. Apparently, less manatee meat is being seen in Mali's markets in recent years but that is attributed to the animals becoming rare and not to tastes changing.

Hippos were a little more common and are possibly harder to kill, in part because they are so dangerous on land. They sometimes even attack boats for no apparent reason. We slowed to watch a couple as they wallowed near the riverbank, only the tops of their heads showing. And later, from the ferry crossing the Niger near Timbuktu, I spotted a large group of them. They were basking and splashing in deep water out from the extensive marshes and rice fields at the river's sides.

Every day at mid-morning, Atanou Saye, our ever-smiling *pinasse* cook, brewed a wine-red tea, a hot fruity drink made from vermillion-coloured wild hibiscus flowers. It was both refreshing and aromatic. And for lunch he would conjure up a fresh salad with tinned tuna, sardines and bread, handed around as we glided through some of the wildest marshes and waterways in Africa.

Every day we passed an occasional Bozo fisherman hand-throwing his net from a *pirogue*, a much smaller, narrower wooden canoe than our *pinasse*. On one such occasion as we passed near, a fishermen was just hauling in a large fish. From its length – about half a metre – and colour – silver with a blue tinge – it was probably a Nile Perch, called *capitaine* here, a very tasty fish to eat. It's found on most menus, either grilled, en brochette, or in a variety of sauces, and is a culinary delight. It's particularly good with green beans or plantain. Atanou signalled to the fisherman that he wanted to buy it so our *pinasse* turned in his direction. Thoughts of fish and chips in the sunset drifted into our minds. But it was not to be. As we approached his pirogue, the huge fish slipped out of his hands back into the muddy Niger. One disappointed Bozo fishermen; 15 disappointed Brits.

It might be one of the poorest countries in the world but food in Mali is surprisingly good, a part legacy from French colonial days. Chicken, though, we found was best avoided, not only because of the Djenne factor but because the scrawny birds provide bones with precious few titbits of tough meat. The availability of fresh fish (and presumably salted fish for the dry months when few if any can be caught) made me wonder why we saw so many young children in Malian villages with obvious kwashiorkor, characterised by a distended abdomen and swollen ankles and feet. Maybe it was a case of parents not knowing that a carbohydrate dominated diet with little or no protein is the cause; including more fish in their diet appeared to us to be an obvious solution.

Having a bunch of friendly, excited children, all bouncing and smiling, often half covered in sand and wanting to hold a 'white' hand while walking through their village is always a lovely experience. But with many of them suffering from kwashiorkor and nasal infections it suggested to me that some of them might not survive even to adolescence.

Nearly a million people depend on the Inner Niger delta for food. Fish are a key part of that resource. So, too, are up to two million cattle that graze its shallower marshes (and even more sheep and goats further inland) for eight months of the year. The aquatic grass that grows naturally in deeper water – known as *bourgou* or Hippo Grass – is harvested and fed to cattle on dry land. Some is stored for the dry season. And some is planted as a crop to harvest.

Extensive crops of rice are grown too; rice is the staple here. The flooding river deposits nutrient-rich silt that aids the growth of other staples like millet and sorghum. In a good year – and this winter has been a very good year with a huge flood – there might even be a surplus of food to sell at the local markets.

Historically, the various ethnic groups living in the delta derived their food very differently. Today, though, that differentiation is less clear. Traditionally, the Bozo fished in shallows using wooden traps. The Somono fished the main river with nets. The Songhay were mostly farmers and traders living near the river's edge. The Fulani were cattle herders, historically nomadic, though now mostly settled in villages. Bartering between the different groups shared produce, and Mali has a history of these different groups co-existing peacefully, at least in times of plenty. 'Since the great droughts in 1974 and 1984, the ancient divisions between fishermen, cattle herders and farmers have disappeared,' Bakary Cone, Director of Wetlands International's Mali office told me after I returned from the trip and wanted to investigate the issue further for *CNN Traveller* magazine. 'Now many fishermen keep a few cows and also grow rice so each family is better able to provide some food if there is a drought. Today this is the farming system that's most prevalent in the Delta.'

A growing issue here is that the natural year-to-year variation in rainfall is compounded by the unpredictability of the impact of climate warming – there have been more drought years in recent decades – and by two reservoirs in the upper part of the Niger: one built for irrigation, the other to supply water to Mali's capital, Bamako. And there are proposals for more reservoirs. Before 1980, drought years were rare. A severe drought in 2005 left over a million people in need of emergency aid. Much the same again happened in 2012. Drought foments conflict here. Tensions rise between fishermen, between farmers cultivating crops and herders trying to get some grazing for their livestock, and all the result of huge shortages of resources to feed a growing human population. In December 1993, these tensions exploded into violent confrontation, leaving 29 dead and 42 wounded. Part of that confrontation was over *bourgou*, the only fodder grass that copes with flood inundation by keeping pace with rising water levels, sometimes reaching 3 m in height. Farmers wanted to harvest and store it for animal feed later in the dry season. Transhumance herders weren't for waiting; they needed to graze it where it grew. Furthermore, because of pollution (sewage entering the river is never treated), because the numbers of fishermen have increased, and because they are using smaller net sizes to catch smaller fish, populations of fish in the Niger Delta have fallen dramatically.

In spite of the superficial serenity as we glide quietly downriver past extensive, wildlife-rich marshes, rice and *bourgou* crops, there are other issues here that are hard to spot. Excessive grazing with livestock, combined with droughts, has degraded a lot of farmland. Erosion of exposed sandy soil is causing the silting up of shallow ponds and streams, once important for fish and other wildlife. Too much tree felling has reduced breeding trees for many of the delta's herons and egrets as well as depriving people of wood, food and shade.

Famine constantly haunts this place because food harvesting is so unpredictable. More predictable are birds; there are always some around though far fewer if the marshes are dry. So everyone kills birds – anything from small wading birds like snipe to large herons – using all manner of homemade traps, nets and slings. Any bird, small or large, adds protein to their otherwise starch-based diet. And better tracks and roads into the Niger Delta are likely to mean more trapping to satisfy the needs of more distant markets.

So far the invasive Water Hyacinth, a native of the Amazon but spreading in waterways worldwide, hasn't made serious inroads in the delta. But it is spreading in other parts of the river both upstream in Mali and downstream in neighbouring Niger. It covers waterways in a dense mat, precluding fishing, elbowing out native plants, seriously disrupting boat traffic and harbouring mosquitoes. Its spread into the delta is inevitable.

With less water in the delta seemingly a more frequent result of climate warming and reservoir construction upstream, bird trapping, tree felling and a gradual takeover of more marshland to grow crops, many of the delta's birds – both breeding species and winter migrants – are declining. Some are holding their own and a few are increasing but, overall, this fabulous wetland is not as wildlife-rich as it was.

The Niger Basin Commission, comprised of representatives from nine countries along the river, is trying to address some of these problems by curbing siltation, encouraging tree planting, clearing Water Hyacinth, re-planting *bourgou* killed off by drought, and modernizing rice growing. But these are poor countries with few resources. They have more people than their land can sustain year-on-year. And they have no control over the most important factor – the seasonal rains – the lifeblood of this river and its inland delta.

The flood in the Niger delta that I witnessed might have been of biblical proportions but the big question remains: when will the next one be?

The Perils of Hiring a Guide

We were struggling through thorny scrub on some very sandy soil. 'You stay here Mark [my name had seemingly proved impossible for my guide to pronounce] and I will call when I find more tracks. He is here very close.' Trouble was, in the thicket of sharp-spined acacia, I could see little of the sandy ground around me. But what I could see was a tad troubling. Burrows in the sand dotted here and there where I stood. Burrows that seemed to be about 10 cm in diameter. For a moment I thought they might be the burrows of a mongoose or some other rodent. But no. Coming out – or going into – several of these burrows was a tell-tale, body-smoothed and winding path as wide as the burrow itself pressed into the hessian-coloured soil. They were python tracks. And it was an Indian Python that my guide Satto Singh, in Rajasthan's fabulous Keoladeo National Park, had just gone off to find.

I just hoped that he knew which way this python was slithering. Or how many pythons there might be. Standing there on my own, and not knowing very much about pythons, I started to wonder how fast one can move if it feels an urge to. And which direction might it come from? If one decided to come out of its burrow – in which, apparently, they lay their eggs – would it simply ignore me and slide away? Or start coiling around my legs and using its undoubtedly substantial powers of constriction? Could I be fighting for my last breath by the time Satto returned?

I thought I should keep still and silent, just in case anything appeared. But do pythons have a good sense of smell? Actually, yes, I found out later; an acute sense of smell to make up for their relatively poor eyesight and hearing. So I stood no chance if one came close. My eyes scanned one hole in the ground after another for what seemed an interminable length of time. I was looking for any movement at any one of those burrows. Maybe 20 minutes later, I heard a call, distant at first, then closer. 'Over here Mark. He is lying here. Come quietly.' What a relief!

A couple of arm-scratching minutes pushing through more acacia thorn and there it was, in a large loose coil in the shade. An Indian Python at least 3 metres long, a rather attractive pattern of golden and mud brown, head up with tongue doing the in and out routine to sense who is about. The snake was an impressive sight. Slowly it slid off into deeper shade. It had been worth the scratched arms. As Satto was quick to point out, this was a small python. They can be over 6 metres long. Killing by squeezing their prey to death, they have been known to kill deer. And devour them whole.

But do they ever kill people? 'Yes, oh yes can kill people,' said Satto with such a degree of certainty that I disbelieved him instantly. I didn't question him too closely but checked up some weeks later. Seemingly, there are recorded cases of humans killed by pythons, though very few, but these are by larger Reticulated Pythons. And there are doubts about whether any such victim has subsequently been eaten by the snake. There are various claims, some lurid photos and much likelihood of hoaxes. But it was a better story for Satto to tell his customers.

What I also found out subsequently was that the Keoladeo National Park has a good population of Indian Pythons. They apparently often take over the burrows of other animals such as mongoose or Asian Porcupine, often killing the burrow-holder first.

We retrieved our bikes on the roadside nearby and cycled off along the road, Satto leading, me – Mark – wobbling behind. It had been years since I had pedalled a bike and re-learning proved to be a bit of a shambolic experience.

I had agreed to hire Satto the evening before. I was staying for a few nights at the rather gloomy Bharatpur Ashok Forest Lodge, the only accommodation within the park boundaries but a rather utilitarian concrete building with little charm. Let's just say that 'location, location' is its best feature. I had met an American couple who had hired Satto for a few days and they recommended him thoroughly. So the deal was done. When I was there he charged 750 rupees (£8) a day.

In India, as in many countries, hiring a guide makes life so much easier though it can be something of a lottery. If you get a good one (and many are not) they know the best wildlife spots and can be extremely good at identifying what you are looking at. Satto was both. Having a guide also reduces hassle. The cycle rickshaw wallahs with yellow national park badges on their bikes who hang around the Bharatpur National Park entrance are authorised guides and they seem to be reasonably knowledgeable about the wildlife, at least the commonly spotted animals. They are certainly good at pressing you to hire them. But it's impossible to know who is good and who is mediocre...or worse.

Competition between guides is pretty severe. That's not surprising; their families depend on the income. In 2002, one man was killed and several seriously injured in a dispute here over under-quoting for guide services. And all over 200 rupees. That's little more than £2.

Booking a guide in advance from the UK is an alternative. In my experience, that doesn't always work out. On one occasion, I'd booked a guide for a day to take me into the tropical forests in the Dominican Republic. Spotting forest birds, often small and not always vividly coloured, high up in tall tree canopies is the most difficult – and neck stiffening – aspect of watching birds I know of. I needed a guide who knew what we might see.

All was arranged, though happily no money was required in advance. But when I got there, he had evaporated. No answer to my phone calls or emails. Presumably, he'd had a better offer and didn't want to admit it. Or he'd left the country. Whatever it was, any other local guide I contacted at short notice was fully booked. My only time in some tropical forest was with the young son of a local villager who, I was told, knew the best paths to use around his village in the Los Haitises National Park, an isolated area of unusual, mostly conical-shaped hills clothed in rainforest. But the forest we walked into, muddy and damp in the humid heat, wasn't especially natural; lots of the trees had been planted by the villagers for fruit and other crops. There were few birds.

I'd got to this isolated village by Jeep with Dr Jose Nunez-Mino, the Field Project Manager for the Hispaniola Endemic Land Mammals Project, funded by the UK's Durrell Wildlife Conservation Trust. It is set up to learn more about the needs of the Hispaniolan Solenodon, a rare rodent that looks like an oversized shrew with a Pinocchio-shaped snout. I didn't see any solenodons (they are nocturnal and difficult to spot anyway) but Jose turned out to be a great guide. Travelling into the national park on rough, wet tracks in the humid heat he stopped where we overlooked a clearing in which the local farmers had planted (illegally) crops in front of some forest.

Jose pointed to a nest in one of the trees. It was the nest of one of the world's rarest birds of prey, a Ridgway's Hawk, down to maybe 100 pairs and all of them now confined to this part of the Dominican Republic. They're in decline mainly because these forests are not protected – even those in the national park – and local communities are slowly clearing them. This slash-and-burn farming to grow crops year-on-year is gradually depleting the very forest that the Los Haitises National Park was created to protect.

With binoculars we could make out a young bird or two in the nest but the adults were nowhere to be seen until, suddenly, the male – slate grey with rusty wing patches and belly – landed in a tree nearby, shortly to be joined by the browner female. It was, I thought, a close-up of a rare bird that might not exist within a human generation.

Making arrangements to meet a guide you have arranged to hire can be much less straightforward than you might imagine too. Preparing for a short visit to the Souss Massa National Park on the west coast of Morocco I contacted Mohamed Bargache, a locally based bird guide who lives in a village within the park. I had read reports saying how good he was. By email I had booked him for a full day.

This national park was primarily set up to protect the sea-cliff breeding areas, and the semi-desert feeding grounds, of one of the world's rarest – though certainly not the most beautiful – birds. The Northern Bald Ibis, the size of a large goose, has a dull red-coloured but bald face, a long down-curved red beak and glossy, slightly iridescent block plumage all over. Ibises are related to spoonbills but, unlike virtually all its relatives, this one eschews wetlands and lives in very arid locations.

Formerly found across North Africa, in Southern Europe and throughout the Middle East, hunting and habitat destruction have rendered it a rarity. Though a few very small populations hang on elsewhere, Morocco now holds the lion's share of the world population. Here they are on the increase. But with around 300 ibises that might be anywhere in this 34,000 ha of arid land where a limited number of very rough stony or sandy tracks are the main means of getting about, I thought it was essential to have a local guide if I was to stand any chance of finding them.

Mohamed, though, backed out just a couple of days before I left for Morocco. He had taken an alternative booking of four days' work. Incomes are low in Morocco so I wasn't surprised. He recommended his younger brother instead. And so it was that I phoned Mustafa when I got to southern Morocco and arranged to meet him at 10 a.m. the following morning. I had Mohamed's original rendezvous instructions and we agreed those. Easy I thought.

Setting off from near the city of Agadir and heading south towards Tiznit on the N1 dual carriageway, I was to turn off right where I saw a 'Camping Massa' sign, a drive of maybe 50 km. And then drive straight to a carpark where we would meet. Eventually I saw the sign, turned right and ended up in Massa village at a T-junction. No mention of that in the instructions. Seeing no obvious signs I took a gamble and turned right. After a kilometre the road, now a track, divided right and left. Stopping to look at some rudimentary signs, a moped pulled up alongside me.

There then followed a conversation in pidgin French, French being the second language here but commonly spoken. The moped rider explained that he was a national park 'guardian'; he wore a cap suggesting that perhaps he was but he could have been anyone. His face, though, lit up when I mentioned Mustafa's name; he immediately made a call on his mobile and proceeded to give me directions to the 'carpark', which I duly followed. And there on a bit of rough gravel stood Mustafa (or someone who claimed to be Mustafa at least). Either way, we got on famously.

Then it was a case of 'find the ibises'. With Mustafa driving my very small hire car (illegally of course), we spent five hours speeding along many tens of kilometres of sandy tracks and bone-shaking, potholed 'roads' peering into the semi-desert on either side – a landscape of pale sand dotted with low spiny bushes – not seeing even one ibis. We had seen other birds of course. But an ibis, no. I thought we were completely out of luck. It wouldn't have been the first time. But Mustafa remained buoyant all day with comments such as 'I never fail' and 'Now I am 26 years old and every day I see the ibis'. I was losing faith rapidly. My belief in Mustafa's optimism was waning.

Then, at 4 p.m. when I had almost given up hope, Mustafa spotted one flying in the distance. Against the bright sunshine I failed to see it. But he knew then where they might be feeding and as we skitted along a sandy track we had travelled along at least twice before that day, we came across a remarkable sight.

A large flock of Northern Bald Ibises no more than 40 m away, casually walking between bits of vegetation picking up whatever they could find in the sandy soil: large beetles, small lizards, seeds from the desert shrubs. I counted 150 ibises; there might have been even more. That's nearly half the world's population of this unusual and rare bird, here in one feeding flock. After maybe 15 minutes they flew up and over my head with a great swooshing of black wings and headed off elsewhere, perhaps to find better pickings. They might not be the prettiest birds in the world but they were an impressive sight. Mustafa had come up trumps. Just as he said he would.

His 600 dirham (about £40) for a day's guiding had been money well spent. I was more convinced than ever that these birds would have been impossible to spot without his local knowledge…and an ability to zip along sandy tracks on which, in many places, it would have been all too easy to get 'bogged down' and spend much of the day digging out the car. We didn't get stuck once, though we came mightily close to it a few times. But Mustafa's wider knowledge of bird identification hadn't been reliable. I wasn't at all convinced that a pair of very uncommon Marbled Ducks he spotted in the distance on the Massa River weren't actually a couple of female (very much more common) Teal! And most small birds we saw exhibiting some red in their plumage were always Moussier's Redstarts – several were, but others were something else entirely. Nevertheless, he found the Bald Ibis and that was what I was primarily interested in seeing.

Satto Singh's bird identification abilities at Keoladeo were in a whole different league. He took me to an extensive, shallow, freshwater marsh that was teeming with birds. It was hard to know where to look first. Without binoculars, Satto started identifying them: three or four species of egrets, all of them white; both Glossy and Black-headed Ibis (but, of course, no Bald!); darters swimming in the water with only their thin necks visible like some prehistoric reptile birds; dozens of Purple Swamp Hens, their iridescent purple plumage contrasting with their scarlet faces and gangly legs and thousands of ducks. Most of them were here for the winter having flown south from their breeding places in cold northern Russia. Satto knew them all.

Originally Keoladeo became famous because of its ducks. A large plaque in the centre of the Park commemorates key events in the Park's history including: '1938: A shooting party headed by the then Viceroy of India Lord Linlithgow shot a maximum of 4,273 birds on 12th November'. It was reckoned to be the best duck shooting in the then British Empire. And you can guess that the Raj exploited it for all that it was worth. As they did here, our Victorian ancestors went around much of the world killing as many animals as they possibly could. And today we lecture most other countries about how they should protect their wildlife.

Keoladeo's freshwater pools and marshes cover up to 10 km^2 of the park's total area of 29 km^2. But their area varies enormously, depending on how prolific the monsoon has been and how much water has been diverted away illegally by farmers. These days quite a lot never gets in the park so the boat trips that used to be an attraction here are a thing of the past.

Ironically these wetlands are manmade. Bharatpur town, just a few kilometres away, used to be prone to flooding during the monsoon. So an earth dam was built to protect it. The hollows from which the earth was removed filled with water. That was in 1760 and Keoladeo's wetlands have been here ever since. Designated a national park in 1982, hunting had been banned – officially anyway – since the 1960s. Away from the wetlands, the rest is dry acacia forest and extensive grasslands have scattered trees more reminiscent of the African savannah.

But even if you had no previous interest in birds or mammals, it's hard not to be entranced by Keoladeo. Out one day sans Satto, I parked my bike among some trees and walked away from the crowds that stick to the single (though thankfully motor vehicle-free) road and just imbibed the atmosphere. I was writing a travel feature for *The Independent* and I wanted to savour the atmosphere of the place. Eagles were soaring in the hot blue sky. Excitable black and white Magpie Robins jumped about on the paths in front of me, dodging into some scrub. Black Drongos with their peculiar lyre-shaped tails were picking insects off the backs of Bluebuck – India's largest antelope – or the many semi-wild cattle that graze the savannah here. And groups of elegant Sarus Cranes, over 5 feet tall, pale grey with blood-red faces, were strutting amongst a plethora of storks and herons. Silence is a distinctly ephemeral experience in Keoladeo, even away from people as a posse of screaming Rose-ringed Parakeets, all lurid green and scarlet-beaked, suddenly do a flypast like jet fighters.

Then there is the occasional blood-curdling, loud, child-like, night-time wailing which gathers momentum as more join the chorus, only to fade away as abruptly as it had begun. A pack of Golden Jackals, more creamy grey than golden, bigger than foxes, wailing to keep in contact with each other. 'Howls, barks, growls, whines and cackles' say the textbooks; in reality it sounds as if a child is being murdered. At night from my balcony at the Ashok Forest Lodge looking out over grassland and forest I could see packs occasionally wandering past, out on night-time patrol.

On most of my trips over the years I have had the very good fortune not to need to hire guides. The experts I was usually meeting were brilliant guides in themselves. Searching for Arabian Oryx in the Empty Quarter of the Saudi desert – the Rub'al-Khali – with Maartin Strauss, a South African mammal expert and Eric Bedin, a French biologist, as guides couldn't have been more informative nor more of a pleasure and a privilege.

Likewise, being out in the woods and pastures of Virginia with Phil West who was then working for the state's Department of Game and Inland Fisheries, gave me a substantial insight into the behaviour and ecological needs of Wild Turkeys even though – much to Phil's irritation – we didn't manage to see one that day.

With Robert Lentaaya, a Dorobo in Kenya, following a honeyguide as the small, noisy bird leads us to a wild bee nest deep in the Mathews Forest, was an experience never to be forgotten. And I was amazed by Robert's almost sixth-sense ability to hear a sound or detect a movement I could never have detected; a family troop of Olive Baboons high up in the forest tree canopy or a White-browed Coucal, skulking but just about visible in some scrub along a river.

An early morning Jeep trip with Michal Krzysiak in Poland's Białowieża Forest spotting deer, Wild Boar and – after a great deal of searching – my first view of a wild European Bison.

Or spending a morning with Wayne Hartley from the *Save the Manatee Club* as we canoed together exceedingly slowly past and over around 100 lumbering Florida Manatees lounging on the bed of the Blue Spring River, most of them individually recognised by Wayne who could often cite their family history from memory.

Being guided by Gabriel Sierra to see Great Bustards for the first time on the wide plains of central Spain near his home village of Moraleja de Matacabras and learning their habits from him. And, some years later, spending time with him watching their incredible 'turn inside out' springtime display, one of the most amazing wildlife spectacles to be seen anywhere.

Or being led by *Butterfly Conservation*'s Caroline Kelly out on Somerset's Collard Hill in midsummer spotting the brilliant flypasts of Large Blue butterflies, now reinstated in England, and searching tiny, purple flowers of thyme to try and find the even tinier Large Blue's eggs.

I could not have wished for better guides. Or better company.

Tales of the Unexpected

I t was Rob Cooke who spotted them and wandered up to me, a perplexed expression on his face. 'I'm not sure about this,' he said in his quiet, unassuming way, 'but there's a couple of birds over there that look a bit like pigeons. You'd better take a look.'

One glance through my binoculars confirmed it: City Pigeons. Nothing odd about that you might think. Except that we weren't in the middle of Solihull or Skegness. We were at a nomadic Tuareg encampment more or less dead centre in the Sahara Desert. Saying that a few City Pigeons here looked pretty incongruous was the understatement of our desert safari.

You don't find many birds in the middle of the Sahara. That might sound a tad obvious. With summer shade (where you can find any) temperatures that soar towards 50°C and an annual rainfall so low that it all but defies measurement, it demands a pretty resilient life-form to survive here at all. I certainly hadn't bargained on Town Pigeons. But these birds are nothing if not adaptable and resilient. They were presumably scrounging spare grain from the Tuaregs' chickens or picking up a few seeds in the dried-up droppings of the goats, that grazed on whatever sharp-spined shrubs they could find in the scatter of wadis.

From where had these pigeons travelled to get here? We were in southwest Libya with no villages for hundreds of kilometres. The closest settlement is 400 km away: Murzuq, a small desert oasis town with a few thousand residents and in one of the driest spots on earth. Maybe these were Murzuq pigeons that fancied a change of scenery. But how would they have found a remote spot comprising arid rocks, small cliffs and sand dunes at the edge of a dried-up wadi temporarily occupied by some goat-grazing nomadic Tuareg families? Could they smell the grain from 400 km away or had they simply taken a long-distance chance – a pigeon reconnaissance flight? Both seem to me to be pretty implausible options. Maybe they followed the semi-nomadic Tuareg in stages, eventually ending up here; leaving anything to chance in such a hostile, arid environment like this would be life threatening.

This wouldn't have been a trip that could be contemplated at any time since the Arab Spring of 2011/12; Libya is now far too dangerous. But I was one of a small group of the so-called 153 Club (see Chapter 6) who had organised guides and 4WD drivers to take us from Tripoli, where we had spent a couple of days, south by road (a very long and tedious minibus trip) via Sabha and out into the heart of the Sahara. Closed to tourists under Libya's repressive regime, in his later years Gaddafi had decided to allow a limited amount of accompanied tourism. But because few Westerners had ventured out into the Libyan Sahara, its animal life was a bit of an unknown quantity. I didn't know what to expect.

You might imagine – most people do – that a huge, often extensively sandy (not rocky) desert like this supports little wildlife. In terms of birds and large mammals that is true; there are only maybe seven bird species out in the Sahara, and even they are very scattered.

One of those species, though, seemed to be with us almost all of the time; whether it was the same pair of ravens following us on our journey or a different pair at each campsite I can't say. Here, the species is the Brown-necked Raven; almost identical to the much more common species found across Europe. Every evening they would turn up somewhere nearby, perched often on a rock outcrop where they would spend the night ready to scour the place for scraps when we left in the morning. Our drivers were very particular cleaning up our campsites so they must have had thin pickings. Still they persisted. There were probably more of them than any other bird, evidence maybe that Libyan Desert expeditions have become a reliable food source.

Camping wild in the Sahara was an absolute delight, especially for a snorer like me. I had a two-person tent all to myself while my fellow travellers pitched in a wide scatter to avoid any such night-time disturbances. Some of our group slept outdoors, probably by choice. Looking up at the night sky with its myriad pinpoints of stars – enough to cast a very dim, slate blue glow over the sand – I would never have slept a wink.

Most nights were wonderfully peaceful save for the jerboas, little long-tailed rodents with big ears, scurrying around the outside of my tent, presumably searching for bits of discarded food to devour. Not that they made any noise. Instead, they would sometimes wake me because they were nudging the side of my tent as they scuffled around. When I opened the tent each morning, the presence of a myriad of tiny footprints confirmed that they had been close to me all night.

Now and again I spotted a bird or two: an elegant little White-crowned Black Wheatear sitting perkily atop a shrub in a wadi; a muddy brown Desert Lark scurrying over boulders or searching the sand between shrubs; a Rock Martin, a grey version of our own Sand Martin, scything the air between some wadi acacias. But not all together. This is the Sahara, not Slimbridge, and birds here have a far harder life trying to find food. And if you wonder what the likes of these wheatears and larks eat in such an arid place, all you need do is to sit by a light in the cool, dark desert evening and just watch all manner of insects that turn up attracted to the light. Small moths, flies, leaf bugs, delicate little lacewings and more. And in the early morning as the sun bursts out horizontally across a wadi, the acacias are draped in a network of dew-doused spiderwebs that get suddenly illuminated.

Gradually, my fellow 153 Club members became better and better versed in alerting me to the desert birds: Lisa invariably 'heard some twittering', Alan had seen something 'small and brown' – though it did take our whole stay before Christiaan from Holland could master the tricky name, White-crowned Black Wheatear. Even our drivers started to take an interest. An arms-wide-apart-flapping gesture from one of them pointing to some distant bush was their usual signal. Towards the end of our trip one of our group was quoting from his travel guidebook on the crows around the Awbari salt lakes. 'No, not crows,' the others said in unison. 'They'll be Brown-necked Ravens!'

Not that all of my tales of the unexpected are about wildlife. Seemingly, it's not impossible, even out here, to encounter a local person when you are least expecting to see anyone. One particular day we had stopped in a particularly arid area of the Akakus at a series of rocky outcrops to see another set of amazing rock drawings from at least 5,000 years ago, a time when the Sahara was more moist and fertile (see Chapter 12).

As we were walking up to the drawings, a Tuareg man appeared suddenly from behind some nearby rocks. It surprised us that he was out here; but what surprised us even more were his spectacles. Dressed in traditional blue robes and a turban, and all smiles, he looked as if he had just come out of Specsavers with the wrong pair of glasses. The nearest Specsavers, incidentally, was an awfully long way away. It seemed likely that some passing European tourist had left them behind on an outcrop. Our friendly Tuareg was determined to wear them whether they improved his eyesight … or more likely not. Beaming with his new bifocals, he shook hands with everyone, although no one could converse with him – our drivers and guide spoke Arabic and at least one Berber dialect but most Tuareg here speak Tamahaq. As we drove off, all of us wishing him (and his specs) well, he walked off to wherever he came from, still all smiles and waving.

Sometimes – though not very often in my experience – you spot the creature you desperately want to see far more quickly than you could hope for. I think my fastest ever bit of spotting was on the Canary Island of Tenerife.

On such islands, some birds have evolved to become quite different from their mainland relatives. Often the differences become so marked over time that experts consider them to be different species. This is presumably what happened with the

Blue Chaffinch, found nowhere else in the world but the Canary Islands of Tenerife and Gran Canaria, where they inhabit the pine forests that grow above about 2000 m on mountain slopes. The vast bulk of the population is on Tenerife, seemingly because most of the pine forest on Gran Canaria has long since been destroyed, along with much other decent wildlife habitat.

Blue Chaffinches are slightly larger than the common European Chaffinch, and the males are quite a vivid slate-blue – the females are duller, more grey than blue. They feed mainly on the cones of the gorgeous Canarian Pine trees; their powerful beaks, a little larger than those of the European Chaffinch, do the job of tearing out the seeds in the cones. But they often congregate around campsites where they can pick up any morsels of food left from human picnics – in that behaviour they are little different from their European cousins!

One such campsite high in the pine forests of northern Tenerife is known to be a good location to see them. But, from bad experiences with other birds supposedly easy to find at other 'good sites' over the years, I was not optimistic. At the campsite, I parked about 50 m away from the nearest picnic table, binoculars at the ready. At best, I thought, these birds will take some patient exploration before I'll see one. And then maybe a glance only. As I got closer, though, I noticed a couple of small birds pootling around on the ground underneath the table. Probably something much more mundane, I thought, such as robins. But a glimpse through my binoculars overturned my disbelief immediately; I could only see their heads as they moved in and out of sight between the picnic table legs, but what I could see was distinctly blue. A pair of Blue Chaffinches! The first I had ever seen. And it had taken about 30 seconds … a personal record.

For the next hour I watched several of them, sometimes in the lower branches of the scattered pines, sometimes searching the ground near a picnic table; brilliant views of a very attractive bird. And later that day as we drove down from some of the highest forests near the ex-volcano of Mount Teide (though the 'ex' is dubious) to lower-elevation pine forest, we stopped by a wooden roadside hut. Within a minute or two, a pair of Blue Chaffinches came close, this time moving through the low branches of the Canarian Pines. There were no picnic tables here, and no food scraps.

Of the up to 4,500 Blue Chaffinches in the world, barely 200 or so of those are on Gran Canaria (in small isolated patches of pine forest), so the population on Tenerife is of huge importance. What is more, their numbers are increasing, due very largely to the forward-looking forestry service on Tenerife, which is extending the forest cover and doing as much as it can to safeguard against fires, probably the biggest threat to this gorgeous bird and the impressive pine forest it inhabits.

I've become a bit of a fan of picnic sites – though only when they are unoccupied – after a holiday on Lesbos, the attractive Greek island out in the eastern Aegean close to the coast of Turkey. Because so many twitchers visit the island in spring – it's a very good, generally accessible place with a variety of habitats that attract a huge range of birds migrating north – every decent bird location on this attractive island is well documented. One of them is a picnic site. Located on a roadside on the edge of some very impressive pine forest in the centre of the island, a tiny bird sometimes makes an appearance after any daytime human hubbub has disappeared. A cousin of the Eurasian Nuthatch that you might be familiar with in British gardens and woods, this is its Aegean cousin, the Krüper's Nuthatch. A bird of pine forests largely confined to Turkey, and declining there because the forests are apparently not managed sympathetically, it's a restless little chap, constantly on the move.

Earlier in the day we had watched – from a distance – a pair of adult Krüper's taking insects to feed youngsters in a nesthole in a rotten pine; we didn't expect to get to see them any closer than this. But hanging around the picnic site where we had parked our car paid off handsomely. A couple of adults soon appeared and made forays from the low branches of pines on to the ground to hoover up any morsels or crumbs left behind from previous picnics. Largely ignoring our presence, they hopped around, no more than 5 m from us, their slate-coloured backs, white eyestripe and chestnut breast patch now very much more obvious than the views at the nesthole had provided. We returned to the picnic site on several more occasions but never saw the tiny Krüper's again. This wildlife watching stuff is nothing if not unpredictable!

With unpredictability in mind, who would ever guess that in extensive, often flat pasture with no trees and scrub to obscure the view, a bird larger than a goose can be virtually impossible to find. The plains of Extremadura in the west of Spain are known to hold one of the highest densities of Great Bustards in the world (see Chapter 15), but it can sometimes takes hours to spot one. The reasons? First, it's not always guaranteed that they will be feeding on any one area of land. They move about. Second, if they sit down, their brown and cream plumage blends them into the surrounding often parched pasture. Third, even when they are walking about (which they spend most of their day doing) they seem to use tussocks of vegetation and slight slopes in the ground to their advantage … and to the disadvantage of the observer!

Finding their slightly smaller cousins, the Houbara of Lanzarote, Fuerteventura and North Africa can be equally difficult. Coloured pale brown, black and white, they blend into their arid, often sandy, stone-strewn habitat. Crouching down in such places, they are almost impossible to spot. Yet, at other times, they seem to make themselves incredibly obvious, walking out in the open not more than 50 m away. One wet day in Lanzarote in an area well known for its good Houbara numbers (though most of the time I saw few or none), we pulled off the road to wait for the rain to pass; there was no point in searching for the bird in such conditions. As the rain catapulted down and formed rivulets down the car windows, I noticed a strange shape on the ground about 30 m away between some clumps of vegetation. The view was pretty murky but binoculars revealed a male Houbara standing bolt still and facing us, sitting out the heavy downpour and looking distinctly bedraggled. Standing about 60 cm high with his distinctive 'mane' of black feathers down each side of his neck and chest, he simply stared in our direction, sometimes turning his head a little.

After an hour the rain had stopped; our bird gave an occasional shake to dislodge water drops and he started to feed. Surprisingly, he didn't seek cover in the vegetation. We drove off. It was one of the closest views of an often timid bird I have ever experienced.

Large birds might be surprisingly difficult to spot; small ones can be almost impossible, especially if there are few of them and even if they are brightly coloured. The Mali Firefinch, a bird the size of a Blue Tit, is one. Firefinches, of which there are about ten species and all found in Africa, are colourful birds, mostly – and this is no surprise – a pinky or orange red, though many have brown upperparts. Some are abundant and have a widespread distribution over several countries; others are very confined. The Mali Firefinch is arguably the most restricted in range, confined to the Niger River zone of Mali (where it inhabits grassy areas on mostly rocky ground) and to a much smaller area of neighbouring Senegal.

The next bit of this story is going to sound rather esoteric and twitcher-like, not adjectives that I take pleasure in using. Whatever, being in Mali (see Chapter 6) I thought I should try to spot one. That, however, is not easy. The Mali Firefinch and the much more common African Firefinch (of which I saw many) are very similar. Extremely similar. The only way to be sure to differentiate them (wait for it) is to look at the extent of brown, or red, on their heads! The African version has a brown back and cap extending right over its head to its beak; the Mali version has the brown head colour ending short of its beak and this frontal part of its cap coloured red. OK? So every time I saw a firefinch I tried to spot this difference. Not easy in a tiny bird not always close by and frequently moving about rather faster than I would have wished. Nevertheless I persevered. And I am not naturally good at perseverance.

So, one afternoon on a trek in Dogon country in southeastern Mali when my fellow trekkers were resting up in the heat of the day (shade temperatures were reaching a punishing 40°C), I decided to sit on the roof of a hut when my companions were snoozing underneath. The habitat outside looked promising; a rocky slope with grassland and scrub. Even in the high heat of the day there were birds about so I thought I would keep watch. I wasn't particularly hopeful. African Firefinches were about; so, too, were slightly larger widowbirds, black with yellow wing patches. And some Neumann's Starlings – larger again and black with burnt-red wing patches – whistling in the rocky scrub. An hour had passed; I'd stared at several African Firefinches but I couldn't see one with a fiery forehead.

Then, yet another came closer, so close that I managed a good look at its head. This time it was unmistakeable; the front of its head above its beak was red not brown. It was a Mali Firefinch. Yes, just another firefinch but, having come all the way to West Africa, it was rewarding to see one of the native birds most restricted to a small part of that great continent. And it was another pleasing tick in my identification book!

Quite often in my experience it's possible to hear a particular mammal or bird but never see it. Pretty frustrating too. For example, I heard the growling bark – more growl than bark – of a leopard in the Mathews Forest, Kenya, (see Chapter 21) at night, but I never saw one, even though their droppings were near to our tents.

Of course, with nocturnal birds such as owls (though not all owls are nocturnal) it's a much more likely occurrence. I've heard diminutive Scops Owls calling at night in France but I had never seen them until a holiday on Lesbos. One of the more unusual but well documented bird locations is a small, inauspicious-seeming grove of tall eucalyptus trees by a sports field on the edge of one of the island's small towns.

Each time we drove past the grove there were at least a couple of birdwatchers replete with telescopes, huge-lens cameras the size of sub-machine guns and binoculars under the trees gazing upwards ardently. One afternoon we succumbed and joined a few Dutch people who had already spotted Scops Owls high in the branches. The owls were fast asleep. And that at least suggested that their almost constant observers hadn't disturbed them. We saw at least three of these very attractive little owls, smaller than Common Blackbirds (though rather different in shape!), brown and cream with black-flecked plumage, dozing serenely on branches close to the tree trunks. We left them to snooze.

Another memorable night-time experience to find a particularly rare bird – one of the rarest in the world – was on the very highest of the rugged mountains of Madeira. I was there to write a feature for *CNN Traveller* magazine (and more recently a chapter in my book, *Back from the Brink* (Whittles, 2015)) about the huge conservation efforts to increase the numbers of Zino's Petrel, a bird of the wide open oceans but which digs a burrow and nests nearly 2,000 m above sea level on Madeira's highest peaks.

It was approaching midnight. And it was cold, dark as pitch, and windy. We had driven up into the mountains with João Nunes, our guide for the evening adventure. Down at lower elevations it had been a typically warm, pleasant evening, warm enough to eat out. Not up here. Cloud swirled around us in eerie sheets making it impossible to see more than a couple of metres in spite of torchlights carried on our heads. We had walked along a narrow, very exposed, summit-top path before João advised that we should stop. And there we huddled behind a few boulders to try and get some shelter from the wind and cold drizzle, high up on a knife-edge mountain ridge. Sudden gusts of wind were blowing squalls of powdered soil that stung our faces.

In the all-enveloping darkness we could barely make out the gloomy shape of the pock-marked cliffs behind us while the precipitous slopes down to the deep gouged valleys way below were thankfully left to our imagination. Aside from the wind, all had been silent since we walked here an hour or so previously. Then, quite suddenly, there was a cry. A ghostly wail from the gloomy cloud swirling around the pinnacles of the mountain peaks alongside us. And another, this one from a different direction. It sounded surreal, as if someone was trying to frighten us as we hunkered down, disorientated by the cloud and wind.

'That's it. That's their call. That's Zino's Petrel,' whispered João. 'The adults are flying in and locating their breeding burrows. They've come in because it's a dark night with no moon.' Such conditions are ideal for a Zino's Petrel to find its burrow and feed its solitary chick which may have had no nourishment for several days. They won't risk flying up here on moonlit nights, as the process of landing on a steep slope and waddling several metres to their burrow puts them at huge risk of attack by marauding gulls.

Said by the shepherds that graze their goats on these slopes to be the cries of their former colleagues who hadn't all survived the stomach-wrenching drops that characterise the island of Madeira's ancient volcanic mountains, what we were witnessing were the calls of Europe's rarest breeding seabird. Having heard their ghostly, wailing calls, I was no longer surprised by the shepherds' explanation.

There might be 80 breeding pairs of Zino's Petrel on this 1160 square kilometre Portuguese island 640 km off the coast of Morocco. Delicate, grey and white seabirds the size of a Jackdaw, though much slimmer, and with long, narrow wings for extended periods of gliding over the deep oceans where they spend the bulk of their lives, they breed nowhere else in the world. They are named after Alec Zino, a Madeiran businessman who discovered them as a new species in the 1960s, after they had been wrongly identified many years earlier and their existence forgotten. It is possible to see Zino's Petrel by day when they are hunting out at sea for small fish, shearing this way and that low over the waves, but they are exceedingly difficult to differentiate in flight from other very similar petrels. I certainly can't distinguish them.

The polar ice caps or the centre of the Sahara Desert, there are no places on earth devoid of wildlife. Certainly not urban areas; visit any industrial complex and you are almost certain to find a few small plants eking out a life in some cracked masonry or path side. Urban foxes will sometimes patrol through such places at night assuming they can get access, underneath a poorly maintained section of perimeter fence perhaps. If there is some dense scrub in a disused corner, foxes might even breed there too. Bomb-damaged houses, industrial sites and docks can provide a breeding habitat for birds such as Black Redstarts who have a penchant for buildings, stony places and mountain screes on the European continent where they are common. Broken masonry, stone ledges and piles of gravel can mimic the natural habitat they are most used to. But these little smoky-black birds with red tails were always rare in Britain. Until, that is, the Luftwaffe bombed London!

But of all the places closely associated with World War II, I had not expected to be listening to birds within the infamous confines of the Majdanek Concentration Camp on the edge of the city of Lublin in eastern Poland. Built originally for forced labour purposes, it became an extermination camp before it was liberated by the Russian army almost intact in July, 1944. Today, those parts of the camp away from the buildings have reverted to grassy meadows, a far cry from the bare mud and soil that covered every piece of ground here when the place was functioning as a living hell. Trying to adjust to the horrors of the place, my wife and I took a walk away from the wooden barracks and gas chambers to get some cool outdoor air. It was then that I heard it; a rough, grating sound muffled by the breeze. Then again from a different spot somewhere on the ground but so hard to know precisely where.

It took me a minute or two to realise what it was. This was a Corncrake, that furtive land bird a bit larger than a Quail, its rasping call the reason why it was given its onomatopoeic Latin name, *Crex*. Walking nearer to the high, once-electrified perimeter camp fence, I could hear several other Corncrakes calling from different parts of the flower-rich meadow grassland. We sat on a bit of discarded concrete and listened. One was calling so close to us, I thought we might see the skulking bird. Others seemed little further in all directions.

It was a surreal moment. In this place of indescribable past horror and suffering, these meadow birds had now found a place to conduct their courtship and breed. Maybe they had bred here when this land was a series of meadows before the Nazi's constructed their site of death. And now they were back, reclaiming their historic home, putting nature back where evil had reigned.

In the Swim of it

'Keep to this side in case there's a cow in here. If she comes out, you need to get on to those rocks at the side out of the way. You'll need to move quickly,' advised Phil in a quiet but firm voice. Wading through tangles of strap-shaped brown kelp we edged along the limpet-encrusted, rock at the side of the gloomy cave lit only by the lights on our helmets, the growling from deep inside becoming louder as the roar of the sea behind us subsided.

Counting Grey Seal pups on their inaccessible, boulder-strewn breeding beaches – even worse, in their dank and dark, musty sea caves – is a hazardous business. Phil Newman, who is in charge of the Skomer Marine Nature Reserve near Marloes in Pembrokeshire, is an old hand at it. He and his team spend much of each autumn locating pups on the rocky coast nearby as part of a Pembrokeshire-wide project monitoring their numbers and breeding success.

I'd arranged to spend a day with them in order to write a feature in *The Independent* about their work and this growing population of Grey Seals. And not by sitting on the sidelines, in some cosy office nearby perhaps, interviewing the people who do the fieldwork. I wanted to participate directly. And so here I was, having struggled and wriggled myself into a rubbery drysuit – more difficult than you might imagine – joining them in their inflatable boat. We set off from the small shingle cove at Martin's Haven and out around the stunningly attractive west Pembrokeshire coast adjacent to Skomer, an island known for its huge numbers of breeding seabirds.

Now I'm not much of a swimmer. While most people relate their swimming prowess in terms of 'lengths', I speak – usually in very hushed tones – about 'widths'. To be more honest, I am careful to refer to a 'width' in the singular and not 'widths'! I sometimes struggle to keep going with my rather basic breast stroke for as much as one width. So I needed that drysuit to keep me afloat when I scrambled over the side of the inflatable and dropped on to – rather than in to – the sea. With an excess of air trapped in the suit to keep me nice and buoyant, thereby more confident in the cold water, I looked like the original Michelin Man. But did I care? Not a bit.

And that's how I found myself, half swimming – kicking my legs to propel me along in a thankfully fairly calm sea – half scrambling over coarse sandpaper-surfaced rocks following Phil into the cave. We eventually approached its furthest reaches and, with our helmet lights shining ahead we could make out two white-furred seal pups lying motionless on a bed of steeply shelving pebbles. One lay on either side of the growling cow, her black globes of eyes fixed on us.

'The pup on the left, we've marked before,' said Phil, whispering to minimize any disturbance to the trio. 'You can just make out the yellow patch we sprayed on it, harmless paint so that we know which pups we've already counted. It must be about three weeks' old because it has patches of grey fur replacing its moulting white baby fur. We try to record numbers of live and dead pups from each breeding beach and cave so that we can track their breeding success year to year. The pup on the right is a new one, perhaps a week or so old, all white. We haven't seen this one before. It's not marked,' he adds. But the wellbeing of the seals, and our safety, come before absolute scientific rigour. Rather than risk more disturbance by trying to approach the unmarked pup or panic the cow (all 150 kg of her or more) into an ungainly dash into the sea, we retreat to our inflatable RIB moored out in the daylight.

A short ride in the boat around another headland and we go overboard again to swim into a small, pebble and boulder-strewn cove backed by cliffs. Scrambling to our feet and almost as ungainly on land as a seal out of water, the first pup we spy is dead. Its small, white and emaciated body is lying in a few feet of water off the beach. It was probably stillborn. Another, lying near the sheer cliff face at the back of the cove was a few days' old when a gull or raven tore open its stomach to pull out coils of pink intestine, its blood-stained white fur a reminder of the harshness of a Grey Seal's environment and its tough struggle of a life in what appears to us such a picturesque and enchanted landscape. The reality is rather different.

But there are plenty of living pups here too. With the southwesterlies blowing shoals of drizzle over the slimy, Bladderwrack-laden boulders, the first, barrel-rotund Grey Seal pup we spot is lying high up the pebble beach and appears almost surreal in its white baby fur, casually glancing up at us with its velvet-black eyes. Newborn, they weigh about 14 kg. Altogether we count six of them, scattered around the cove. They are surprisingly difficult to spot, lying motionless amongst pale grey rocks or hidden behind larger boulders. Each one gets a blast with a can of spray paint somewhere along its back; a yellow splodge on otherwise pristine white fur.

The mothers are in the sea just off the edge of the cove, lying in the shallow water and keeping an eye on what we're up to. Having given birth, they leave their newborn pups onshore and come in to feed them four to six times a day. Once they're a few days' old, they're perfectly safe left lying there for hours on end.

From the cliff-top path a couple of hundred feet above, these coves backed by steep, sometimes near-vertical rock faces in multiple shades of ochre and grey look as nature intended. Down amongst the giant boulders and lying on the beds of crunching pebbles, it's a slightly different picture. Here are the reminders of the jetsam of everyday shipping: plastic bottles, sheets of plywood, cardboard boxes and a lot else. Maybe some of it comes from holidaymakers a little further along the coast. But much of it clearly originates from further afield – hence the Cyrillic or Chinese writing on some of the containers – almost certainly dropped off ships that passed nearby. Like most people, I find this litter an affront to the natural beauty of the place. To the seals, of course, it matters not a jot. Unless, that is, an inquisitive pup – and these pups can be very inquisitive – ingests some discarded fishing hooks or gets tangled up in discarded fragments of fishing net or line. Then this jetsam can very easily be lethal.

On the far side of the damp cove, lying on a thick, oily-brown bed of kelp we spot a grey and white cow seal suckling her week old, blubbery, milk-surfeited pup. We walk, more correctly stumble, that way. 'We won't go too close; the cows can be very aggressive if they get cornered,' warns Phil. Mostly, if they're disturbed, a cow will waddle surprisingly fast down the beach and into the sea where they keep watch. But this one was different; she stayed put, snarling loudly when we get too close. And those teeth that can snap a large fish in half could easily snap off some human fingers.

On a sunny day with a calm sea, these coves look deceptively peaceful and idyllic. The rhythmic thuds of the surf mix with the haunting, human baby-like wail of young seal pups and the raucous, echoing calls of crow-like, black Choughs feeding on the yellow and blue flower-spattered clifftop turf. But stand here and witness a storm that tosses and smashes boulders into these cliffs as if they were toys and you might wonder how a podgy, metre long seal pup can survive at all. 'Every year,' says Phil, 'about one in five pups die before they are weaned. Some of that's natural mortality and some due to predators and storms. Once they are old enough to go to sea and fend for themselves, we don't know how many more die; it depends on the weather conditions and food availability.'

About 1300 pups are born around the Pembrokeshire coast each season, 40% of them in sea caves and 60% on inaccessible shingle beaches like the ones we struggled on to. The seals have learnt to avoid pupping on most beaches that people can get access to. During the autumn breeding season peak when I joined them, the team were at a heightened pitch of anxiety. Phocine distemper virus (PDV), a natural seal disease something like a virulent influenza outbreak in humans, had spread to the UK from Scandinavia. It was already decimating Common Seals in The Wash on the east of England; the Common is a smaller species than the Grey, and seemingly more susceptible to PDV. Tests on the few Greys found dead off the Welsh coast had not yet found the virus. On Skomer Island, a mile offshore from where we were, Grey Seal numbers have been monitored for more than a quarter century – one of the longest such studies in the world – and pup numbers are increasing by about 10% per annum. There are some apparently suitable, inaccessible beaches hardly used by seals for breeding unless, that is, they avoid these sites for reasons we don't understand. So, potentially, their numbers might increase even further.

Choosing a suitable cave or breeding beach must be a tricky business. There has to be enough shingle left dry for the young pups above any normal high tide, otherwise newborn pups will be carried out to sea and drown. And the distance from the sea at low tide to the top end of the rocky cove where many of the pups lie can't be too great or the fasting cows will use up too much energy struggling up and down to feed them.

That first month for the pup, mostly left alone, is a crucial time. While they might only be susceptible to predators such as ravens or gulls while still a day or two old, they have no protection against storm battering for that vital first month. They cannot swim until they are at least a month old so entering the sea is certain death. Pups need to treble their birth weight in their first few weeks. So they need every feed going. After that, they have to fend for themselves out at sea. Outside the breeding season, this population of Greys – numbering around 5,000 and the southernmost in Europe – swim far out to sea; north towards the Isle of Man, west to the Irish coast and south maybe to Cornwall and edging out into the vast Atlantic Ocean.

Getting close to a week old, milk-surfeited white pup with its doe eyes, it is all too easy to assume that they are as cuddly as they look. But as soon as Phil and I get too close, this cuteness immediately proves illusory. The docile pup in front of us transforms itself as it lurches forward, growling and gurgling aggressively, its jaw wide open, globules of saliva dripping between its needle-sharp teeth. No predator would have an easy time of it with one of these maritime Rottweilers. We step back a little.

From the cliff path above these coves, it's natural for many people to assume, wrongly, that motionless pups lying alone, flippers-up amongst the boulders are ill or maybe even dead. 'We get lots of phone calls from concerned members of the public,' says Phil. 'The pups sleep or lie motionless most of the time. The cows come ashore to suckle them only a few times a day. So they just lie there for hours on end all on their own. It's good that people are concerned about them. But disturbance is still a concern. We need people to make themselves inconspicuous and to be quiet on the clifftops above the breeding beaches. Dogs need to be kept under control. Otherwise, the lactating cows will stay in the sea and the pups will miss feeds. And that could easily weaken them,' he adds.

Spotting seal pups from the clifftops high above their breeding coves isn't as easy as it might seem. I've done it many times and binoculars always prove essential.

The motionless pups blend in with the gently sloping canvas of mud grey, burnt red and quartz-white pebbles, rocks and giant boulders way down below. You may at first only spot one or two pups. But scan carefully and I'll guarantee you'll find several more. Watching a cove from above for a couple of hours is an interesting and very relaxing experience. Eventually, you'll spot a 300 kg potential milk tanker lumbering very slowly from the sea shallows on to the shingle. Struggling up the shelving beach, she takes several minutes to reach her 'crying' pup. The crying stops as the pup nuzzles into its mother's side to get at a nipple. Warm, thick, fat-rich milk at last!

The first time I walked this part of the coastal path in autumn, the sounds echoing around the cliff amphitheatres below were incredibly eerie, almost alarming. They take some getting used to. An unmistakeable, almost human baby cry from the lounging pups mixes with the rhythmical thud of waves breaking on the stony shore. It's a disconcerting sound; a cry needing to be answered; an urgent appeal for food. It sets off what I can only describe as rather visceral alarm bells; little wonder that many people don't realise that the crying pup is perfectly ok. It's merely hoping for a milk top-up and alerting its mother.

Tourists often walk the coastal path above these rocky headlands especially to watch and listen to the sounds and events in these open-plan, maritime maternity wards. Today the Pembrokeshire Coastal Path is a key part of the Wales Coast Path – all 1,400 km of it – and Wales (the country of my birth) is the first country in the world to have a signposted footpath around its whole national boundary. It's a fantastic asset. Tourist boat trips have burgeoned over the last couple of decades as more people visit this part of Wales to spot an array of sea wildlife: dolphins, seabirds like Puffins and Gannets and, of course, these Grey Seals. The tourist boats stick to an agreed code of conduct so that they cause little or no disturbance and, so far, the arrangements seem to be working well.

Competition with fishermen, though, could become a much more serious problem. Some of the local fishermen, making a living from their catches of lobster, crab, rays and bass complain that they are now 'more endangered than seals'. I can understand their concern; the seals have a somewhat similar fishy diet in mind! Similar, yes, but far from identical because research has found that, overall, only a few percent of a seal's diet consists of commercially important fish while perhaps 60% of it consists of tiny sand eels. But try telling that to a fisherman. They will quickly retort that seals frequently try to feed out of their fishing nets after anything that's easy to catch. They are even sometimes congregating around a fishing boat before any fishing begins. And although its legal with a special licence for fishermen to kill seals in the vicinity of nets to protect a fishery outside the seal breeding season, most fishermen hereabouts tolerate them, at least at present. After all, they know that any calls for a cull of Pembrokeshire's Grey Seals would be certain to provoke a huge public outcry and damage its all-important tourist industry.

Tourism and fishing aside, it has always seemed to me that the Grey Seals of west Wales are arguably some of the most vulnerable anywhere. They breed cheek-by-jowl with one of the busiest oil ports – Milford Haven – in Europe. The *Sea Empress*' huge leak of deadly oil (see Chapter 28) only missed them in 1996 because the tanker grounded near the shore in February when the seals were well away from their breeding beaches out at sea. Had the *Sea Empress* run aground in September or October, the impact on these magnificent and endearing mammals would have been too awful to contemplate.

As I left Martin's Haven after my day with Phil Newman, the ominous bulk of an oil tanker moored a few miles away out in the bay was just visible through the descending grey haze of drizzle.

The Body Eaters

It wasn't long before the metronome-like rhythm of the prayer chanting, led by the two white-robed priests in their tall hats, became soporific in the leaden heat of the late afternoon. A Nassesalar – a corpse bearer – also dressed in a white cotton tunic, trousers and cap sat reverently at the side of the dead man on the cool stone floor. The sacred dog, a small tan and white mongrel, was led in, sniffed around the body to check that there was no life remaining, and was led out again in a ritual as important to the Parsis – the followers of Zoroastrianism, one of the world's oldest religions – as what would follow later.

Outside the low, whitewashed building occupied by the family and close friends of the old man who had died the previous night, gardeners in their mud-brown uniforms went about their everyday business, watering exotic shrubs and scarlet-flowering climbers while the heady aroma of cypress trees hung heavy in the air. To me, hardly used to such events, it all seemed rather surreal.

I had come to Mumbai to research a feature for *The Telegraph Magazine* about the enormous die-off of nearly all the vultures across India and its adjacent countries. It had been totally unexpected. What had caused it was a common and very cheap painkiller, diclofenac (marketed usually as Voltarol for human use), administered to cattle and water buffalo – the most abundant livestock in India – to treat lameness and mastitis. What no one could have predicted was that many species of vulture are particularly sensitive to the drug; it gives them severe gout and they die, almost certainly – and ironically – in pain due to kidney failure. Before diclofenac was marketed, there were an estimated 40 million of the most common species of vulture, the Oriental White-backed Vulture, in India alone. Now it's hard to find one.

The link between the cattle and buffalo, the painkiller and vultures was simple enough. In India and adjacent countries, whenever a cow or water buffalo dies, they are left for vultures to eat. Constantly soaring in the sky on the lookout for some carrion to devour, a pack of a hundred or so would reduce the dead beast to bones in less than an hour. It was free, there was no fuss and because disease didn't have a chance to spread courtesy of flies, rats or other vectors, it was hygienic. The farmer only had the bones to get rid of. No vultures equals no cattle corpse consumption. And, in a hot and often humid climate, that means decomposing cattle or water buffalo corpses attract a plethora of rats, feral dogs (that often here carry rabies) and diseases ranging from plague to typhus. In recent years, the feral dog population in India has burgeoned and become a widespread problem; some nasty diseases have almost certainly increased too, although documentation is shambolic.

So what, you might well be thinking, does this have to do with attending a Parsi funeral as I was invited to do?

Indian farmers weren't the only people to make use of the ability of vultures to eat bodies rapidly and, therefore, hygienically. The Parsis – adherents of Zoroastrianism founded in what is now Iran in the 6th century – believe that their dead must not pollute air, water or land. And while Parsis in other parts of the world do things differently, their largest single community, in Mumbai, has always used vultures to consume their dead. The process became ritualised at the so-called Towers of Silence at Malabar Hill in central Mumbai, a peaceful, wooded area of land, and the largest green lung in this overcrowded, noisy, sprawling and – too often – squalid city.

To understand the traditional process of dealing with the Parsi dead in Mumbai, my Parsi hosts suggested I go and talk to a draper who makes traditional Parsi clothes not far from Malabar Hill. I find Noshir Mulla in his small shop, a man bursting with energy who is more than keen to describe for me what happens – more correctly, what used to happen – at the squat stone towers hidden away in the woodland. He remembers his grandmother's funeral in 1957 as if it had just taken place. Tears well up in his dark eyes as he recalls the occasion.

'I was 14 then and asking lots of questions,' he says. 'When the Nassesalars carried her body on the bier and we walked behind in procession, there were many vultures in the air. They seemed to follow us to the tower, landing on the stone parapet around its edge. There must have been 70 or more. Once the Nassesalars had left her body on the tower, they clapped their hands. It was the sign for the vultures to descend to gorge themselves. They took less than an hour. They had done their work perfectly according to our Parsi tradition,' he added.

Exactly the same funeral ritual has taken place at Mumbai's Towers of Silence, sometimes as many as three or four times a day, almost every day since. It is a rare example of the interdependence of birds and people; the Parsis are dependent on the vultures to quickly, and hygienically, dispose of their dead and the vultures are reliant on an easy – and regular – meal. Both the vultures and the Parsis gain.

The day I attended the Parsi funeral, Black Kites swirled high above, and the raucous, grating calls of scraggy black House Crows were interrupted by the occasional shriek of a parakeet in the lush gardens. After perhaps half an hour, the prayers were over. The priests came out into the scorching sun, removed their hats and chatted to the deceased man's family. It was the cue for the mourners to file slowly past his body, the last time for the family to see him. When they had finished, the body, covered entirely now by a white sheet and raised on a metal bier at shoulder height by the four Nassesalars – one at each corner – was taken down the steps and out into the blaze of the late afternoon sun.

As I watch, I'm struck by how dignified this all is. No pomp and circumstance. No elaborate dress code. No music. And it's never any different whether the dead person comes from a rich background or a poor one. Only Parsis can join the procession to the open-topped towers. And when they reach the tower allocated for their particular loved one, they can go no further. Only the Nassesalars can enter inside to lay the body, face upward and naked, on the stone surface of the tower top. The only time these Parsis will ever enter the tower, they will already be dead.

But what Noshir Mulla described to me hasn't been possible here for some years. All of Malabar Hill's vultures, just like their millions sub-continent wide, have died off. For over a decade there has not been a single vulture at Malabar Hill to consume the Parsi dead. They have disappeared, too, from their nesting colonies outside Mumbai from where they used to fly in every morning.

In ancient Persia where the religion was founded, pre-Islam, it was almost certainly the custom to leave dead bodies untended on some open ground where they would be eaten rapidly by wolves, jackals and vultures. The alternatives were impractical anyway. Presumably, wood for funeral pyres would have been scarce. Rivers would have been seasonal. And the often arid, rocky ground would not have lent itself to easy burial. In India, where most Parsis settled in the 8th century having been ousted from Persia, the process became ritualised at stone towers built specially for the purpose of encouraging vultures to consume their dead quickly. After all, vultures were then incredibly abundant, perfect for the form of body disposal central to their faith. Nor would the vultures have needed much encouragement to stay around. Because, in Mumbai, the Parsi community is slowly depleting as its population ages and because it doesn't usually accept converts to the faith. You have to be born a Parsi. And not enough are being born; up to 900 of them die annually in the city.

When vultures were abundant at the towers, after each laying of a body its flesh would have been consumed within an hour, leaving the skeleton to desiccate in the hot sun. After a few weeks the corpse bearers would return to sweep the brittle, powdering bones into the tower's central pit where they would join those of thousands of other Parsis. The process was rapid, hygienic and non-polluting. Earth, air and water had not been defiled; it offered natural food to nature's scavengers; it produced no false sentimentality, no fuss, no monuments, no epitaphs, no urns … and it was cost-free. It couldn't have fitted their traditions better.

I had come to Mumbai to try and understand the implications of the loss of India's vultures and it soon became obvious to me that its impact on the Parsi community was not only huge but divisive. Mumbai's nearly 46,000 Parsis – their largest single community in the world – still carry on the Zoroastrian tradition of laying out their dead on the towers. But they were now relying on the sun's heat to desiccate the corpses because the only other carrion eaters still around – Black Kites and House Crows – were taking far too long to devour the bodies. And this lingering was producing odours, anathema to Parsis.

I talked to Khojeste Mistree, a leading Parsi academic of Iranian descent living in Mumbai. 'When the vultures disappeared, I suggested that we should construct a large netted aviary around one or more of the towers. With the necessary licences to capture a few remaining birds we would have bred vultures there and kept them on site so that our traditional practices could continue,' he said. 'But the Bombay Parsi Punchayet [their ruling body] eventually turned down the idea because of concerns that diclofenac residues in human bodies might kill the vultures. It's very disappointing.'

Vulture experts I talked to mostly agree that although diclofenac breaks down within days in any animal, further breakdown stops at death. So livestock or humans given the drug shortly before death to relieve pain might retain enough in their vital organs to kill vultures. And that's a risk if vultures were reintroduced and kept here because diclofenac (as Voltarol) is still marketed for human use even though it has been banned now for animal treatment in India and its neighbouring countries.

The Punchayet has a novel – and controversial – solution: solar reflectors installed on three of the four towers concentrate the sun's heat on the bodies in order to desiccate them more rapidly so that there is no smell of slow decomposition. But Mumbai's Parsi community is divided. Some think the solar reflectors are a practical response to the fix they're in. Others like Mistree disagree. 'I contend that the bodies must burn, contrary to our beliefs,' he told me. 'They get heated to 125°C. It's like a grill. It's heretical. It's so hot that the crows and kites can't even land there until sundown. Then in the monsoon months, of course, the reflectors don't work at all. Allowing kites and crows to eat the bodies, albeit much more slowly than vultures, would be acceptable. Most of the priests agree with me but their views have been marginalised. It is so wrong.'

To get another view I spent a morning on Malabar Hill with Dr Viraf Kapadia, a Mumbai Parsi and homeopath. 'Most Parsis are concerned that using the reflectors isn't appropriate but they feel it's inevitable,' he explains. 'They want the bodies to dry rapidly to eliminate any decomposition odours that they fear if slow consumption by kites and crows is the only alternative.'

The massive loss of millions of vultures has dismayed conservationists. Luckily, a few of each rapidly declining species were captured in order to breed from them in purpose-built aviaries, mostly in India, Nepal and Pakistan. This captive breeding is going well and the first releases of vultures back into the wild are expected soon providing large areas of land can be guaranteed to have no traces of diclofenac in any water buffalo or cattle corpses. But it is unlikely that these scavengers, which everyone took for granted for centuries, will ever again become commonplace. They haven't gone the way of the infamous Dodo, but it has been a close-run thing and their decline has been even more rapid than the Dodo's.

No one, though, had given any thought to the implications of the vultures' disappearance on the Parsi community, not even the Parsis themselves, until they had gone. And their loss has precipitated what might well become a rethink of their long-held traditions. Will it ever again be possible to dispose of their dead as they had for millennia? Is it anyway feasible to do so within a large and sprawling urban conurbation? And do they have to consider whether – like some Parsis in other parts of the world – they adapt their traditions and consider burying their dead as a more practical alternative?

Vultures aren't the most attractive birds to look at and they don't have many admirers. But they do perform a free, efficient and hygienic disposal service in many tropical and subtropical countries around the world, a service that many developing countries cannot replicate in their absence, with huge implications for limiting disease spread. Without them, rat, feral dog and insect-borne diseases affecting humans are very likely to proliferate. And who would have guessed that the demise of these scavengers would have had such a profound impact on one of the world's very oldest religions?

The Bird that Guides

I can't blame Google. Type the words 'bird guide' or 'bird guiding' into its search facility and up come reams of wildlife holiday companies and other guided birdwatching holidays. But something else appears too, though maybe not until the second or third page. Honeyguides.

I had known a little about these unusual birds for years – that they can guide people to wild bee nests – but that was about all. When I was researching my book, *Life with Birds: A Story of Mutual Exploitation* (Whittles, 2011), I needed to tell the whole story because they are arguably the only birds in the world that do guide people to a food resource, one that benefits them (because, very unusually, they eat bee honeycomb) and the person it leads because us humans have a rather soft spot for honey.

There is one other bird in the world that, it is claimed, will act as a guide: the Northern Raven. Found across the northern half of the globe throughout Europe, northern Asia, the USA and Canada as well as the even more northerly Arctic area, ravens are very successful – and very intelligent – birds. What is undisputed is that the brains of ravens count among the largest of any bird species and that they display considerable ability in problem solving, as well as other cognitive processes such as imitation and insight. A biologist, Bernd Heinrich at the University of Vermont in the USA, has catalogued the evidence to support the notion that ravens sometimes guide hunters. After all, the birds are as keen to get to a caribou kill as the hunter that has just shot one. Butchered on the spot, the entrails are usually dumped for ravens to feed on. In his book *Mind of the Raven* (Harper Perennial, 2006) he suggests that ravens in the Arctic signal to the hunters – by tucking in one wing momentarily as they fly or by making a certain call – to indicate that prey such as caribou are nearby. If the signalling raven then flies off in a certain direction, the hunters might rightly presume that the animals are that way. He doesn't have objective proof but, if Heinrich is right, and his idea is based on anecdotes from Inuit hunters on ice-bound Baffin Island in the Arctic between Greenland and the very north of Canada, then both the ravens and the hunters gain. Heinrich writes:

> Abe Okpik, an elderly man who was no longer a hunter … later had told me that when out on the land hunting caribou, or out on the ice hunting polar bear, a hunter seeing a raven fly over used to look up and call its name loudly three times: 'Tulugaq, tulugaq, tulugaq'. Having the bird's attention, he would then yell to it, telling it to tumble out of the sky in the direction of the prey. If the raven gave its gong-like call three times in succession, then the hunters went in that direction. 'They believed in the raven strongly, and followed it,' said Okpik. 'And after they killed the caribou or the bear, they always left the raven the choicest tidbits of meat as a reward.'

Far-fetched? Don't believe it? I wasn't sure either. Until, that is, I spent time with a Kenyan Dorobo tribesman who frequently uses honeyguides to get to wild bee nests.

I had made contact with Luca Borghesio, an Italian biologist who was researching how subtle changes to a huge, isolated and not well known forest in the Mathews Range of Central Kenya was affecting its bird population. Working with him was a Dorobo tribesman called Robert Lentaaya who had considerable experience of using honeyguides. And, in a series of emails, Luca passed on to me a considerable amount of first-hand information from Lentaaya, including some experience never before recorded. But more of that later! I used a great deal of what Robert Lentaaya told me via Luca in my book, *Life With Birds*.

In the partly forested hill country a few hundred kilometres north of Kenya's capital Nairobi, the Ndorobo people have retained much of their hunting and hunter-gatherer culture. Moved out of their traditional forest environment in the 1970s to try and force them to settle and become cattle farmers like their Samburu neighbours, many have clung to living closely with the wildlife they have always exploited sustainably.

Robert, a Ndorobo with a family to support, lives in the Karissia Hills about 300 km north of Nairobi. Like all Dorobo, he isn't at all sure when he was born (time is not important) but he knows precisely in which forest cave he was born because a sense of place is what matters. So Robert isn't able to say precisely how old he is but he appears to be in his forties. His animal tracking skills, his knowledge of edible plants and his ability to identify a wide range of forest creatures is second to none. And like many Dorobo people, he frequently makes use of honeyguides – rather drab, thrush-sized, olive-green and brown birds – to guide him to bee nests.

My opportunity to participate in this amazing bird/human partnership came about a couple of years later. Luca had invited me to their summer camp in the

Mathews forests; Robert Lentaaya was to be there too. I spent ten days with them camping in one of the most isolated locations – apart from the Sahara – I've ever camped in.

A couple of days into my forest visit and I had staggered back to the campsite after a morning's hard walking (accompanied, as always away from camp, by two of our Samburu helpers, one of them armed in case we encountered anything dangerous such as African Wild Cattle). Lentaaya, as everyone referred to him (rather than his Christian name), was agitated. 'Ah, Malcolm, it is a pity you were not here because a honeyguide came to the camp and stayed all morning calling to me. But I told him we could not go with him until you were back. And now he has gone. We will go to see if we can find him,' he said.

So began one of the more surreal half hours I have experienced. We traipsed around the forest just behind our camp with Lentaaya talking loudly and shouting in all directions in his Dorobo language. He explained to me that he was asking the honeyguide for forgiveness; we were apologising for not helping him, for making him stay around the camp when he wanted to lead us. Unfortunately, the appeals didn't work. This honeyguide had clearly taken the huff. After half an hour of trying to coax him back, Lentaaya gave up.

We were to wait another couple of days before we would encounter another. It happened as a small group of us were well away from camp sitting down for a rest on some boulders at the side of the little Ngeng River. The only sound I could hear was from the water tumbling over a jumble of stones. Lentaaya, with his much more acute hearing, sensed a very different sound.

'Malcolm, a honeyguide; look up there in that tree'. And just a couple of metres above us, there it was. Clearly agitated, the bird was hopping excitedly from one twig to another, flicking its white-edged tail and calling incessantly, a persistent, double call to attract attention, a harsh, rattling chatter of a noise. It is the sort of noise, close-by, that's hard to ignore. Suddenly, it was all I could hear; the noise of the stream had somehow faded out of my senses. We didn't delay. We were up and off; the honeyguide led, all the while chattering and flicking; flitting ahead from branch to branch, past trees encased in vine stems and other climbers. And throughout, Lentaaya was calling back to the bird, keeping in touch with it as it led the way.

Not once did we lose sight of the honeyguide. And not once did we fail to hear it call. Never more than 10 m or so ahead of us, this bird had no intention of losing us amongst the trees and shrubs en route to the bee nest I presumed it needed us to open. Lentaaya led with me in tow crunching through the brown leaf litter for maybe 300 m until we reached a big forest tree, perhaps 30 m high. It was certainly very tall.

The honeyguide was a bit less agitated; it had changed its call – softer in tone and much less persistent – and the bird stayed put on low branches next to this formidable tree. No longer was it flashing its white tail feathers; it had reached its destination … and seemingly ours. Lentaaya's responses became muted, and from high in the tree canopy above us we could hear the loud hum of wild bees like a not-too-distant moped at full throttle. Unlike a moped, this hum sounded distinctly vicious.

But the huge tree with its smooth vertical trunk was impossible to climb without ropes and other equipment. Lentaaya was clearly disappointed. My response was more mixed; I was desperate to experience a bee nest being opened and the honeyguide being given some honeycomb as its 'reward' but I have to admit to some fear of a horde of aggressive wild bees descending in my direction.

Our honeyguide, though, was much more single-minded. It was very obviously irritated at our ineptitude. Big style! As we walked away reluctantly, Lentaaya talking to it all the while, it flew from branch to branch just above our heads, calling wildly and incessantly, flicking its wings and tail again, trying its level best to entice us back to the bees. We had the audacity to leave this clever bird in the lurch; we were walking away and nothing Lentaaya said to it – and he talked to it all the time – was going to soften the blow. The honeyguide followed us, keeping up its noisy appeal until we had walked more than 50 m away. And we could still hear it chattering in the distance as we headed slowly back to camp. I felt we had let it down.

The honeyguide/human relationship has probably been in existence for thousands of years, though its origins are a mystery. And there is an awful lot that isn't well known about this unusual family of birds. There are 17 different species, all but two of them found in Africa south of the Sahara. The other two occur in Southern Asia south of the Himalayas. Some of the African honeyguides that live only in forests are so rarely seen, even though they might not be uncommon, that very little is known about them. And two of the species were only discovered during the last 50 years. The best known is the Greater Honeyguide, the one we had been following; a brown, black and dirty cream colour, similar to a very large sparrow, and with the male possessing a slightly chubby pink beak. Most experts believe that this is the only honeyguide known to guide people to a bee's nest. Lentaaya's day-to-day experience, though, is very different. He told me that while every Samburu knows about the *lodokotuk* (Greater Honeyguide) and its guiding behaviour, only Dorobo people can use other honeyguides, the *silasili* (Scaly-throated Honeyguide) and the *airiguti* (Lesser Honeyguide) as they are known to the Samburu.

'When we meet a *giochoroi* [the general Samburu name for all honeyguides] the Dorobo start singing a particular song to invite the bird to show them the way to the nearest bee nest. We have a different song for each species. The song for the *lodokotuk* is a joke that asks the bird to lead us to the bees and requests it not to show the way to other Dorobos. The song for the *silasili* and the *airiguti* refers to them as a girl because their voices are softer than that of the *lodokotuk*,' he said. It is this differentiation between the responses used by the Dorobo – depending on which species of honeyguide turns up – that I can't find any mention of in the scientific literature. 'But,' Lentaaya added, 'the *lodokotuk* is the best guide. The other two we use but they are not as accurate because they don't take us close to the bee's nest entrance and because they are less reliable at guiding. I collect about ten litres of honey in a year and sell it for about 2000 Kenyan shillings [£15] so I can pay for school fees for my children.'

What has long been established is that honeyguides are always attracted by human sounds, whether it is talking, chopping wood, cooking or something else. At a campsite they will often come very close, inspecting the tents and other equipment. They are certainly extremely curious birds.

But why, you might reasonably ask, does a honeyguide need people to break into the bee's nest in the first place? It is because they don't have large, strong beaks capable of doing the job themselves and because, in spite of having thickened skin, presumably to give them some protection, they are still vulnerable to being stung. Often, too, the bee's nest is in an awkward spot; a cleft in some rocks for instance which is hard enough for a person to get access to and to which a honeyguide stands no chance of breaking in alone. Honeyguides have been seen in the cool early morning scraping bits of honeycomb at a nest they can partly access, presumably only then when the bees are still rather cool and dopey. But they have sometimes been found dead, too, and always close to a bee's nest, killed by an overwhelming bout of bee stings. Meddling with wild bees can be a dangerous business.

So why eat bee honeycomb in the first place? For some unknown reason, honeyguides are particularly keen on a meal of wax and they are some of the few birds in the world that can digest it. They do eat other things, mainly spiders and a wide range of insects, including scale insects which have a waxy covering, as well as some fruits like figs. And when they gorge on honeycomb they are, of course, also eating quite a lot of bee eggs and grubs at the same time.

Dr Hussein Isack, an ornithologist at the National Museum of Kenya, Nairobi, is a honeyguide expert. He told me about his three-year research in northern Kenya in the mid-1980s where he found that 96% of wild honeybee nests were accessible to the birds only after people had opened them up first. So these birds have a lot to gain from their human relationship. He also found that tribesmen took an average of nearly nine hours to find a bee's nest without any help from the birds but just over three hours when guided. And that was a conservative estimate of the time difference because it didn't include days on which no nest was found, something that was rare indeed when the birds were doing the guiding.

This close inter-relationship between birds and people has probably been in existence for thousands of years. There are written accounts of it in the 17th century and early religious missionaries in Africa were surprised by birds that came to their altars and took pieces of wax from their beeswax candles. In Asia, 3rd century Chinese scribes wrote of 'little birds of the wax combs' based on reports about the Yellow-rumped Honeyguide of the Himalayas, though they are not known to guide.

So how might their guiding habits have begun? There have been suggestions that the honeyguide/human link-up derived from a similar relationship between honeyguides and Ratels (Honey Badgers), attractive grey and black badgers common in much of Southern Africa. Very fierce mammals, Ratels can easily kill snakes, even venomous ones, amongst other animals. But they also have a liking for beehives and wild bee nests. Many experts doubt the badger/honeyguides mutualism because there are few or no confirmed sightings, at least not confirmed by Western eyes! Robert Lentaaya, though, is quite sure; he told me that he has seen a Greater Honeyguide leading a Ratel on several occasions. And I most certainly have no reason to disbelieve him.

A couple of days before I was due to leave the Mathews Range, another honeyguide made a chattering appearance very close to our campsite. And Lentaaya started talking to it, calling me over at the same time. We were off! This time I could more easily see the flicking tail as we walked fast under the forest trees and around some patches of impenetrable scrub. We even had to cross the Ngeng River to follow it, hopping from boulder to boulder but never losing contact with our guide. The bird very obviously slowed down at times to wait for us to catch up. Another couple of hundred metres, up a steep, wooded slope on the far side of the river and the chattering eased, the bird stayed in one spot and the characteristically loud hum of a colony of bees began to dominate the stillness. We spotted their nest only a metre or so above the ground on a rocky outcrop under the forest canopy. And, as Lentaaya cut a large branch from a nearby tree and trimmed it with his knife to make a sturdy straight pole, the honeyguide watched from some low branches just above us.

But first, the vital task of pacifying the bees. Lentaaya gathered together a large bunch of twigs and dry vegetation, tied it into a torch-shaped bundle, lit the end of it with a lighter he carried and blew out the flame. Carrying the smoking firebrand to the rock cleft where the bees were, he wafted it to and fro, subduing them just as a commercial beekeeper would. The humming quietened.

Then it was time for more physical action. He quickly jammed the pole into the nest entrance between pieces of rock, prised it suddenly to one side and, with an audible crack, the rock split open to reveal a cloud of highly agitated bees. I stepped back, fearful of stings. Lentaaya, smoking firebrand in hand and seemingly oblivious to any stinging, thrust it into the nest, drugging the bees quicker than I dared imagine was possible.

Quickly, he grabbed most of the honeycomb, depositing it in a bag he had carried with him. A small piece he threw on the ground nearby, and off we went. By now the bees had recovered; they were distinctly agitated once again, the smoke drugging rapidly wearing off. Their collective hum had become a threateningly loud drum-roll, and I for one was relieved that retreat was the distinctly more sensible form of valour. A little distance away we stopped to look back at the bee nest site. With binoculars we could see the honeyguide on the ground pecking away at its piece of honeycomb; silent now as it ate its fill of the food. The only sound was that of the highly agitated bees, their nest largely destroyed and a rebuilding or relocating task in store for them. No wonder they were buzzing loudly.

It had been an amazing experience; a huge privilege accompanying Lentaaya. Within a generation, though, this astounding and unique relationship between honeyguides and people might well be confined to history and story-telling. Few people, even among the Dorobo, now bother to follow the birds to honeycombs because many people now raise bees in hives at home. As people the world over become more and more distanced from a way of life in which nature is part of their everyday existence, such close relationships will become rarer still. Most will die out.

The birds themselves, too, might well decline as more and more woodland is felled for fuelwood and not enough is planted to replace it, although the best guider, the Greater Honeyguide, is a bird not of forest as much as more open ground with scattered trees. Nevertheless, trees are essential for these birds. They are often the location for the bee nests they crave. And older trees with rot holes and other cavities are the breeding places for barbets, starlings and woodpeckers in whose nests honeyguides lay their eggs, cuckoo-like, and let these foster families do all the hard work of raising their young for them.

No parental responsibilities, helpers to get much of their food, and lots of honey to eat into the bargain. Maybe it's not a bad life being a honeyguide after all.

A Rocky Road for Saharan Art

I must admit that it was a very far cry from a normal art gallery. In the scorching desert heat, the sandy wadi behind me as dry as dust and the nearby sun-drenched rocks too hot to touch, I'm admiring walls covered in artistic images of crocodiles, giraffes, elephants, herds of antelope and hunters giving chase with spears and clubs. It's a pretty unlikely location for any of these images. Because here in Libya's Akakus Mountains (the Jebel Akakus) in the very centre of the Sahara Desert there is no chance of a giraffe surviving in today's arid conditions. And there are no streams for many hundreds of kilometres that could possibly nurture a crocodile or encourage a hunter to lie in wait for large game to kill.

Here on sun-shaded rock faces, while they probably took a bit of a rest from their everyday work, one-time local inhabitants decided to make a few drawings. They left no written records, but their legacy of vibrant rock drawings and carvings provides evidence of the savannah, marshes and rivers that once occupied today's desert. Some are in outline only. Others are coloured. There are amazing images of crocodiles, giraffes, elephants, herds of antelope, and of hunters giving chase. There are people herding domesticated livestock, riding in chariots, of adults and children. Of a couple holding hands as if attending some ritual. Even of a young woman having her hair combed by another, ready for her wedding perhaps.

Incredible though it seems in today's Sahara – at over 9 million km², by far the largest of the world's deserts – all of these animals, and others, were once its common inhabitants. And not really that long ago either. These exquisite images date from a time, between 8000 and 5000 BC when the Sahara was not a desert but a lush, fertile land capable of supporting a vibrant and extensive human community more akin to the savannahs of Africa today. It wasn't the enormous arid barrier that migrating birds now have to endure flying over twice a year. When the Sahara was more akin to a fertile grassland dotted with trees and watered by streams and rivers, most migrating birds would have been able to stop and feed, fuelling up for the remainder of their enormous journey. Today, that's virtually impossible.

But this incredible resource of rock art, distributed across about 1,300 scattered rocky sites, is not solely a unique record of early life in the Sahara. It is also a documentation of a past era of climate change and its human impacts having a resonance for life on our planet today.

Some years before the rather optimistically named Arab Spring delivered chaos and armed conflict amongst a myriad competing factions to post-Gaddafi Libya, I was with a group from the 153 Club (a club for enthusiasts and travellers within the Sahara) doing a 750 km minibus drive from Tripoli to Sabha in the southwest of Libya. From there we transferred to four Toyota 4WDs with Arab drivers and our Libyan guide, Aref Salim, who had a special knowledge of these artistic artefacts.

Also with us on the minibus to Sabha, but no further, was an armed, plain clothes guard supplied compulsorily by the Libyan police. Dressed in casuals, he spent much of his time asleep, playing games on his mobile phone or chatting up one or two of the women in our group. Whatever function he was with us to perform, his presence was obligatory. It seemed to consist of bobbing up and down excitedly every time we encountered a police roadside checkpoint (there are many, so much bobbing) while our driver handed the friendly police a copy of our itinerary and, maybe, some cash to oil the wheels of travel and to help the police who otherwise here scratch a living. Whatever his function, the roadblocks proved no barrier to our progress.

Today's Jebel Akakus is an arid scene of dark, unvegetated, rocky mountains interspersed with gravel plains; terracotta-coloured, sandy wadis with a scatter of shrubs; and massive, wind-carved dunes in which very few people are today able to eke out a difficult and nomadic existence based on grazing a few goats. The remaining desert inhabitants, the Tuareg – a few families of which are still semi-nomadic here – are incredibly proud of the rock drawings which they treat as a precious inheritance handed down to them by their forebears.

Arid and inhospitable, with summer temperatures approaching 50°C and an annual rainfall so low that it all but defies measurement, the Jebel Akakus – eroded sandstone mountains in the far southwest corner of Libya – is a demanding environment today. But it is most certainly a stunning place. Tolkien-like sandstone pillars, arches, chasms and monster-cut shapes eroded by sandstorms crouch high over wide wadis, the pancake-flat valleys of pale terracotta sand – where water flows if it ever rains – with their scatter of viciously thorny acacias, scrubby bushes and ground-creeping Wild Gourds which tantalisingly resemble melons but are dry and inedible.

As you might imagine, in spite of the Tuareg having been very familiar for generations with these drawings and carvings, they were 'discovered' – as it's always expressed – by Western explorers, in this case two German explorers, Heinrich Barth and Gustav Nachtigal, in the late 19th century. To add insult to injury, these two gentlemen were firmly of the view that only Europeans – and not 'barbarians' as they so indelicately put it at the time – could have drawn them! It wasn't until 1955 that this injustice was put right by Professor Fabrizio Mori, a palaeoethnologist at Rome University who began the first systematic studies of the drawings.

Most experts agree that the paintings were done using crude brushes made of feathers or animal hair or by using a stick, a bone spatula, or just fingers. The outlines are thought to have been done first, then coloured in. Some are realistically proportioned, others not. Most of the drawings are red in colour. To make the 'paint', it's thought that the artists ground and burnt iron-rich rock, then mixed this with a binder such as egg white, milk, perhaps urine, animal fat or blood. By serendipity, it's these binders that give the drawings their longevity. The much fewer white-coloured drawings that we saw used some mix of white clay or rock, perhaps with vegetable dyes and binders such as egg albumen.

The carved drawings in the rock must have taken far more effort. Cut with stone tools, chipped and smoothed, they are realistic and often incredibly life-like images of wild cattle, elephants, giraffe, huge wild buffalo and crocodile. Some are so large that they reflect the size of the animal itself. They are certainly not carvings that could be completed in an afternoon; maybe, Aref Salim thought, they were done by communal effort. Others show hunting scenes depicting thorn branch leg traps (carved as circles with spokes) attached by ropes to specially shaped boulders that would slow down the movements of a large mammal and allow the hunters to kill it more easily.

Incredibly, in Wadi Matkhandouch, a shallow, acacia-lined, sandy ravine on the eastern edge of the Akakus, some of the boulders, with a waistline-like cut to hold the rope, are still scattered about on the ground. I picked up one or two; it was an almost surreal experience imagining that these were maybe 7,000 years old and had lain here on the ground ever since, left behind on a pasture-like savannah and now in the same spot in arid, stony desert. In many countries such amazing artefacts would be housed in a museum and treated with due reverence. Here they were available for anyone – or anyone getting this far – to pick up and examine.

Who were these people with these albeit primitive artistic skills? And what did their drawings tell us about everyday life before the North African climate dried out so catastrophically? I needed to consult some experts to get the answers.

The sequence of events seems to have been that people settled originally in the Sahara around 10,000 BC when the climate there was more humid, perhaps getting ten or fifteen times the quantity of rain it receives today. The first colonists were hunter-gatherers. They collected grasses and wild cereals like sorghum and millet; they fished and hunted river animals including crocodile, hippopotamus and turtles as well as savannah animals such as antelopes and Barbary sheep. By 5000 BC the hunter-gatherers were combining hunting, fishing and gathering with pastoralism, herding cattle, sheep and goats to graze more extensive grasslands. Archaeologists searching the Akakus region have found the remains of domestic animal stalls as well as partially ground grass seed in the fossilised animal faeces of Barbary sheep, all of which indicates that they were being fed.

These early Saharan native people may have been the first in the world to domesticate cattle. Today the semi-nomadic Tuareg still build small rock shelters against shaded cliffs to contain young goats they rear. 'Around this time there was a drier climate period which might have stimulated their move from hunting and gathering to more livestock domestication,' Jeremy Keenan, a Visiting Professor of Archaeology and Anthropology at Bristol and Exeter Universities tells me. 'It could be that water, becoming scarcer, was concentrated at fewer lakes. And there were probably lower flows in the rivers. So animals would more naturally concentrate up.'

And it is this climatic drying that's thought to explain the presence of horses, chariots and camels, together with signs of a more Egyptian-style culture in the drawings. Camels (more correctly, dromedaries, because they have one hump not two!) are known to have been introduced as pack animals to North Africa from the Middle East around 200 BC, roughly the time that the area dried up and became desert-like.

And as the land became drier, so a more mobile culture probably became necessary. Hence the dromedaries; their use in long-distance trade became a necessity, the forerunner of the once commonplace south-north 'camel' trains across the Sahara – now replaced by fume-spluttering lorries. This market was based on salt, critical for preserving meat and other foods. Found in dried up lake basins in the Sahara as more and more lakes dried up, it was exported south to tropical Africa where it is naturally scarce. The desert peoples traded it for gold from the Niger basin, for slaves and exotic goods which they then transported back north to the Mediterranean coast.

'The main drying of the climate started around 3000 BC,' Jeremy Keenan told me. 'By 1000 BC the Sahara would have been as arid as it is today. It forced people to gather into communities where there was at least some water left, around oases where they could grow date palms and some other crops.' Some climate scientists think that this change from lushness to aridity happened much more suddenly: Peter de Menocal, Associate Professor at the Lamont-Doherty Earth Observatory of Columbia University, New York is one. He and his colleagues detected an abrupt end to the humid period at around 3500 BC in Mauritania (about 2,400 km west of the Akakus). And there is evidence that many African lakes dried up abruptly then too, perhaps as rapidly as over a century. In other places the transition was more gradual. And other experts like Professor Martin Claussen, Director of the Max Planck Institute for Meteorology in Hamburg agree. 'In what's now the western Sahara our computer modelling of the climate shows an abrupt change but it seems to have been more gradual in the eastern Sahara,' Claussen told me. The Jebel Akakus is in the middle.

But how, you might ask, when there most certainly wasn't the production of greenhouses gases we record today, could the climate flip so rapidly? My enquiries found that there are several possibilities: perhaps the changing tilt of the Earth relative to the Sun – a cyclical process that occurs naturally – could have reduced the amount of heat hitting the ground, thereby causing less hot air to rise and northern Africa to suck in less moisture-laden air from the Atlantic; or perhaps changes in solar pulses, which would have had a similar effect – deprived of water, the vegetation would soon have withered.

Slow change, or rapid, more catastrophic change, these amazing rock drawings and carvings are almost all that remains of an early civilisation that lived out its many generations in a landscape that is hard to imagine in the middle of today's Sahara.

Designated in 1985 by UNESCO as a World Heritage Site, the "Rock-Art Sites of Tadrart Acacus", is listed for its 'thousands of cave paintings in very different styles dating from 12,000 BC to AD 100 reflecting marked changes in the fauna and flora, and also the different ways of life of the populations that succeeded one another in this region of the Sahara'. At the main locations of rock drawings and carvings we came across signs erected by the Libyan Government to show that they are protected by its Department of Antiquities. But the locations are in isolated areas well away from any roads or habitation. So practical protection seemingly relies on specialist tour guides like ours acting responsibly and the few local Tuareg keeping an eye on what's happening out here.

When we went there – at a time when the Gaddafi Government was just opening up the country to limited tourism – visitors to the Jebel Akakus had to be accompanied by an authorised guide, a measure introduced and enforced by the government after some amateur European archaeologists had attempted to make silicon rubber replicas of some of the rock drawings. It almost obliterated the images they targeted. We saw other evidence of damage too. At some sites, pieces of rock had been removed, presumably with their drawings intact. At Wadi Matkhandouch, a few of the exquisite animal carvings have modern, chiselled hacking marks as if someone has tried to deface them. At Tin Chalaga, one of the most important protected rock drawing sites, someone had even carved his sweetheart's name in Arabic next to a painted rhino. In the recent past some unscrupulous guides have wetted the painted images so that they show up better for tourists to see and photograph. But any wetting slowly dissolves out the colour pigments so the images become increasingly faded.

Depressing though all this is, the ultimate safeguard is perhaps the sheer number of sites with drawings and, maybe, the presence of some yet undiscovered, known to the Tuareg but no Westerners with tendencies to remove or copy them. One day when our group was taking a long midday break to cool off in the shade of some shallow cliffs, I wandered off to another set of rock outcrops a kilometre or so distant. There were no vehicle tracks nearby so I assumed they were off any hardy tourist's trail. To my surprise, as I examined much of the rock surface, there were oodles of rock drawings here too, many of them coloured; drawings of cattle, of herders with sticks, of animals including ostrich and hippos. Maybe this is their best safeguard; that they are so widely distributed – and so abundant – that many or most are virtually bound to survive. I hope so.

At least most of the turmoil and armed faction fighting post Gaddafi – and the country's virtually total lack of governance – is less likely to impact on rock drawings in the middle of the Sahara than it obviously is in the more populated coastal areas of Libya where the destruction of archaeological and historic sites has been substantial. Italian archaeologists – many of whom have followed in Fabrizio Mori's footsteps – were proposing that the Libyans designate the Akakus as a national park and introduce better practical protection using the local Tuareg, by training responsible guards and by controlling any developments that could cause damage. But, because of Libya's descent into virtual anarchy, that's all pie in the sky for some considerable time to come!

We might never be sure whether the Saharan climate flipped suddenly or gradually; from providing a land of plenty to an arid desert where few people can eke out a living of sorts. But change it did. And drastically. The rock art of the Akakus is a lesson we need to take heed of when we weigh up the potential impact of today's changing climate.

Pigeons Galore

City (or Town) Pigeons are one of the most successful birds in the world. And they are the one bird that more people on this planet see every day than any other. They are so commonplace in towns and cities across the world, most people pay them little or no attention. Unless, that is, one flutters up too close for comfort or manages to drop a small, white package on your new jacket. But there are a few people who pay them a great deal of attention: a small band of diehards who persist in feeding them, usually much to the annoyance of city authorities trying to keep building ledges, park benches and other places free of pigeon poo.

Descended long ago from Rock Doves that breed on sea-cliffs – and interbred with already domesticated pigeons (such as homing pigeons and show pigeons) – City Pigeons have adapted to breeding on the urban 'cliffs' of concrete, brick and stone buildings in villages, towns and cities virtually worldwide. There they have adapted equally to an abundance of urban food, most of it dropped or dumped by us untidy humans. The world over, there are maybe 260 million City Pigeons.

Their adaptability seems to have virtually no limits. Watch the television replays of the enormous flooding caused in New Orleans when Hurricane Katrina passed close to the city on 29 August 2005 and you will see whole sections of the city underwater with few human residents in sight. Most had been evacuated. But look carefully at the film. Occasionally, a bird or two can be spotted, on rooftops, on walls, in trees or flying from one bit of dry urban construction to another. They are, of course, Town Pigeons. Presumably able to find enough food, they often survived the apocalyptic flooding better than people did.

And when you next see television film of a bomb-shattered town – in Syria for instance – you are almost certain to spot a group of City Pigeons picking about on the ground, then flying up when the next explosion shatters yet another couple of buildings, only to land again within seconds and resume foraging. They are some of the most adaptable birds on earth.

So you might reasonably assume that all this highly successful adaptation has attracted the attention of ornithologists around the world. Not a bit of it. Like most urban workers hurrying their way to their city office, few self-respecting ornithologists give the ubiquitous town or city pigeon a second glance, let alone study its success. It is as if this humble but hugely successful bird is somehow impure, not worthy of serious study, condemned because it is not a real species (it's impossible now to distinguish Rock Doves from many City Pigeons), because it has become rather tame and, maybe, because it waddles about our urban areas picking up the detritus of human society. It's a 'Heinz 57' of the bird world.

But one ornithologist who did study the Town Pigeon was John Tully, a retired school schoolteacher who lived near Bristol (he has since died). A few years ago I had the pleasure of spending a morning with him to chat about his research so that I could summarise his findings in my book, *Life With Birds: A Story of Mutual Exploitation* (Whittles, 2011). He is one of the many amateur naturalists I have met over the years; people who give up hours of their personal time to follow their interest but who very often come up with new, sometimes crucial information on what's happening to some of our wildlife and why. John Tully was one of those committed individuals whose work on Town Pigeons, House Sparrows and other species produced information on them that was unique. A delightful man, he was exceedingly helpful and great fun. In 2009, he had received a national award for services to ornithology at the annual conference of the British Trust for Ornithology. In part it recognised his key work on city pigeons.

This is some of what I wrote after our chat:

John Tully is a breath of fresh air. An active amateur ornithologist, Mr Tully is putting the City Pigeon on the ornithological map for the first time. Over the last couple of decades he has become the leading world expert on these successful birds.

'Birdwatchers want wild birds to look at,' comments Tully. 'I suppose they think that City Pigeons are sort of tainted but I think their success makes them even more worth studying. They are arguably the bird that has best adapted itself to live our urban life.'

'It's pretty easy to count them in winter because almost all of them are in towns and cities then,' he says. 'In summer, when they're breeding, they make forays out into the countryside for food so it's harder then to get accurate counts. But unlike counting most birds, you don't even have to get up early in the morning. Pigeons rise late and roost early. That suits me! They even line up on building ledges like well-behaved schoolchildren,' he adds wistfully.

'In the 1991/2 winter when I retired,' he says, 'I counted 108 pigeon flocks in Bristol totalling 7,440 birds. I repeated the count ten years later and the total came to between 7,500 and 8,000 birds so it hadn't changed much, if at all. A few flocks had disappeared but many of the others had increased in number, some markedly. But they have declined a bit since then.'

But what John Tully had spotted in his repeat survey was a big change in where the pigeons were living. No longer were they predominantly in the city centre where they were concentrated in 1991/2. Many of them had moved further out, not to the outer suburbs with their bigger gardens and leafy green spaces, but as far as the inner suburbs – still very built up – closer to the centre. Often where there are shopping centres, pavement cafes and other places where people drop food.

'Where houses are pretty tightly packed as they are in some parts of Bristol,' comments Tully, 'There don't seem to be as many pigeons. It may be that, by coincidence perhaps, there are less food scraps or there are more cats to kill them off'.

'But I also think the pigeons like shopping places and piazzas, places where they can also get an open view. It might be something to do with spotting predators like cats, or Peregrines that hunt them or even Sparrowhawks, the females of which are big enough to kill them and carry them off. They don't seem to like being confined too much where they can't see what's happening around them,' he adds.

And the reason for Town Pigeons moving out to pastures – or more correctly buildings – new? John Tully reckons that it's because much more aggressive gulls have moved into city centres to grab all the scraps and to breed on warm city roofs and ledges where they are little disturbed.

But land-filling of domestic refuse is declining as more Local Authorities and consumer groups promote recycling and composting. So their food sources will decline, probably drastically. Their abundance might yet be short-lived and City Pigeons might even re-take 'their' city centres!

City Pigeons, much more delicate and more easily deterred birds, never great squabblers, wouldn't stand a chance of success competing with a noisy, beak-stabbing, bellicose Herring Gull at a newly discarded burger and fries.

'You get around one Town Pigeon for every 50 people in most cities,' comments Tully. 'I suspect it's higher in tourist areas. I did counts in Bath, a popular tourist destination, several years ago and there the ratio was one pigeon for every 44 people though in Weston-Super-Mare it was only one for every 58, perhaps because, as a seaside resort, Weston isn't exactly popular in winter when I did the counts. Or the pigeons don't like the sea air,' he adds.

'So much depends on how free of food scraps and other rubbish a town is,' says Tully. 'Nailsea in North Somerset (population 18,000) has a pretty reasonable pigeon population and it isn't too spick and span,' he comments. 'Thornbury in South Gloucestershire (population 12,000), on the other hand, has cleaner streets and better waste collection. There are almost no pigeons there'.

Tully has estimated the numbers of human city and large town dwellers in Britain to be about 30 million out of the UK's total population and used his average of about fifty people for each pigeon. That gives a total of around 600,000 City Pigeons in the UK! It might even be more.

To anyone who slips headlong on their slimy droppings or has their drying washing stained with the stuff, City Pigeons are a pest. But they have their attributes too. Tully estimates that the Bristol lot consume between one and two tonnes of waste food every week, anything from discarded apple cores to Kentucky Fried Chicken.

'They don't re-deposit most of it where they feed either,' he says. 'Most of their droppings are at their roost sites, mainly dilapidated buildings with a plethora of holes in their roofs and smashed windows. It's only the demolition workers that need worry! Most city people don't come into contact with it,' he adds.

But their diet doesn't consist entirely of human society's waste. City Pigeons, like their wild counterparts, will also take seeds of garden plants and weeds growing in urban areas. And they make forays into the countryside in order to feed on grain or other plant seeds too. They pick up grit from roads and pavements, sometimes even small pieces of mortar as a source of calcium and to help physically in their crops to break down the food they eat. After all, British fish and chips can take some digesting.

This unprecedented success of City Pigeons virtually worldwide – they even get into the centre of the Sahara at times (see Chapter 8) – has given many people the idea that all species of wild pigeon anywhere in the world are a pretty mundane, even boring lot. It's as if they are all rather dull and uninspiring whereas, in truth, pigeons are some of the most versatile and adaptable birds known. Some are exceedingly attractively coloured, probably contrary to the assumption many people make that most pigeons in the world are kitted out in various dull shades of grey and brown.

A few years back, I remember waiting at a garage forecourt north of Nairobi in Kenya for our vehicle to have a tyre repaired, when a small flock of plump birds landed in a nearby fruit tree and started feeding. They turned out to be African Green Pigeons; with their bright green backs and blue-grey fronts, red legs and bright white eyes, they were exquisite. I had seen a similar species in India previously; the Yellow-footed Green Pigeon is similar to its African cousin but is maybe even more attractive because the blue-grey front is replaced with a vibrant yellow. In India they are commonplace in forests and anywhere there are fruit trees.

Now for another surprise: pigeons are most closely related to parrots. And the green pigeons I saw, clambering about after fruit in trees, looked remarkably like a small flock of parrots as they fed. And, in case you think my African and Indian Greens are exceptional and that most pigeons in the world are rather more conservatively attired, these most certainly are not the most colourful pigeons!

There are several others in more vivid shades of green: the wonderfully named and widespread Wompoo Fruit Dove of Australia and New Guinea has a bright green back, violet underparts and a red beak. Even so, the bird is apparently not easy to spot amongst the foliage of fruit trees. The White-crowned Pigeon of Central America and the West Indies is dark grey all over, almost black, with a white crown, while the gorgeous Namaqua Dove of the most arid African savannahs and semi-deserts in the Middle East, all pale grey and black with a long pointed tail, is such a delicate-looking bird in flight that I've sometimes assumed it's something more like a parakeet.

There's no point, of course, in my pretending that wild pigeons of all types are gorgeous creatures and admired by everyone. Many are not. Take, for instance, the super-abundant, stockily built Wood Pigeon found across the whole of Europe and east into the western part of Asia. Despised by farmers everywhere, Wood Pigeons delight in descending in huge flocks on to fields of grain, peas, beans and many others to devour as much of the crop as they can. Modern, intensive farming has indirectly and unintentionally encouraged them by growing extensive areas of such crops. And although numbers of Wood Pigeons with their plump breasts are shot for the table – and good eating they make too – the birds remain as abundant as ever.

In recent years, particularly in the UK, Wood Pigeons have quite suddenly realised that our gardens provide a very good food supply too, especially the bits of food that drop from the bird feeders that many gardeners put out to feed smaller garden birds, many of whom dislodge and scatter seeds and suet as they feed. For Wood Pigeons, the clumsier these smaller birds are, the more food that drops to the ground for them to hoover up. Combine that with seeds found naturally in many gardens, tall trees to roost in and no firecrackers or shotguns to molest them, and our gardens are a Wood Pigeon nirvana. We have them in our garden, though only in the last few years. With us they have established themselves like old friends. Our resident pair nest in a large cypress tree and the two of them waddle about, seemingly well fed, like a pair of very elderly, slightly corpulent pensioners on a day trip to the seaside.

Dove or pigeon, the names are really interchangeable, though many of the smaller, more demure species tend to be called doves; the plumper larger ones are nearly always pigeons. Of the 300 or so pigeon species in the world, 26 are endangered. That's the result of habitat destruction (many are forest birds) and hunting (so many, especially the plumper ones, make a good meal) but also because some are confined to islands.

On Madeira, the popular tourist island off the northwest coast of Africa, the Trocaz Pigeon is to be found in its laurel forests but nowhere else in the world. Probably a descendent of a Wood Pigeon-like ancestor, it's rather more colourful: grey and pink with a silvery neck patch. Isolated on Madeira it has evolved in its own way; today there might be as many as 10,000 there and they are quite easy to spot from vantage points on mountain slopes overlooking forested areas. The main problem is that the Madeiran laurel forests can sometimes be shrouded in mist. I was lucky; a clear day with good views from a mountain-top vantage point over extensive areas of forest and it wasn't long before I saw one flying from one patch of forest to another. Then another. And within an hour I had seen several Trocaz Pigeons.

Much the same has happened on the Canary Islands south of Madeira where, on Tenerife, I recently waited – and waited – looking out over the laurel-forested Ruiz Gorge on its north coast until, on different occasions, I had glimpses of an occasional Laurel Pigeon and Bolle's Laurel Pigeon fly past and dive into a tree irritatingly out of sight. These two have evolved in isolation (no pigeons fly large distances so they're unlikely to make it to the African coast or from Tenerife to Madeira) and differ from each other and from the Trocaz too. Why two different pigeon species should have evolved on Tenerife, and just one on Madeira, no one knows. All three are protected; their forests are generally conserved, some are even being expanded by more tree planting and illegal hunting is seemingly minimal. So their future seems secure … albeit naturally restricted.

Times were very different for one much more famous bird; one that gave us a very commonly used saying but one that most people would never know was a pigeon. Long extinct, it too is 'as dead as a Dodo'! I had researched the Dodo story when I was writing a chapter for *Back from the Brink* (Whittles, 2015) about the Mauritius Kestrel, a bird for which enormous conservation efforts had recovered it from the very brink of extinction. The same didn't happen for its one-time fellow islander, the Dodo, also an inhabitant of Mauritius.

The curiously named Dodo was a metre-tall pigeon, probably brownish grey, and named perhaps after its pigeon-like call or from a mispronunciation of Portuguese or Dutch words such as *dodoor* for 'sluggard' but more probably from *Dodaars* which means either 'fat-arse' or 'knot-arse', referring to the knot of feathers on its hind end. Whichever, neither origin is very complimentary! They lived only on this one large island. Contemporary drawings suggest that Dodos were plump, somewhat ungainly and covered in plenty of meat. But current thinking is that their ungainliness and obesity were exaggerated in contemporary drawings and descriptions though it's not clear why. More importantly, they couldn't fly and they nested on the ground, a rather fatal combination if there are hungry people about. Before humans started encroaching, there were probably no predators capable of killing them.

First mentioned by a Dutchman, Vice-Admiral Wybrand van Warwijck who visited the island in 1598, various accounts from the time give mixed reports about Dodo meat, some describing it as tasty, others as nasty and tough. Tasty or not, there are scattered reports of mass killings of Dodos for provisioning of ships for long voyages and, like many animals that evolved in isolation from significant predators, the Dodo was entirely fearless of humans. Combined with their inability to fly, it made the Dodo easy prey for sailors who clubbed them to death mercilessly. If they weren't bludgeoned for food, their ground nests were almost certainly deprived of their eggs by animals such as rats, cats and pigs introduced by Mauritius's early settlers. At the same time, people started felling the island's forests where the Dodos nested and fed.

The last widely accepted record of a Dodo sighting is the 1662 report by shipwrecked mariner Volkert Evertsz of the Dutch ship *Arnhem* who described birds caught on a small islet off Mauritius. There's also a description from around 1680 by Benjamin Harry, chief mate on the *Berkley Castle*. And a sighting was reported in the hunting records of Isaac Johannes Lamotius in 1688. Regardless, the Dodo must have been rare for some time before that and it's unlikely that any survived past the last decades of the 17th century, just a century after it was discovered.

For a long time this rather odd-looking pigeon was forgotten. Not though by Lewis Carroll who immortalised it in *Alice's Adventures in Wonderland* (1865). The Dodo of his stories is supposedly a caricature of the author whose real name was Charles Dodgson. A popular but unsubstantiated belief is that Dodgson chose it because of his stammer, and thus would accidentally introduce himself as 'Do-do-Dodgson'.

I have another interest in this story too. For the last 30 or more years I have lived near Llandudno, one of the most pleasant and attractive coastal resort towns in Britain. Llandudno was the holiday destination of the real Alice in Wonderland, Alice Liddell, the girl who inspired Lewis Carroll and on whom he based Alice in Wonderland. She first came to the town with her family on holiday in 1861 aged eight. Carroll became a close friend of the family and it is believed by some that it was Alice's exploits in Llandudno that provided inspiration for his Alice books.

With the popularity of the book, the Dodo became a well-known and easily recognisable icon of extinction. But probably hardly anyone today would ever guess that the hapless Dodo was a pigeon.

The Forest Emperor in the Mist

Our alarm buzzed at 4 a.m. The night's darkness was just giving way to a distant slit of light and in half an hour came the knock on the door. Michal Krzysiak was distinctly brighter and more cheery than my wife and I. A well-built vet with excellent English and working for the Białowieża National Park, we had arranged for him to take us on a dawn tour searching for Europe's largest land animal, the European Bison, cousin of the arguably better known American Buffalo.

Białowieża is the largest remaining primeval forest in Europe, well over 600 km² of it in Poland and much the same on the Belarus side of the border. We were staying in the pretty Polish village of the same name located in a large clearing well inside the forest. With around 500 European Bison roaming the Polish side of this forest, animals weighing up to a tonne and the size of large cattle, it's all too easy to assume that they can't be difficult to locate. But optimism can wear thin.

Driving out of the village along rough tracks in Michal's Jeep, we soon realised that the extensive bison-height band of post-dawn mist was not going to make our search any easier. Suddenly, an animal scuttled across the track in front of us, diving hurriedly into tree cover. It was a Wild Boar, caught out before it retired for the day in some quiet woodland cover to sleep with the peace only pigs can.

We drove on, scanning left and right. A few deer, out in clearings for some undisturbed night-time grazing, veered out of the way much like the boar. But no bison. A few hundred bison secreted away somewhere in this massive forest suddenly seemed rather like the veritable needle in a haystack. After two hours of searching, peering across little meadows through the low band of mist and driving along narrow forest tracks squeezed between dense-growing oaks, hornbeams and spruce, we had almost given up hope.

'I think the mist this morning is causing us difficulties to see any. But this is nature; sometimes we see several, other times none,' says Michal rather philosophically. Our early morning search – a good time to spot bison because they usually come out of the forest by night to graze pastures in clearings and don't return till after dawn – was not proving very fruitful at all. Then, very suddenly, our luck changed. And rather dramatically too. Bumping slowly along yet another spruce and oak-shaded track, we suddenly lurched to a standstill. It's Michal who spots it first and can't hide his pleasure.

'There. Look, just there, a three- or four-year-old bull bison!' he splutters. And what a magnificent sight it was, Europe's largest land animal 30 m away, his massive, horned head turned towards us. Watching us watching him. Moist clouds of air being expelled from his nostrils in the damp morning mists. And he doesn't move for what seems like a couple of minutes, giving us a superb, close-up view. Then slowly, very slowly, he walks away, nonchalantly looking back to check us out as we creep a little further along the track to try not to lose sight of him. For such a huge animal he makes little noise as he picks his way over the bronzed carpet of twigs and leaves on the forest floor.

Then, a strange thing happened. Almost as suddenly as this huge animal appeared, he disappeared from view not even 50 metres away. Camouflaged by the scatter of forest trees and the shadows they cast in the early morning sunlight, he had faded from sight, his dark, chocolate brown body hidden by the shrubby infant trees that will someday become this forest's giants. He had faded away like the stars in the morning light. For a few seconds it felt as if what we had seen was an apparition.

So, in spite of the post-dawn mist, our early start had been well rewarded, eventually, by a wonderful view of a magnificent animal. It was by far the closest encounter with a wild bison we were to get.

A little under a century ago, it would not have been possible to find any bison in this huge forest; they had all been shot. European Bison had been driven to extinction in the wild. Historically, their range extended over most of lowland Europe from the French Massif Central as far east as western and southern Russia, maybe further east still. But that range decreased as human populations expanded, felling forests as they went and farming larger and larger areas of land, confining bison to what forests remained and to more remote regions of Eastern Europe.

By the 8th century they were largely gone from France, the Low Countries and the western part of today's Germany except for some isolated populations in less inhabited regions such as the Vosges in the east of France where they lasted maybe until the 15th century. In the 11th century they became extinct in Sweden and the last European Bison in what is now Romania died in 1790. In Poland, however, bison in the Białowieża Forest were the property of the Polish kings, at least until 1795 when Poland was unceremoniously wiped off the map by its neighbouring countries.

'By the 14th century, Białowieża had been set aside as a royal forest [rather like England's New Forest; see Chapter 4] and by the 16th century 300 royal wardens were employed to keep it free of intruders, to prevent illegal logging and to stop any animal poaching by the locals,' Professor Tomasz Wesołowski of Wroclaw University told me. He has been studying the place for 30 years.

Draconian measures were introduced to protect it. In 1538, King Sigismund II Augustus (1548–1569) instituted the death penalty for poaching a European Bison here. And in the early 19th century when the forest was part of Russia, its tzars also retained old Polish laws protecting them.

So why did bison decline? Habitat degradation and fragmentation caused by agricultural development together with forest logging and illegal hunting were the probable reasons for a steady decline in bison numbers through the 19th century. A burgeoning deer population probably didn't help either; there's a finite amount of ground vegetation and shrubs to graze even in a forest as large as this. Only the Białowieza population – numbering maybe 700 – and one population in the Caucasus (today part of the Russian Federation) survived into the 20th century but the 1917 Russian Revolution and World War I finished them off, albeit indirectly. Occupying German troops killed 600 bison in the Białowieża Forest for sport and for their meat, hides and horns while, at the end of the war, retreating German soldiers shot all but nine animals. The last wild European Bison in Poland was killed in 1919 and the last one living wild anywhere in Europe was killed by poachers in 1927 in the western Caucasus.

By then fewer than 50 remained in zoos and private collections. Only seven of these were guaranteed pure-bred animals of the type found in Białowieża, and they formed the founders of a captive breeding programme. By 1929, bison were again in the Białowieża forest, albeit in a small, confined reserve where they were kept for breeding; ten years later there were sixteen of them and releases into the forest began. Despite losses in World War II, by the early 1970s successful breeding and more releases had brought the population here up to 200. By 2013, 500 bison were roaming the Polish part of the great forest at Białowieża with another 450 in the Belarus half of the forest. 'Europe-wide today there are approximately 4,663 bison, about 40% of them in zoos and other breeding centres, the rest wild though some are within large confined areas of land,' Katarzyna Daleszczyk, a bison expert at the Białowieża National Park tells me when I interview her for my book, *Back from the Brink* (Whittles, 2015). They all originate from the Białowieża herd.

But Białowieża is a divided forest. Since the early 1980s, the border between the two countries within it (a length of more than 50 km) has been fenced, making mixing of the two bison populations impossible, a situation that will only change if there is substantial political revision at some future time. On both sides of the border, sections of the forest are designated as national parks. And while much larger areas are subject to commercial forestry, which is highly controversial and the subject of a great deal of criticism from conservationists, forestry interests claim that it is managed sympathetically with wildlife a priority. There is no evidence that any forestry practices here are causing bison a problem.

Having talked to Kararzyna and other bison experts working in this part of Poland to get information about their behaviour and ecology, we thought we might ourselves try finding some bison at dusk when a few come out of the forest to graze in hay meadows and other clearings. So one evening we drove west a few kilometres to Teremiski village, really just a small hamlet surrounded by hay meadows and pasture cut out of the forest a very long time ago; one of several hamlets in the area burnt down by the Nazis in World War II. They cleared people out of the whole area, shooting any members of Jewish families who had lived here for generations. The villages were re-built after the war.

We had stopped in a spot where we could see some forest edge after sunset but before the evening's light had faded. And there we waited, constantly scanning from side to side. A scatter of moving lumps in the short-cropped meadows turned out to be hares. A few deer came into sight at the forest's edge, obviously coming out for some rather different night-time grazing. The only other wildlife we could spot in the gathering gloom – more correctly they spotted us – were mosquitoes and some other undetermined biting insects. We waited, but no bison appeared. By now the light was fading steadily and we changed position, stopping where we had a view in a different direction and where we could see a longer length of forest edge. Wisps of mist were starting to form ghostly strands near the damp ground; it was a reminder of our previous après-dawn trip.

Then we spotted one. It had walked out of the forest some distance away but its ominous bulk was perfectly recognisable with binoculars in the darkening gloom. First one bison, then another and, eventually, a third; walking slowly out from the trees about 400 m away to graze on the lush, succulent meadow flowers and grasses unobtainable in most of the forest. The hay crop was high but we could still see their huge bodies with their enormous, bearded, triangular-shaped heads hanging down. After a few minutes the mist was thickening, the light extinguished and we could only just make out some bison shapes. We left them there, spending their dark hours grazing while we retreated to the comfort of our small, family-run hotel in Białowieża village.

There is a lot more wildlife interest at Białowieża than just the bison. In essence this is the best preserved lowland natural forest in Europe with an exceptionally rich range of plants and animals that have survived nearly unchanged ever since the forest first grew up. Białowieża boasts well over 1,000 different plant species, over 4,000 different fungi, and more than 700 lichens, mosses, liverworts and slime moulds. Many of the fungi are rare or extinct in other managed forests because they are utterly dependent on dead timber which is usually cleared away. Although some of it is managed commercially, one large section is left completely natural with no forest management. Here, any old-age trees that fall, any storm damage, or any other changes that take place naturally are allowed to happen without interference. It is one of the very few areas of forest in Europe left to its own devices.

I arranged to visit this sector with a guide to have an early morning walk. One of the most obvious features was the sheer amount of decomposing timber, the richest habitat in any forest. There was a scatter of dead standing trees and several particularly old denizens that had fallen to the forest floor and were rotting away steadily. It is because of all this dead timber that a cornucopia of fungi and vast numbers of wood-boring beetles and other invertebrates burgeon. The split-open tree stumps and fallen tree trunks might look like battlefield corpses but these are the basis for much of the forest's wildlife, something that's often in very short supply in most forests across Europe, Britain included. Pock-marked by beetle boreholes and sporting clumps of bracket fungi in several colours, this dead timber supports a vast array of species. Somewhere around 10,000 different species of invertebrate live here, my guide told me, maybe more. No one's checked them all out. Seemingly, though, that total does include well over twenty different mosquito species and I can vouch personally for some of them testing out their annoying biting behaviour.

In places, the towering tree canopy of oaks, limes, ash and spruce soared to 40–50 m and some of the largest trees are thought to be well over half a millennium old. They were an impressive sight though I found it virtually impossible to identify any small birds so high up in the canopy … and got a very stiff neck trying to do so. We saw several of the nearly 30 different tree species here, from poplar and hornbeam to alder and hazel; streamside marshes, open pools, sedge beds, glades and small meadows added to the diversity leaving me in little doubt that this is one of the wildlife wonders of Eastern Europe.

I was at Białowieża in mid-summer, not the best time to see most of the forest birds. They had finished breeding and long ceased singing to advertise their territories. But the flute-like, rather exotic calls of the striking, primrose and green Golden Orioles rang out in places and I spotted a family group of Common Rosefinches, including an adult male with his bright, scarlet-flushed head and breast. All of Europe's woodpeckers are here and, on various walks, we had heard the loud calls of a Black Woodpecker in the distance and had good views of both the Great Spotted and Middle Spotted Woodpecker, all species I had seen before. The one that eluded me was that much rarer species apparently confined to forests with a generous supply of rotting timber and mature trees: the White-backed Woodpecker. So where better than Białowieża!

Then one day, I was walking along a path in the forest adjacent to some waterlogged ground and shallow pools in which there were a good proportion of standing dead trees, mainly birch. It was maybe a couple of kilometres into the forest from Białowieża village towards the Belarus border. I was aware of something landing on one of these stems, stopped and searched with binoculars and – somewhat crestfallen – realised that it was a Great Spotted Woodpecker. I kept looking around and I noticed another woodpecker, or so I thought, a few trees away. I assumed it might be the Great Spotted's mate. But this one seemed a little larger. I suddenly had a clear view of both of them with their backs facing me, each of them climbing up a different tree stem. The larger one had the tell-tale 'ladder-back' pattern of white rather than the larger white patches of the Great Spotted. It was a White-backed.

I don't doubt that in spring the forest here is alive with the harsh calls and drumming of woodpeckers, with the songs of warblers and the evocative flutes of shy Golden Orioles. Like the orioles, they are not frequently seen but Białowieża is also home to Elk, Red and Roe Deer, Wild Boar, Pine Martens, numerous bats and many other mammals … as well as to European Bison. Today, Białowieża Forest (both the Polish and Belarus sides) is a World Heritage Site, a Biosphere Reserve and the Polish half is a Special Area of Conservation designated by the EU Habitats Directive, all designations that emphasise that this magnificent place is not only of Polish or Belarusian importance; it's of European and world heritage value, a precious asset that must never be squandered.

But in this place of beauty and wildlife riches there is conflict too. 'In Poland conservationists are uncommon beings,' Adam Wajrak, nature correspondent for Poland's biggest daily paper, *Gazeta Wyborcza* and a Białowieża village resident, tells me. 'Polish people are very different to those in the west. They don't save energy. But they are very connected to nature. Most of us have grandparents living in the countryside, some farmers, some foresters, and we spend holidays there. I am surprised how much emotion comes out. If they tried to cull wolves here, as they did in Sweden, there would be demonstrations in the street.'

'The Białowieża Forest is public property; it belongs to all citizens of Poland and not to local communities and foresters,' Professor Wesołowski explains. 'The conflict is not between conservationists and foresters as foresters love to frame it but between stakeholders at large [70% of Poles want the Białowieża Forest to be protected] and a small group of people with vested interests in timber exploitation, mainly local foresters and loggers. We propose to protect the whole area as a national park [only a sixth of the Polish side is national park now] and we see no place for commercial timber production or exploitation here.'

'The creation of a national park doesn't mean that no exploitation would be allowed. No one proposes to make the whole forest a strictly protected area. There would be some 'no enter' zones but otherwise the forest would be open for low impact use (collection of fungi and berries, tourism, research). We also propose to allow limited fuel wood extraction to cover the needs of local communities,' he says. So far, the Polish Government, harangued by foresters and local interests on one side and by conservationists and academics, plus international pressure on the other, is seemingly doing nothing about it.

Wesolowski is far from optimistic. 'It is impossible to enlarge the park in our current legal system in which local community councils have a veto right. They can block establishment or enlargement of the park forever, without giving any reason. It takes only eight people, the majority of the Białowieża commune council, to block enlargement of the park against the will of the rest of society. This is democracy Polish way. We are trying to change this stupid law in the parliament, but so far without success.'

Wesołowski likes to compare the forest with the Hubble space telescope. 'Hubble revolutionised astronomy by allowing scientists to peer back in time with unprecedented clarity but there's a key difference with Białowieża,' he says. 'If Hubble gets damaged, it can be replaced. This primeval forest cannot be bought or reconstructed.' And Adam Wajrak echoes this view. 'We are a country destroyed by wars and here there is not much heritage left apart from nature. This is the one unique thing we can give to the world.'

The Bird that Inspired Flamenco

I can watch an expertly executed waltz and admire its elegance. And I can appreciate the more lively dramatic style of a pasodoble, modelled apparently on the sound, drama and movement of the Spanish and Portuguese bullfight. But the only style of dance – more accurately a dance and dramatic music combination – that I find utterly mesmerising is flamenco, a popular form of Spanish folk music and dance from Andalusia in southern Spain. It includes *cante* (singing), *toque* (guitar playing), *baile* (dance) and *palmas* (handclaps) all blended together in a unique and tantalising combination. I've watched performances in places ranging from plush theatres in Seville to backyard bars in Ronda and I never tire of it.

First mentioned in literature in 1774, flamenco is thought to have grown out of Andalusian and Romani music and dance styles and it's usually associated with the Gitanos – the Romani people of Spain – and a number of famous flamenco artists with this ethnicity. There are more styles than I can describe … and certainly more than I have experienced. In recent years flamenco has become popular all over the world and is taught in many countries; in Japan there are more flamenco academies than there are in Spain. In 2010 UNESCO declared flamenco one of the Masterpieces of the Oral and Intangible Heritage of Humanity.

So what do I find so entrancing about it? I suppose it's the drama, the sensuality of the dancing, the rustle of the castanets, the deep-down, earthy wailing of song, the energy, the volcanic yet controlled crescendos, the strumming of the guitar accompaniment and the formality and striking beauty of the costumes. In *A Rose for Winter* (Hogarth Press, 1955), Laurie Lee, the English poet and novelist who adored Spain, wrote a description of a flamenco session he had watched in Algeciras in the very south of the country. It is the best, most impassioned description I have read. This is what he wrote:

> First comes the guitarist, a neutral, dark-suited figure, carrying his instrument in one hand and a kitchen chair in another … He strikes a

few chords in the darkness, speculatively, warming his hands and his imagination together. Presently the music becomes more confident and free, the crisp strokes of the rhythms more challenging. At that moment the singer walks into the light, stands with closed eyes, and begins to moan in the back of his throat as though testing the muscles of his voice. The audience goes deathly quiet for what is coming has never been heard before and will never be heard again. Suddenly the singer takes a gasp of breath, throws back his head and hits a high, barbaric note, a naked wail of sand and desert, serpentine, prehensile. Shuddering then, with contorted and screwed-up face, he moves into the first verse of his song. It is a lament of passion, an animal cry, thrown out, as it were, over burning rocks, a call half-lost in air, but imperative and terrible.

At last, the awful solitude of his cry is answered by a dry shiver of castanets, the rustle of an awakened cicada, stirred by the man's hot voice. Gradually the pulse grows more staccato, stronger, louder, nearer. Then slow as a creeping fire, her huge eyes smoking, her red dress trailing like flames behind her, the girl appears from the wings. Her white arms are raised like snakes above her, her head is thrown back, her breasts and belly taut, while from her snapping, flickering fingers the black mouths of the castanets hiss and rattle, a tropic tongue, eloquent and savage. The man remains motionless, his arms outstretched, throwing forth loops of song around her and drawing her close towards him. And slowly, on drumming feet, she advances, tossing her head and uttering little cries. Once caught within his orbit she begins to circle him, weaving and writhing, stamping and turning; her castanets chatter, tremble, whisper; her limbs are entangled in his song, coiled in it, reflecting each parched and tortured phrase by the voluptuous postures of her body. And so they act out together long tales of love; singing, dancing, joined but never touching.

And if you find Lee's sensual and dramatic prose somewhat exhausting in itself, imagine the energy expended by the flamenco dancer and her guitarist in the oven-warmth and heavy, aromatic herb-aroma of an Andalusian summer evening. Researching the origins of this culturally important piece of southern Spanish heritage doesn't get you very far; its origins are pretty much unknown. An array of reasons are usually given to try and explain why that should be, and these include the following: flamenco originated in the 'lower levels' of Andalusian society, which lacked the prestige of art forms developed by 'higher classes'; times were turbulent for the people involved in flamenco culture – the Moors, the Gitanos and the Jews were all persecuted, and the Moors and Jews were expelled by the Spanish Inquisition in

1492; the Gitanos have been fundamental in maintaining flamenco but they have an oral culture while the non-gypsy Andalusian poorer classes were mostly illiterate; and there was a lack of interest in the past from historians and musicologists.

But what about its original inspiration? What was it that inspired flamenco? Did the natural world provide some, maybe all, of that inspiration? Most of the Gitanos, the Moors and the others would have spent their days labouring out in the fields, on the great Spanish plains. Could at least a small part of its origins arise from one of the most unusual and extravagant courtship displays of any bird in the world? And one that can be seen up to a couple of kilometres away. Workers toiling away in the fields would have been very familiar with it; maybe even awe-struck by its extravagance. It's that of the Great Bustard.

Spain and Portugal hold the largest global population of this magnificent ground bird. I've watched them in many parts of both countries on several occasions and they never fail to impress me. Arguably the heaviest flying bird in the world, the male is the size of a large goose, the female smaller. They are shy and inhabit a very open habitat, making it almost impossible to get close to them. Both sexes have black-flecked, rich chestnut brown backs, grey heads and white bellies. As they strut slowly across the ground they pick at the vegetation, take seeds, large insects, maybe a rodent or two and much else that they can find. They are such large birds inhabiting very open, flat or slightly undulating landscapes that it's even possible to mistake them at a distance for a small flock of sheep. Until a few years ago, I had not managed to see the incredible display that a male Great Bustard puts on to woo nearby females. Either our Iberian visit was a little too late that year … or a little early. On one visit, though, we must have hit it at its displaying peak.

I met up with a good friend, Gabriel Sierra, at a bar in Madrigal de las Atlas Torres, a village about 50 km from Salamanca in central Spain. Its sole claim to fame is that Isabella I of Castille was born here in 1451. A formidable monarch, she brought unity and stability to Spain, substantially reducing crime; but with her husband Ferdinand II of Aragon she also exiled the Moors and Jews that had settled in the country too.

Gabi and I had met some years before when I was researching Great Bustards for a feature in *The Independent on Sunday*. He had been extremely helpful. The good news this particular morning was that he had just been out to see a large flock of Great Bustards not far away … and some males were displaying. We were off!

Driving along dusty, sandy tracks we stopped well out of sight of where he knew the birds were and where we had a rare opportunity: a small plantation of conifers – planted years ago as a windbreak in this open landscape – between us and them. It was a rare opportunity to get relatively close to them so that we could watch the display I had yet to see but had heard and read so much about.

Most of the land around Madrigal is flat and uninspiring; its grasslands were long ago ploughed up to grow wheat and barley plus a little lucerne as an animal fodder crop. The bustards, birds that would have inhabited the original grassy plains around here, have taken to the replacement crop-growing habitat because the local farmers use very little pesticide and not much fertilizer. Crop yields are low but the cereal varieties they use are more sustainable and appropriate for the very dry summer conditions. Their way of farming allows insects to survive. Birds follow. It is the antithesis of the intensive wheat and barley growing we have in Britain and much of the rest of Europe in which any weeds and pests are killed off with pesticides and the crop is lavished with fertiliser to bulk up its yield; about as far removed from being wildlife sympathetic as a tarmac-surfaced carpark.

We walked quietly a couple of hundred yards into the conifers, then moved behind one tree after another until we were near the far side of the plantation. And the birds were still there; about 100 m away stood 50 or so bustards, mostly females but with a scatter of the larger males. It was the closest I have ever been (it still is) and it was a magnificent viewpoint. We kept very quiet, communicating with hand signals rather than whispers.

Almost immediately, Gabi started pointing to the left. A male was beginning his display. He was puffing out his throat pouches, inflating them with air until his neck had blown up to the size of a small football, his head disappearing 'into' it. He fanned his chestnut tail and inverted it over his back. He did the same with his wings, inverting them to form huge white rosettes of feathers from under his body that bulged out on either side and completely covered his back in a flurry of pure white. He appeared to have turned himself inside out just as some of the descriptions of this amazing transition claim.

It was incredible. This rich chestnut-brown bird had metamorphosed into a shimmering white mass. And he now proceeded to show off while most of the female bustards around got on with their feeding! Rhythmically shaking his now white plumage, he seemed to billow like a ship in full sail as he strutted a couple of paces in one direction, then another.

In less than a minute it was all over. His tail and wings returned to their normal positions, his neck deflated and suddenly I was looking at a large brown bird once more. And he returned to feeding, nonchalantly picking here and there on the ground as if dissatisfied with the whole transformational act. The experience was surreal; it was as if some magician had performed a trick so convincing in front of my very eyes that I couldn't be sure whether this rather plain bird had transformed itself into a Persil-white foaming bundle or not. The speed with which this incredible transition is accomplished is such that, from a distance, many observers describe what they see as something akin to a bush covered in white spring blossom that's present one minute, then disappears.

But why have such an extravagant display at all? Why not just do a few bows, flutter their wings a little, sing some fabulous song or raise a few feathers on their head to attract a mate just like many other birds do? A good voice is not much use on the large, open and frequently windswept plains they live on. The sound of the wind would drown it out and no other bustard would hear it. The only way to attract a mate is to be seen … and bustards (there are 26 different species worldwide and all of them have amazing displays) have become masters of the catwalk, modelling some of the most eye-catching bird fashions in the world. Don't bother with a bit of crest-raising or tail flicking; what female bustard is going to notice that out here on these vast, flat expanses. Instead, the message seems to be: if you've got it, then flaunt it; bustard displays are designed to be seen!

Gabi, helpful as ever, pointed out more males – some close, others distant – that displayed just as thoroughly as the first. We watched them for an hour or more. It was spellbinding; I had had a ringside seat to an awe-inspiring ritual. Later that day, from tracks and small roads, we could see other, much more distant Great Bustard males performing their magic; some were maybe a couple of kilometres away. The white shimmering, caught in the afternoon sunlight, appeared for a few seconds, sometimes perhaps nearer a minute, then disappeared as if it was a mirage, not really there at all.

So what would the Gitanos, the Romani people of Andalusia – many of them working long hours in the countryside – have made of this visual display of nuptial spring extravagance? They must have noticed it every year on the spring-chilled plains of southern Spain where these birds were almost certainly more abundant in the past. How could they not? And they would have been very familiar with these birds for another, very different reason – food. Well before the days of bird protection, country people would have trapped or shot the occasional bustard. A bird of this proportion would feed a family for days and the meat, by all accounts, was very tasty indeed.

It was one of the reasons why they declined – to eventual extinction – in England through the 17th and 18th centuries. Until then they were not uncommon, especially in southern England. Hunting and habitat change, especially the increasingly intensive use of farmland, has caused their decline across much of Europe but Spain and Portugal still have large populations. In the UK, the English enclosures divided up the large tracts of open land they favour with hedges and other structures, effectively destroying their habitat. The last pair of Great Bustards bred in England in 1832 though in the last decade or so a population has been reintroduced to the Wiltshire downs but is struggling to re-establish itself in any numbers.

With such familiarity with these birds on the Spanish plains, is there not a chance that the Gitanos might have adopted some of its flamboyance, combined it with the brightly coloured, extravagant dresses the women wore traditionally for special occasions, and added in a heady mix of sensuality and passion that's part of life for these people? Did the strutting male bustard, thrusting his head haughtily one way, then the other, an intense mass of white feathers, trying to attract the attention of his female harem, help inspire the weaving and writhing, the stamping and turning of the tightly clad flamenco dancer, her body in one voluptuous posture after another?

In the flamenco it's the girl that does the alluring, sensual writhing. How else can it possibly be? For the bustard it's the male showing off all his manly attributes to any females willing to watch. Flamenco perhaps just reversed those roles. They added in the clicking castanets and the rhythmical hand clapping – reminiscent of the metronome-tempo calls of cicadas in the heady summer warmth maybe – and the crisp, vibrant rhythms of the guitar, their traditional instrument. And then you have it: the elegant, supreme, passionate, voluptuous invocation that's called flamenco.

Go and imbibe it. You won't be disappointed. But, when you do, imagine that amazing 'brown bird to shimmering, spring-blossomed bush transformation' that takes place every spring across these warm, soporific Iberian plains.

Those Simple Bear Necessities

Softly spoken and charming, François Arcangeli is a most unlikely recipient of death threats. And Arbas, the tranquil and somewhat forlorn village tucked away in the foothills of the French Pyrenees, seems an unlikely location for violent demonstrations. Testing the boundaries of incredulity yet further, the cause of this violence is an animal that inspired the cuddly teddy.

Arcangeli, an architect, has been Mayor for many years in Arbas, 80 km east of Lourdes, and we met in his Mairie (Town Hall) where I interviewed him for a *Telegraph* Magazine feature about the huge and often vicious fracas a few bears were causing. Perhaps 20 bears survive in these forests and mountains that divide Spain and France. It's a population that is likely to die out unless it is better protected and its numbers get bolstered by bears introduced from Eastern Europe's larger, much more stable populations.

'In the spring of 2006, the French Government arranged for three bears from Slovenia to be released into our forests near Arbas. Two others were released near other villages,' he tells me. 'Gendarmerie intelligence warned us that there might be a few protestors, mostly farmers worried about their sheep being attacked by bears. But 250 turned up, smashing anything they could find outside the Mairie, trying to break in, spraying paint and throwing bottles of blood. Eighty gendarmes tried to keep order. It was terrible. Most of them came from the Ariège Département [Arbas is in adjacent Haute-Garonne]. Augustin Bonrepaux, the President of Ariège and a Deputy in the French Parliament paid them 20,000 Euros to come and protest violently. He's strongly anti-bear,' he says. Many local politicians seem to have similar views.

The plan, agreed between Spain, France and Andorra, had been to introduce 15 bears over three years, but no attempt has been made to release any bears since those Arbas riots. Seemingly, successive French Governments have backed down in the face of threats from a hardcore of farmers who won't tolerate bears. The latest releases were planned in 2013 in the western Pyrenees, Arcangeli (now Conseiller Régional in the

Midi-Pyrénées Regional Government, where he represents the Green Party) told me more recently. But he reckons the French Government backed out yet again with no rational explanation. It seems they are running scared of some thuggish farmers.

Of the five Brown Bears from Slovenia introduced in 2006, one gave birth to two cubs. Two bears, both females, subsequently died. One fell from a cliff in a rare freak accident. The other was killed by a car on a road outside Lourdes, much to the delight of many local farmers and the sorrow of conservationists. The strength of anti-bear feeling is best summarised by Marie-Lise Broueilh, President of the Association Interprofessionnelle du Mouton Barèges Gavarnie, an organisation promoting mountain sheep meat. She told me: 'We are immensely satisfied that this bear was killed. This is a great relief for local farmers.'

Bears are shy creatures, easily frightened by people. And while claims of aggressive bears are often promoted by anti-bear interests, there are virtually no records of anyone being attacked anywhere in Western Europe. So forest walking in bear country is perfectly safe. In most Eastern European countries where Brown Bears are much more common, people working in forests or walking for recreation don't give bear attacks a second thought.

In any case Brown Bears are largely vegetarian. In spring they feed on flowering plants and grasses, adding in fruits and berries during summer. In autumn, preparing for hibernation, they need to eat fat-rich foods. So acorns, beechnuts and hazelnuts figure highly. Hibernating in dens they dig or in natural rock cavities for three to six months of winter – the time that they give birth and feed their cubs on fat-rich milk – bears are active mainly at night, and around dawn and dusk, for the rest of the year. And, in true Winnie-the-Pooh tradition, bears really do love honey; hence their liking for wild bee nests and beehives. A wooden beehive is never any match for a strong bear; if it decides to do a break-in, it can tear a hive apart in seconds to get at the honeycomb.

Honey-making is an artisan industry in the Pyrenees. Beehives are easy to protect from marauding bears by using electric fences or by elevating hives on tripods out of their reach. And government compensation is available if such measures fail. But they will sometimes attack animals to add to their diet; hence Pyrenean farmers' concerns. Powerfully built, they are quite capable of killing large deer. Sheep, though, are easier prey. And therein lies the source of most of the conflict.

The trouble is, few farmers will take any note of the statistics. These show that bear kills pale into insignificance compared with other factors. 'Of the half million sheep in the French Pyrenees, around 15,000 die naturally each year because of disease, bad weather and falls,' Frédéric Decaluwe of ONCFS, the Office National de la Chasse et de la Faune Sauvage – the French Government agency that oversees hunting – tells me when we meet in his office. 'But only 200 to 300 a year are killed by bears and the farmers are compensated for those kills.' He is clearly exasperated that farmers won't take any notice of such figures.

To me the compensation on offer seemed pretty generous. When I was there interviewing the protagonists, it amounted to upwards of three times the market value of a sheep killed by a bear, maybe as much as ten times its value depending on the quality of the animal at the time it was killed. Similar compensation schemes were operating on the Spanish side of the Pyrenees too. 'It's a quick process. We usually get the compensation to the farmer within three weeks. If there's doubt about what killed the sheep [wolves, stray dogs and even the farmers' own dogs are other possibilities] a Commission on which farmers are represented meets at the end of each season to assess the evidence. If there's any doubt, the compensation is paid,' adds Decaluwe. François Arcangeli, who is also President of Pays de l'ours-ADET, an organisation promoting bear conservation, likewise thinks the farmers do well from the system. 'Before the compensation for bear kills, farmers used to complain that stray dogs killed their sheep. But they never claim that now, only bears. It's always bears!' he says rocking with laughter.

Brown Bears are still reasonably common across North America, Russia and northern and central Asia. Their range once covered the whole of Europe too. But that was before forest clearance steadily reduced their habitat. By the Middle Ages, Europe's Brown Bears were confined to the less accessible mountain areas. Hunting finished most of them off and they were extinct in Britain before the Norman Conquest. Today, their European stronghold is in western Russia and northern Scandinavia where thousands still live. They fare reasonably well in some Eastern European countries such as Romania, Slovenia and Croatia too. In Western Europe, where they are strictly protected, their populations are fragmented, very small and vulnerable to extinction. Most are confined to inaccessible forested mountain ranges.

Spotting one is far from easy. It's no good walking through forests you know they inhabit and hoping to come across one. However quiet you are, they'll hear you coming and be away before you even know there was one close by.

Slovenia, though, has one of the larger, more stable Brown Bear populations in Western Europe – at least a few hundred – the reason why bears introduced to the Pyrenees have been captured in Slovenia's extensive forests. Here, in the Jelen Hunting Reserve near the Croatian border, I had been lucky to have help from Miro Uljan, a local hunter and game warden working for the Slovenian Forest Service. But it was a cool summer's evening with puffs of mist and no moon to brighten the night-time gloom; Miro was not confident that we would see one. Our concerns about the weather conditions, though, evaporated rapidly. Not long after settling into the hide overlooking a clearing, two Brown Bears came sauntering out between the trees. It was an almost surreal experience.

For the next three hours, until the coal-night darkness rendered it impossible, we watched, awe-struck, as these two magnificent animals, a large, chocolate-brown male perhaps weighing 300 kg and a paler brown and grey, three-quarter grown cub came within 30 m of our hide. They had come out of the forest to feed on grain scattered to attract them – so close, we could hear them munching it – bounded up grassy slopes alongside and, occasionally, retreated into the inky-dark safety of the forest. When time came for us to leave, we moved out quietly, up a path and on to the forest track we'd left three hours earlier. And as we walked away we could still hear the bears sitting on the damp ground eating the grain.

'People are used to living alongside bears in Slovenia,' Aleksandra Majic Skrbinšek at the University of Ljubljana tells me when we meet in her office. She was studying public attitudes to large carnivores (bears, lynx and wolves) in several European countries. 'Each year our government licences a number of bears to be hunted. Most of the hunting is done by local people and they take a responsible attitude. Bears are shot for trophies and the meat is sold so the local economy benefits. Although some people believe there should be no bear hunting, it means that country people value their bears and have a personal investment in maintaining the population,' she says.

It's not an attitude I found to be prevalent in much of the Pyrenees. In the 1930s there were perhaps 200 bears in these part-forested mountains. By the mid-1990s, just six are thought to have remained even though hunting had been banned – in theory but not so in practice – in Spain and France. Three bears from Slovenia were introduced in 1996 plus the five in 2006 in an attempt to bolster their numbers. One of the few remaining native Pyrenean bears, a female, was shot trying to defend its cubs against a hunter's dog in 2004, an incident the then President Jacques Chirac called 'a great loss for France and Europe' and which galvanised public opinion in favour of better protection. But, 'great loss' or not, the French Government has done nothing to boost their dwindling population ever since. The current population, less than 20 spread over a huge land area, is too small to be self-sustaining.

Recognising that Pyrenean farmers have to change the way they farm if they are to co-exist with bears, payments are available to encourage them to adapt. Most of this cash is channelled through local voluntary organisations and comes from the Spanish and French Governments. I went to meet Catherine Lacroix, a farmer in the tiny village of Barjac, a few kilometres north of St Girons, and a founder member of the Association pour la Cohabitation Pastorale (ACP). She has changed the way she farms. Walking with her on her farm's lush fields framed by beechwoods on the hill slopes around, it's not easy to spot the white Pyrenean Mountain Dog – known here as a Patou – amongst her sheep flock as they thunder towards us across the flower-specked turf.

A Patou can weigh over 50 kg and stand 80 cm high, the height of a small sheep. It's a very old breed that has been used for hundreds of years by shepherds, including many in and around the Pyrenees on both the French and Spanish sides. One of the first descriptions of the breed dates from 1407, and from 1675 they were a favourite of the Grand Dauphin and other members of the French aristocracy. By the early 19th century there was a thriving market for the dogs in mountain towns, from where they would be taken to other parts of France. The breed was developed to be agile in order to guard sheep on steep, mountainous slopes.

'The Patou lives out with the sheep whatever the weather, day and night,' says Lacroix. 'He's here to protect the flock and if the flock is in danger – from a bear perhaps or wolves or a feral dog – the Patou will become aggressive, barking loudly. They have to be brought up with the sheep as puppies and they are never treated like pets. Otherwise they couldn't do their job.' Lacroix's Patou looked friendly enough but that was entirely because she was with me; on well used footpaths throughout the Pyrenees the Patous are the reason why leaflets are now commonplace telling walkers not to venture into a field with sheep and not to get close to a flock grazing the open mountain pastures. A Patou might be guarding them and a guarding Patou is of far greater danger to a walker than a bear would ever be.

Using government grants paid by ACP as enticement, several hundred farmers now use the Patou. They receive a one-off payment once the dog has been trained to the correct standard (to offset its purchase cost plus the time to train it) and annual payments after that. Surveys of farmers using these dogs have found a reduction in the number of sheep killed by bears of more than 90%. But not all farmers are happy to accept Patous and the cash that goes with them. Some, Lacroix acknowledges, are unwilling to accept the extra work required to train and keep a Patou and are resentful that they have to change the way they manage their sheep.

EU cash is also available here to employ shepherds and to accommodate them in mountain huts when sheep flocks are taken up to the high summer pastures. Watching over their charges by day, with or without a Patou, the sheep are then rounded up at night using a collie and often brought within a temporary enclosure protected by an electric fence. I arranged to meet Robert Wojciechowski who runs a small company designing such temporary electric fences and other bear deterrents including lights, pyrotechnics, and harmless lasers that can be triggered if a bear approaches. In the mountains they can be run using solar panels. Farmers buying such devices can receive government grants to defray their cost. 'There are about 200 farmers in the three valleys I work in,' says Wojciecowski. 'Forty have bought my fences but even they are not happy knowing that they have to protect their sheep against bears. Not that it's always bears; feral dogs are just as much of a problem.'

But Wojciecowski is not convinced that the French Government's determination to bolster bear numbers while giving money to farmers to reflect their extra cost is going to work. 'Paris imposes bears in the Pyrenees. They don't ask the farmers; they have no understanding of the issue from the farmers' viewpoint. Most farmers won't even come to a meeting to discuss bears because they are afraid to appear that they agree with the policy. It's a war between farmers and bears; city people who like to think there are bears here and country people who don't want them,' he argues.

Wanting to get the farmer's perspective I also arranged to meet Olivier Maurin, a young man who farms 200 sheep to produce cheese at Agnos about 20 km southwest of Pau. He's typical of many farmers in the area. 'I love bears but I don't want to have to live with them. For us farmers it's not about compensation, it's changing our way of life, our way of farming,' says Maurin who adds, contradicting himself, 'I know we get EU subsidies to farm but we would have to get much more money before we accept bears here.'

And while most farmers are implacably anti-bear, organisations like ACP quote public attitude surveys such as one done in the Haute-Garonne in 2005 showing 80% of residents in this part of the Pyrenees in favour of retaining them. There is much less conflict in Slovenia between bears and farmers than here in the Pyrenees. In Slovenia, sheep have always been gathered into enclosures at night to protect them. In other countries where bears have been introduced, in Trentino in Italy for instance, the state authorities talk directly to the local people about the options. In France they just talk to the local politicians and other representatives. So local people, farmers especially, feel that things are imposed on them.

It isn't an argument that Frédéric Decaluwe accepts. 'We try hard to talk to farmers. Every summer we have nine people outdoors doing just that. The main problem is that farmers don't want to talk about bears because they don't want bears. They say they want bears removed not more brought here,' he says. 'The French Government has all the facts,' says Decaluwe. 'We have perhaps 20 bears in the Pyrenees. It's not a sustainable population. Our farmers are compensated well for any problems and they get EU subsidies to farm. We have a detailed action plan that includes introducing more bears. But it's all so slow. It's local politics.'

Slowly, opposition is declining according to François Arcangeli. 'Farmers are less and less opposed. The measures to protect sheep flocks are being put in place gradually and bear kills are stable or even decreasing. The opposition is a minority. There has been some successful breeding so the number of bears has increased a little,' he says.

But not everyone is so positive. 'Ultimately, I think the cash incentives have perhaps softened some hearts but overall, the programme is still meeting with stubborn resistance,' Julia Stagg, a writer and, for several years a resident of the Ariège Département, told me more recently. 'Now that the reintroduction programme has been stopped for a few years, it will be even harder to get going again. I'm not sure about changes in attitudes over the intervening years. I think some of the recent "calm" surrounding the issue of bears has been created by the temporary suspension of the reintroductions. There have been fewer protests. But as soon as there is any suggestion that a bear has attacked sheep, it all flares up again,' she tells me. Dr Pierre-Yves Quenette of ONCFS, who is head of the project to manage bears in the French side of the Pyrenees, says that there'll be no more introductions of bears at least over the next two or three years and, while farmer opposition seems less strong, he agrees with Julia Stagg that it can flare up at any time.

If the French Authorities fail to reintroduce more bears, the isolated population in the Pyrenees will struggle to survive. Since I visited the region, Brown Bear numbers have risen to around 25, ironically almost all of them on the French side of the mountains. Both the French and the Spanish Governments seem to be able to side-step their legal responsibilities under the EU's Habitats Directive which requires them to get their Brown Bear populations into a viable state. Politically, instead, both governments seem willing to go along with the often irrational views of Pyrenean farmers rather than confront the issue itself. Seemingly, more introductions won't go ahead until these concerns are very largely overcome. Whether all the talking and the compensation packages will reduce this opposition only time will tell. Meanwhile, any future that Brown Bears have in the Pyrenees continues to teeter in the balance.

The Curse of Stein Erik

Stein Erik's buoyant optimism was sinking fast. We had been grinding along dusty forest tracks in first gear for nearly two hours, the minibus lurching to a gravel-spraying halt whenever anyone thought they saw something vaguely resembling a large animal in the increasingly murky forest clearings on either side. The trip was becoming a tad boring. In the descending late evening gloom, the silhouettes of trees were playing Elk-shaped tricks with our eyes. But we hadn't even spotted a squirrel.

Earlier that evening I had assembled with five or six others in a somewhat nondescript, shop-lined square in Trysil, an otherwise delightful little Norwegian town about 240 km northeast of Oslo. The surrounding pine forests are excellent walking country. What's more, they are supposed to teem with Elk, those earth-brown critters with antlers like spreading oak trees. They are actually a species of deer. We were going on an Elk safari with The Wildlife Company's local expert, Stein Erik. And we had set off with a feeling of obvious excitement. 'We will travel slowly once we are in the forest. We must look for anything large and grey, the size of a small cow,' he announced in carefully measured, somewhat hushed phrases, as if we were about to be ushered into the presence of royalty. Now we were excitedly optimistic.

By around 11 p.m. – and in southern Norway in late summer that means it isn't dark, just very dull – we ground to yet another, rubber-searing halt. One of our eagle-eyed, fellow safari punters had spotted a massive, grey backside beating a hasty retreat into the black as coal forest. Stein Erik reckoned it was a five-feet-tall female Elk. We managed a split second grey blur. A little later someone spotted another, the minibus lurched again, and we had a flash view of two more Elk bums, one very large, the other small. Apparently a full-grown female with a three-foot youngster. We took Stein Erik's word for it.

By the end of the trip as we got back to Trysil's town square, our guide was more downbeat, trying to come up with explanations for why we were the poor sods that were destined to have such pathetic views of these otherwise impressive animals.

Apparently, almost all other such safaris get stupendous views. I suppose he was bothered that for 200 Kroner (£17) a person, three fast moving bums wasn't much of a memory to return home with. He was dead right.

Elk avoided us for the whole week in southern Norway, much of it spent within or close to forest. In fact, it's not easy to avoid being in or close to forest in most of Norway. It was one of those frustrating trips when what you assume will be one of the most common and instantly recognisable animals Scandinavia can offer suddenly goes shy. The country supposedly has at least 120,000 Elk. You might have thought that just one of them could have put in a decent appearance for my week, but no. And this in spite of several evenings spent sitting around on forest tracks in places where the locals in Trysil reckoned we would definitely see them when they came out of the forest at night to graze. We had walked past heaps of their rich brown, rugby ball-shaped droppings the size of ten-pence pieces on forest paths. But no Elk.

There were compensations though. One evening, a couple more hours of sitting and standing quietly in the cover of a group of trees did provide a superb close-up view of one of the most attractive owls in Europe; the Northern Hawk Owl is mainly a daytime owl with a longish tail and a dark brown –virtually black – striped appearance on white plumage. This one landed just above us on an exposed branch of a pine and gave us an occasional downward glance with its bright yellow eyes. In flight especially, Hawk Owls look more like Sparrowhawks than owls, hence its name.

Compensation, too, came in the shape of European Beavers. In Ljordalen, a tiny agglomeration of wooden houses, farms and a couple of general stores which passes muster for a village about 40 km east of Trysil near the Swedish border, the Ljora River has a good population of beavers. Apparently, so did most rivers around here. My wife and I hired a dark green (nicely camouflaged), two-seater canoe from Norvald Doksrud, an incredibly helpful and informative local builder. There were always beavers on the river he told us and the best time to see them was in the evening. We put our mammal-searching trust in him and hoped that he didn't have the curse of Stein Erik upon him.

So, sprayed copiously with insect repellent, an essential summer evening precaution in Scandinavian forests, we set off with a push and a wave into the sluggish but crystal clear water. We glided downstream on the imperceptible current, hardly using our paddles except to guide us a touch left or right away from the riverbanks. It was an almost dreamlike experience under a cloudless, evening-blue sky, upside-down trees in their perfect leafy detail reflected in the cool stillness of the water's surface. An occasional silver-grey fish noisily broke through the reflection of a tree, sending out a little circle of ripples and momentarily destroying the surreal image that mesmerised us.

Regimentally spaced flotillas of grey-brown female Goldeneye Ducks with their entourage of bobbing, brown, down-covered ducklings swam ahead of us, the elegant males black and white with their large green heads and white beak spot, the females greyer with a chestnut head. They would have raised their ducklings in holes high up in the old boles of bankside trees, holes often chopped out and vacated by breeding Black Woodpeckers. And when the chicks are ready to leave their nest-hole – just a few days old – they flutter down to the ground like trainee parachutists, hoping to land safely, shake themselves off and waddle into the water where they are safer from predators than they are on land.

Bunches of leathery, green-stemmed Water Crowfoot plants rooted in the shallow, gravel riffles, floating their gorgeous, white-as-snow flowers on the water's surface, decorated our idyllic riverine route. Straining ahead to distinguish river from sky, we suddenly spotted a tiny bow wave reflecting the evening sun, a bow wave followed by V-shaped ripples heading across the river. The canoe yawing wildly as we grabbed our binoculars and dropped the paddles (thankfully, inside the boat), a full-grown beaver came into focus.

It eyed us cautiously, circled in the water, its metre-long, chestnut-brown body hardly breaking the surface. It swam off downstream and we paddled hard to try and keep up. Then, as if aware that we were in hot pursuit, it circled once more in the river, its marbles of dark eyes fixed on us. Suddenly, it arched its back, dived headfirst underwater and slapped its large flat tail on the water's surface with a loud whack, a beaver alarm signal to warn others of hostility afoot. It didn't work. As we drifted further on our four-mile downriver trip, we spotted another three beavers, all of them keeping their distance, swimming and diving in the clear, cool water, their little, sun-reflecting bow waves a giveaway. Thankfully, the curse of Stein Erik hadn't followed us into the river.

It wasn't until a few years later that we were driving along a track in the Baxter State Park in Maine in the northeast USA, just south of the Canada border, that I saw my first Elk, or Moose as it is known in North America. In true Stein Erik tradition, I lurched to a sudden halt, spraying gravel this way and that. Just to our left in a small lake, a pair of huge, tell-tale antlers were rising out of the water, parts of them draped in green weed. It was something of a John the Baptist moment. And here was one, then another, emerging from feeding on the lake bed greenery, coming up for air now and again, their huge spreading antlers followed by their overly long, barrel-shaped head and snout. If the water gets too deep for them, Moose are surprisingly good swimmers.

They are not the best looking of the deer family. In fact they look as if they have had a nose job which has gone very badly wrong. Their affinity with water is three-fold: because they graze the floating and bottom-growing vegetation; because it cools them in summer; and because it gets them away from the blackflies that pester them. Most of the vegetation they eat on land tends to be short of sodium so Moose make up for that by consuming water plants, apparently a richer source of the mineral they need.

Unlike almost all deer, Moose are solitary animals, never living in groups. Maybe they don't like the look of each other. And they always seem rather ponderous and slow moving. But don't be fooled. Angered, they can put on an impressive show of speed. What they do have in common with other deer, males only, are their antlers. And it would be difficult to beat the sheer size of a full grown bull Moose's huge pair. They can be up to 200 cm wide (that's nearly seven feet); they are dropped prior to each winter to conserve energy, then re-grown each spring when a bull feeds voraciously to nurture their growth. Moose antlers are sexy appendages, to cow Moose anyway; the cows actually select male partners based on their antler size.

Since the 1990s, Moose populations have declined dramatically in virtually every part of North America. No one is sure why. It appears to be a combination of factors, from changes in habitat and heat stress caused by global warming, liver flukes, brain worms, unregulated hunting to the reintroduction of wolves and winter tick infestations. In Europe, though, especially in Scandinavia and Russia, they are abundant and doing well in spite of my difficulty seeing them with Stein Erik.

Moose can be a lethal hazard when they cross roads, especially at night when they are often hard to spot. It can be a deadly experience both for the animal and for the vehicle's occupants. That's because of the Moose's shape: rather thin spindly legs and a very heavy body. Generally, when colliding with it at speed, a saloon car's front bumper and grille will break the Moose's legs, causing its body to crash through the windscreen and crush the front seat passengers. A full-grown bull Moose can weigh up to 700 kg, the weight of a small car. Seatbelts or airbags will give you no protection. Which is why most forest roads in Scandinavia have frequent Elk warning signs and most main roads are fenced to prevent them crossing.

Baxter State Park made up for Stein Erik's safari. But it had its own frustrations all the same. One of the common mammals of this mainly forested, nearly 900 km² area, is the Black Bear. They are not large bears; adults can weigh as little as 50 kg, much less than Brown Bears, though some are larger. But could we spot one? Each time we arrived at the State Park visitor centre, the staff had recently spotted one nearby. They soon got to know us – the visitor centre staff, most certainly not the bears – and seemed genuinely sorry every time we turned up and had just missed yet another impressive viewing. I should have explained that it was the curse of Stein Erik all over again. But I didn't. And I have still never seen a Black Bear.

Forests – often with extensive bogs associated with them – anywhere in the northern extremities of our planet from Russia to Canada and Alaska (where it's called 'muskeg') can be exciting places for a variety of wildlife. Store Mosse is the largest, partly pine-forested mire in southern Sweden; 10,000 ha of marsh, lakes and conifer forest near the southernmost world limit of this kind of habitat. Walking out on the extensive track network provided by the Park Authorities gets you into what feels very quickly like a huge wilderness. Red Squirrels rustle in the trees; in one clearing around an abandoned hut we came across a family of them, the youngsters maybe two-thirds grown but already sporting bushy russet-red tails that seemed larger than their bodies and little ear tufts too. Without doubt, they really are very endearing mammals. Scurrying this way and that, the youngsters kept bobbing under the wooden foundations of the shack, then coming out and tearing about on the open ground around. It was difficult to count them but there were definitely more that the average three or four that's normal in a single brood. So perhaps we had stumbled across a squirrel crèche. Whoever was in charge was not having much success corralling them!

Getting an overview of a huge, flat wetland like this is always difficult, so the attraction of a three-storey viewing platform was obvious. It gave us commanding views over a very large area of the national park including some of the breeding area for Common Cranes. And what a view that turned out to be. About a kilometre away (they need undisturbed places for successful breeding) we could see them standing on boggy ground between scattered pines and spruces, their nesting platforms – piles of branches and vegetation built up on the bog surface – obvious too. Some of the cranes were incubating, sitting tight on their nests.

Then things got a little lively. A couple of the non-incubating birds, males presumably, started to do their characteristic dance, something I hadn't seen before. As if choreographed by some silent orchestra, the birds opened their wings, jumped up into the air, bobbed about, bowing and pirouetting … then stopped as if an imaginary ballet teacher had suggested that their effort wasn't quite up to muster and they should try repeating those movements again. And so they did. Several times we watched their amazing dances, and several times it seemed to stop unnecessarily abruptly. Maybe they were just showing off to their incubating females, lending encouragement on a beautifully sunny early summer's day and looking forward to the offspring they would soon have. More prosaically – and more realistically – they were probably doing what biologists usually say under these circumstances: they were re-enforcing the pair bond between breeding males and females. Cranes usually mate for life but their courtship rituals are re-enacted every spring. Their loud unison call involves the female holding her head up and gradually lowering it down as she calls while the male follows with a longer scream in a similar posture – more pair bonding.

Just like most crane species worldwide, the dances have complex social meanings and may occur at almost any time of year. And while we didn't see it here at Store Mosse, – though I have seen it in winter in the dehesas of Extremadura in Spain (see Chapter 3), cranes also do aggressive displays which can include ruffling their wing feathers, throwing vegetation in the air and pointing the bare red patch on their heads at each other.

It was something of a wrench to turn away from the Store Mosse cranes and scan further out into the open bog. But in the distance we could see small birds flying several tens of metres above the Sphagnum surface, then seemingly dropping down on to it. But what were they? And what were they doing? It took a while for me to realise that they were waders, little Wood Sandpipers we see in Britain on passage at estuaries or at inland pools but breeding here on the open bog amongst the sweet odour of Bog Myrtle and Dwarf Willows growing on the Sphagnum moss surface. These were their display flights, presumably by the males (though, seemingly, females do them too), who fly up into the air with their wings angled sharply backwards like jet fighters, circle above their nesting area on the ground below while fluttering their wings in bursts, before gliding on outspread wings and tail to descend back on to the ground. An energetic business, they repeat the whole display at frequent intervals.

Later on that day, having seen a White-tailed Eagle fly past in the distance, its huge wing-span and splayed-out white tail obvious, another of Store Mosse's specialities made its presence felt. And I don't mean mosquitoes. At first I couldn't see what was making the loud, yodelling or ringing call coming from some spruces at the edge of a boggy area a couple of hundred metres ahead of us. Eventually we spotted the source: a small wading bird that we, in Britain and much of southern Europe, are used to seeing feeding on muddy shorelines in estuaries and around little freshwater pools. But certainly not in the breeding season. That's not where Green Sandpipers – waders a little smaller than Redshank – are to be found when they're breeding. And this one was most definitely in its characteristic habitat. Perched half way up a spruce tree on a branch overlooking the bog, it was singing, an incongruous sight if you only ever see them in winter walking around on a muddy shoreline. Nearby, I assume, it had its nest; not on the ground but up in a tree where these unusual birds purloin an old thrush or Fieldfare nest to use as its own. When the youngsters are raised and ready to leave home, they half fly, half flutter to the boggy ground below rather like hole-nesting ducks such as the Goldeneye near the Ljora River. With their nesting trees usually growing on a thick mat of spongy bogmoss, the Green Sandpiper chicks are more likely to be guaranteed a cushioned landing.

There was, though, one much larger animal that occurs in good numbers at Store Mosse but which we didn't see. It was the Elk. Though we scanned large areas of the bog and walked – quietly – through much boggy forest, we failed to find one. The Norwegians and the Swedes don't always see eye to eye and I reckon that Stein Erik had made his presence felt over here in Sweden too.

Stepping Out on the Steppes

As we walked along the rutted path, olive and brown striped frogs, from tiny to large, legs stretched out behind them like free-fall parachutists, dived headlong into the murky ditch water a couple of metres below. All we could hear was a rhythmical 'plop, plop'; it even drowned out most of the bird song around. It was as if someone had fired the starting pistol for a staggered amphibian Olympic swimming final.

Most summers in the Hortobágy – the vast, pancake-flat plain or *puszta* (meaning 'bare' or 'bereft', though in reality it's neither) of eastern Hungary – the heat keeps the frogs slouching in the cooler water, croaking with tubercular grunts. It can be so hot that atmospheric tricks cause mirages of inviting blue water to appear here, shimmering on the sun-bleached grasses of the crispbread plains. No mirages for us. We saw the real thing: too much rain. Shallow pools of mucky water dotted the flower-speckled landscape. Most afternoons we were grateful for the occasional plum tree. Not just to gorge on the free fruit, but for shelter from the thundery downpours. It was why the frogs were content to lounge in the damp vegetation; they had no need of total immersion.

The *puszta* is a wide open landscape where it's easy to imagine that there's no protection when winter sets in and an incredibly icy wind blows from yet further east. It was less easy to imagine the baking hot summers with no shade from the glare of the East European sun ... except in the summer I was there. Much of the *puszta*, 800 km², though that's not all of it, was designated a national park in 1973 but not solely for its wildlife or because it's the largest fairly natural area of flower-rich grassland in lowland Europe. The *puszta* is of equal importance for its folklore and cultural history. And I was here in 2004 to write a travel feature about the area for *The Independent*.

It used to be reckoned that these grassy plains must have been created when extensive forests were felled, perhaps in the Middle Ages, and the whole land put over to grazing livestock. But more recent evidence suggests that it's much older still, dating from the last Ice Age 10,000 years ago when, with the ice retreat, the land remained treeless due to the grazing of wild animals and the Tisza River forming wetlands too marshy for trees to grow in. Most of the wild grazers were gradually killed off and replaced with sheep and cattle as humankind exerted its increasing influence, introducing special breeds to withstand the rigours of such a climate.

But the *puszta* isn't all grassland, coloured – especially in spring – with a generous assemblage of flowers; it is also dotted with numerous fishponds, many small but several of them really quite large. They were dug mainly during World War I to cultivate fish as a protein-rich food that local people needed badly. There are plenty of fish in them today too and the margins of many sport reedbeds and other marsh vegetation where Great Bitterns lurk, those long-necked heron-like birds known for their curious, far-reaching springtime courtship calls. Always described as 'booming', this peculiar sound, heard mainly around dawn and dusk, is more like the sudden deflation of a football or a sharp blow across the top of a large and empty glass bottle. It carries for maybe 2 km and although it's never loud, it is an unmistakable sound. Not surprisingly, the fishponds I saw were full to the brim with water, their beds of man-high reed alive with the rattling, vibrating – and rather monotonous – songs of Savi's Warblers and the twanging calls of baby Bearded Reedlings.

These are two birds that couldn't be more different. Savi's is a plain reddish-brown and cream warbler, skulking in the reeds except when the males are singing to secure a mate. And that monotonous, mechanical, insect-like reeling reminiscent of a cricket calling on a hot summer's day – and rarely stopping – could have been designed to drive someone to despair. Though presumably not a female Savi's Warbler who must think the most monotonous and persistent buzzer she can hear is the most macho and the best mate she could possibly have. The Bearded Reedling or Bearded Tit is a much showier chap; deep straw/orange-brown in colour with a long tail, a grey head and impressive black moustache markings down the face (though the female, obviously, lacks the moustache). They are drop dead gorgeous. Always on the move, they have a range of twanging and chirping calls, sometimes hard to locate but not in the least monotonous. But these two birds do at least have something in common; they are both often very difficult to spot in swaying reeds.

Incredibly, a third of the Hortobágy National Park – still the most impressive part of the Hungarian *puszta* – consists of fishponds and the extensive reedbeds that have grown up around them. Some, like those at Hortobágy-halast, with its ancient, nine-arch river bridge much visited by tourists, have hides or viewing platforms to look out over them. It may sound obvious, but with reeds too tall to see over, and 25 km² of reedbed and ponds just in this one place, it's important to try to keep a sense of direction if you want to return to where you started. For someone with a generally poor sense of direction like me, that was pretty well essential.

And what a profusion of wildlife they reveal for anyone equipped with binoculars on one of the platforms. Flotillas of ducks, including the chestnut-coloured

Ferruginous Duck, swim by, occasionally diving in the shallow waters to find bottom-living invertebrates to savour. This is a duck confined to eastern and southern Europe, commonplace here. Now and again I managed to spot a svelte black and white, aptly named Black-crowned Night Heron perching motionless at the edge of the reeds waiting to plunge its beak into the murky water and pierce a small fish or frog. Usually making an appearance around dawn and dusk, and more active at night as their name suggests, these herons were out in full daylight. Lined up on some dead branches in the reeds were a group of jet-black Pygmy Cormorants with their characteristic brown heads, resting I presumed after a spot of successful fishing. Birds of Eastern Europe and Asia, they are half the size of the cormorant common in the UK and most of Western Europe.

Out on the vast, flat *puszta* you no longer see long-cloaked cowboys – *csikós* – riding their horses to round up herds of the rather odd-looking, but traditional corkscrew-horned Racka (pronounced 'ratchka') sheep. Today's *csikós* wear jeans though it's possible to see them dressed up in their finery in the more touristy spots where you can hire horses and do some riding with them if you feel confident enough. Traditionally, though, they wore black, high boots; ornately buttoned, blue waistcoats; black, tricorn hats and long flowing, pleated skirts (again, blue) worn over their breeches, an operatically flamboyant outfit that gives every impression of being a tad impractical. Nevertheless, that was their traditional garb. These days I'm sure they're relieved to sally forth in a pair of comfortable jeans.

But the *csikós* did, of course, have well-honed survival skills out here where sudden thundery downpours of cold rain could bring on hypothermia in less time than it takes to round up a few Rackas. To keep dry under such conditions a *csikó* would sit his horse down and tuck himself in underneath its stomach between its front legs as if in a sentry box to shelter from the fierce *puszta* rain storms.

The first Rackas I saw, pale brown in colour, were pretty startling. Both the males and females have a pair of outward pointing spiral horns, I suppose about 60 cm long. They are the only breed of sheep in the world with such horns. What use they are to the animals I have no idea; what I do know is that this is a hardy breed (it has to be here) and they are kept for milk as well as for their wool and meat.

More interesting still are the traditional creamy-white, retriever-like Puli sheepdogs and their huge cousin, the Komondor. Pulis are usually black but the examples I saw on the *puszta* were always creamy white for some reason. Standing just 40 cm high, they are the canid version of a Rastafarian. With deeply matted floor-length hair enveloping them from head to toe, it isn't until they bark that it's obvious which end is the front. Trained for herding and protecting the Racka sheep, they need to be cosy and warm in winter, and waterproof when it pours with rain. The Puli is an ancient sheepdog breed introduced here by the immigration of the

Magyars from Central Asia more than 1,000 years ago. Traditionally, the Puli would work together with the much larger, white-haired Komondor, a Hungarian breed of livestock guarding dog. The Komondor is altogether different and more intimidating. It's a large, solidly built dog, powerful and athletic – also with a Rastafarian coat hanging down to the ground in great twisted cords – but much larger, a metre tall or sometimes more. Stand them together and they look as if they've been crocheted out of hanks of wool and sisal by bored grandmothers passing away long winter evenings when it's too cold and dark for a walk in the *puszta*.

The Komondor (or several Komondors if there was a large amount of livestock) guarded the sheep or cattle particularly at night, while the Puli herded and guarded them during the day. When wolves or bears attacked the livestock, the Puli would alert the pack and the powerful Komondors would come and fight the intruders. Seemingly, the little Pulis were also good at fighting off wolves because their thick coat protects their skin from bites. The Komondors usually rested during daytime but at night walked around the flock, constantly moving, patrolling the area. The dogs were so vital that nomadic shepherds of the Hungarian plains used to pay as much as a year's salary for a Puli. Bears and wolves were killed off in these parts long ago, though wolves are spreading once again across Europe and nowadays there are a couple of hundred in Hungary (though probably none in the Hortobágy). So the dogs' presence these days is almost solely for herding and as a key part of the culture and traditional land use. Imported into the USA, though, they have undergone a renaissance in their use; there they are valued to protect sheep from the bears, wolves, coyotes and other predators that most certainly do still exist.

Sometimes this canine pairing can get too close for comfort. One day I spotted a distant little-and-large pair competing for the title of best barker of the *puszta*, making steady progress towards me as I tried, in vain, to concentrate on watching a gorgeous orange and grey Red-footed Falcon, perched on a distant tree. I'm sure I could have brazened it out with the Puli. But the Komondor with its long swags of matted brown hair swaying from side to side as it galloped towards me like a Rastafarian bull at full charge, was a different matter. They are known to be unpredictable and aggressive. Never very keen on large dogs, retreat seemed the best option; I jumped in the car and fled the scene.

Calmer circumstances prevailed when I visited the Puszta Animal Park, a rare breeds conservation centre within the national park. We eyeballed muddy Mangalica pigs, Racka sheep, a very ugly breed of chicken with a scraggy bare neck, and huge, off-white Hungarian Grey cattle. And all at close quarters in pens. There were a couple of Puli sheepdogs, too. But, thankfully, no Komondors. They also had some of the wild species that used to inhabit the *puszta* before they were hunted to extinction: wolves and jackals for instance, in a setting that's a kind of hybrid between a zoo and a safari park.

The *puszta* is the place, say local people, where sky and land meet. You can sometimes see so far over this flat-as-a-pancake landscape, interrupted only by the occasional tree, it seems to extend to the end of the earth. But out here on a typically hot summer's day it's not possible to see a great distance because of heat shimmer. Ironically, with so much rain before and during my visit, the shimmer was much worse than usual. The occasional viewing platform provided by the national park proved particularly useful; at least it gave me a chance to see a little further. One such day revealed a large flock of distant – and shimmering – Common Cranes, early arrivals on their way south, I assumed, from their breeding grounds in Poland and the Baltic states to southern Europe for the winter. Through the evaporating moisture, the elegant, tall, slate-grey birds seemed to flicker and dance, their Edwardian bustle-like tails flicking this way and that, their long necks bending and scything upwards as if the birds were framed in a speeded up series of cartoon drawings.

Here and there on the grassland, small mounds of soil and stones lie dug out on the surface. They're a bit like large molehills and they can be commonplace. It doesn't usually take long before you spot their architects. Walking along a path one day I heard a distant whistle, then another. There was no one about so I stopped and looked around; standing on its back legs on top of one of these little mounds not far away, surveying the scene – and having spotted me before I saw it – was a European Souslik, Europe's answer to the equally delightful meerkat of Southern African deserts. It was giving its alarm whistle to warn other sousliks to get into their underground tunnels and out of sight. Sharpish.

Days later I happened to spot a small family group of them outside their burrows and before they saw me. I hid behind some scrub to watch their antics. Delightful little mammals, they scurried about, often several metres from where I could see they had burrow entrances, seemingly finding seeds to eat and whatever else they could. And all the time, the duty souslik did his lookout job. After half an hour I thought I'd test their reactions. Moving out of the scrub, the sentinel spotted me, whistled several times and in seconds all the sousliks had disappeared underground. You can't hang around on the surface in full view if you are this vulnerable to whatever ground predator might be lurking nearby or soaring silently just above in the sky. Their sentinels are absolutely essential; a whole range of animals prey on them. After all, a full-grown souslik makes a very filling meal: for weasels, foxes, wandering domestic cats, buzzards and other birds of prey for starters. Sousliks need eyes not just in the backs of their heads, but on top of them too. Otherwise, their life is not likely to be a long one.

Up to 20 cm long and yellow-grey in colour with a lighter abdomen, sousliks are active outside their burrows by day and live in colonies consisting of a set of burrows and chambers dug into the soil up to 2 m below the surface. Feeding on seeds, plant shoots and roots and on flightless invertebrates, all of the colonies maintain sentinels that whistle at the sight of a predator, bringing the pack scurrying back to safety. Out here on the *puszta* is ideal souslik habitat: short-cropped grassland that isn't being ploughed (which has caused substantial souslik declines elsewhere in Eastern Europe) but is kept scrub-free by grazing sheep and cattle. It's too iced up and snow covered for them to find food in the ferocious winters here so sousliks hibernate for maybe half the year, snoozing away underground where it's much warmer.

One of the characteristic manmade features of the *puszta* apart from the fish ponds is the scatter of pivoted, wooden-beam wells used in summertime for bringing water to the surface from deep below ground for the livestock to drink. Having had plenty of rain in recent weeks, all the wooden beams I saw were eerily still. In normally dry summers, they apparently grunt and squeak as they pivot up and down like nodding donkeys to draw up vital water.

It's difficult to imagine today in such a tranquil environment but these fabulous plains once played a horrific role in Hungarian history; a role that has been acknowledged officially only in recent years. In the 1950s the tragic fate of several thousand deported Hungarian families, maybe as many as 10,000, was played out on the *puszta*; whole families held in captivity in 12 labour camps to which they were transported in cattle cars. They were treated like slaves in their own country. It was only in the mid-1990s that documents were released to show the outrages that had taken place here.

The purpose? Because of Stalin's influential doctrine to liquidate the urban and agricultural middle classes and to terrify the whole of society, thereby guaranteeing obedience to the communist philosophy. Anybody could have been on the depor-tee list; it was enough to have a big, well-equipped farmhouse, or a nice spacious apartment in the city, or to have an influential enemy. People were rounded up at night with no warning, their property and belongings confiscated. Children, the elderly and the sick were taken too. After their arrival in the *puszta* they were crowded into sheep-folds in groups of one or two hundred where they could only sleep on the ground. Forced to work long hours under terrible conditions, their documents were confiscated and they were forbidden to have contact with the outside world. Medical treatment was almost non-existent; they were taken to hospital only in cases of severe emergency. None knew how long they would remain.

Not until after Stalin's death in 1953 were the camps gradually closed and everyone released. Many of the incumbents had died; others were too weakened and ill to resume a normal life … and no one received their property back. In 1990 at least 1,000 former Hortobágy deportees gathered to celebrate the erection of a memorial, the Hortobágy Cross, made of railway track rails, to commemorate the deportees. Today, it's a place of pilgrimage for their descendants.

Ironically, many of these slave labourers changed the face of the *puszta* through being forced by the governing Communists to dig a huge network of ditches to dry out the marshes. As a result, the habitat was degraded and wildlife declined. Restoration began in 2002, filling in many of the ditches and removing huge amounts of concrete used to build dykes. Slowly the water levels have been rising to restore marshes that are once more attracting bitterns, egrets, cranes and much other wildlife too; another kind of memorial in this fabulous place of stark beauty with dark secrets.

Journeys to Remember

Rakesh seemed a reliable fellow, though it was almost impossible to communicate because he spoke no English (or so I thought) and I spoke no Hindi. What worried me more was that he was too old for the task in hand.

As the taxi driver I was relying on to get me from the hotel in Keoladeo National Park (about 150 km south of New Delhi) to Bharatpur rail station, his age might have been an advantage had he been driving a car. But, according to the rather basic information at the hotel's reception desk (it was not a plush hotel), only a cycle rickshaw was possible. I booked Rakesh.

For a journey that would take half an hour or so, I arranged to meet him nearly two hours before my train was due, plenty of time in case he wasn't a very fast cyclist I thought. I paid my bill, picked up my rucksack and small suitcase. Rakesh was waiting outside the hotel entrance. It couldn't have been a better start. With my bags crushed in beside me in the tiny rickshaw, he started peddling. It was mid evening but pitch dark.

Out on the Keoloadev Road, there are no lights. And Rakesh had such a dim version on the front of his bike, no blackout wardens in wartime London would have objected to it. It was powered, I suppose, by one of those old dynamos that used to be fitted to push bikes in the 1950s and 1960s. I could see no more than a metre in front of his bike. I just hoped no Golden Jackals were crossing the road in front of him (they were often near the hotel). If they were, there was no chance he would see them.

After about ten minutes of cycling, Rakesh made it to the edge of the town. A cycle ride on level roads, it was probably harder work than I realised; his bike had no gears and he had me and my clobber to drag along behind. Seeing the edge of Bharatpur, I relaxed a little: it can't be far now I thought and at least there was dim street lighting to help us on our way more safely. But now we began jostling with cars, lorries, the occasional cow and herds of goats; all on a busy road and many of them showing no special aptitude for lane discipline, rights of way at junctions or even travelling on the correct side of the road: on the left in India (a former British colony). By now, Rakesh was all too frequently wiping the sweat off his forehead. He was looking distinctly tired.

I wasn't sure how far it was to the rail station. I didn't recall the journey to the hotel several days back taking too long, though that was in daylight and in an auto rickshaw, a three-wheeler with a tiny engine. What started to get disconcerting, though, was that Rakesh was now heading out of town into the countryside in some other direction. I had no idea where he was going. Soon we were on a poorly lit country road again; this time complete with cows, herds of goats and more panic on my part.

'Where are we?' I said to Rakesh in vain. So I said 'station' and pointed ahead. He nodded: 'Bharatpur station,' he said and pointed ahead again. Presumably we were going the right way. I relaxed … a little. I didn't want to miss this train; I had sleeper tickets to Mumbai and it ran only once a day. On we went. It became darker and I got yet more anxious. Then Rakesh, in an unexpected burst of English, turned around. 'You want old station or new station?'

Old or new? As far as I knew there was just one Bharatpur station. I desperately tried to recall the afternoon I had arrived there. Did it look old or new? In India, such things are often hard to gauge. There are plenty of fairly new buildings here that look tired and old. Yet a really 'old' station, I guessed, would look ultra-old and badly worn. I didn't think the place I arrived at looked that decrepit. I plumped for 'new station'.

Then I discover that Rakesh speaks more English than he at first let on! 'Ah,' he said, 'New station too far. You get other rickshaw. I take you to my brother.' I stifled any swearing. His brother? Where was he? Would I make it to the station and, if I did, was it the correct station anyway?

On he cycled, struggling now to keep going. Sweat was dripping: his through physical activity; mine through anxiety. He pointed ahead again but all I could see were a few dim lights. As we biked closer, the lights turned out to be a multi-shaw or multi-rick – whatever is the correct collective noun for an agglomeration of cycle rickshaws – and, thank goodness, of auto rickshaws too. I paid Rakesh more rupees than he asked for and before I had realised, my case and rucksack were transferred to an auto and I was off at a faster rate. This was Rakesh's all smiling (and younger) brother, or so he said, though I never did get his name.

Within ten minutes I saw the station – it was definitely the one I'd walked out of a few days back – when I was surrounded immediately by a mob of lads all of whom wanted to carry my belongings. My relief was palpable. I paid Rakesh's brother and thanked him. I could have hugged him but thought I shouldn't. I walked quickly into the station. The express to Mumbai was running an hour late!

There have been many other anxiety-provoking journeys over the years too; it's inevitable when you sometimes have to rely on a variety of people to get you to – and, hopefully from – some rather far-flung spot. So it was with someone I shall call Abdullah. It isn't his real name. He was our Saudi driver on a visit arranged some years back through government channels to parts of the Saudi desert including the legendary Empty Quarter, the Rub'al-Khali. At the time I was Chief Scientist at the Countryside Council for Wales; two of us were there to look at the successful, Saudi-led reintroduction and management programme for Arabian Oryx in the Empty Quarter. The full story of the Arabian Oryx and the enormous effort put into its recovery is told in my book, *Back from the Brink* (Whittles, 2015).

Abdullah had driven us there in a large 4WD all the way from a reserve near Taif, a journey that had taken us most of the day. In the dark, we turned off the tarmac road on to stony tracks into quite mountainous, rocky desert and then drove maybe 30 km to the Saudi out-station – a group of portacabins and tents – on the western edge of the Rub'al-Khali.

Some days later we were leaving along the same track, though this time in daylight, to get to the southernmost Saudi town, Najran, close to the Yemen border. Abdullah could probably best be described as not the best at concentrating on his driving, spending more time loading his CDs of Arabic music and talking excitedly. We bumped along the track which was cut into a steep, arid hillside giving us stupendous views out over folded orange-pink sand dunes and small gravel plains, the kind of habitat suited to Arabian Oryx.

Suddenly, he pulled the vehicle over to the trackside overlooking the steep slope down, ostensibly to give us a better view. We crunched to a halt with the front of the car very close to the edge. After a couple of minutes admiring the scene falling away steeply – very steeply – below us, Abdullah tried to reverse back on to the track. No such luck. After several attempts he had to give up. 4WDs aren't all they are cracked up to be; at least this one wasn't.

'No problem', said Abdullah with glee written all over his face. 'We go down instead'. Before we could remonstrate, we were over the edge of the track and at a frighteningly steep angle starting to accelerate and careering down the sandy slope. The slope was so steep, we were hanging forward in our seat belts and holding on to anything in the car we could grab. Dotted here and there downslope in front of us were rock outcrops, the kind of obstacles that would have torn into the vehicle and catapulted us into probable oblivion had we hit one. Somehow, Abdullah managed to steer us between them, staying on the sand and half sliding, half driving down the snowless equivalent of the Cresta Run.

Gradually the slope eased, we slowed, and Abdullah somehow got the vehicle under full control and drove us back to the original track much lower down where it had meandered its way off the hillside. Relief is an understatement. Abdullah was overjoyed, shouting about his driving abilities and telling us that there had been 'no problem' at all. We were glad to have survived unscathed.

Sometimes, of course, you have no one else to blame but yourself for getting into an impossibly difficult situation. Getting hopelessly lost in the Mid Wales hill country close to where I was brought up is one such situation, though I do have to plead youth and a great deal of hill mist in my defence. Plus a wide open, undulating, boggy landscape with few discernible features … fewer still when mist comes down and envelopes you.

On one occasion, aged about 14 and walking these hills on my own, I was heading north from the highest point, Drygarn Fawr (at 644 m not exactly a high peak) aiming to get to a tucked-away gem of a small mountain lake, Llyn Carw. (Now that's an odd Welsh name for these parts; *carw* means 'deer' so I have no idea how long it has been since there were any such animals in these inhospitable hills. Certainly not within living memory.) This shallow lake, set in a depression in the blanket of boggy moor grass and sedges that clothes most of the country here, is the source of the Afon Elan, a delightful mountain stream that runs down over mossy boulders and peat-cushioned soils to the Elan Valley reservoirs, a huge Victorian construction built to supply Welsh water to Birmingham. It's a hard 5 km walk from Drygarn to Llyn Carw; the route takes you down into wet, peat-soaked depressions and up again – seemingly endlessly – on to the drab, sedgy surface of the peat that clothes almost every square metre of land here and is the vast sponge that holds more water than all the reservoirs of Britain, releasing it slowly into the streams that gradually drain from it.

But the direct route between these two features crosses a much more dangerous bog in which the few farmers who graze sheep here tell of horses sinking over their heads, even horses and carts – complete with their shepherd – disappearing into its thick, black, peat-stained waters never to be seen again. It is called Cors yr Hwch. It means 'The Pig's Bog' (actually the female pig, a sow!). But a pig of a bog all the same. Even though most of these bog horror stories, maybe all of them, are fiction, common sense rather than courage dictates that it's sensible to divert from the straight route to skirt its edges … just in case. But mist plays tricks.

And it was most certainly such a day for misty tricks to be played. Before I realised that the vegetation was getting increasingly sparse and the peat-blackened water more abundant, I found myself in mild panic stepping, sometimes almost jumping, from one clump of Moor Grass to the next, trying to avoid stepping into the blackened mire water of unknown depth. As I performed these steps – an amalgam of dainty ballet in which I am not best practiced and balanced jumps – the vibration caused the whole bog around me to heave up and down; I was crossing what would be more correctly defined as a lake (at least horse and cart deep I assumed) though with a layer, hopefully thick, of vegetation comprised mainly of Sphagnum moss covering its surface like a tablecloth covers a table. What is best left to the imagination is the depth of water and peat slurry underneath this carpet … and how strong the carpet actually is. I was glad to reach the carpet's edge. To bog experts these places are known as 'quaking bogs' or by the German term *schwingmoor*, translated as 'swinging moorland' although such places quake more than swing in my experience.

You might assume, even in mist, that a lake that's a hectare in area is not difficult to find, especially if you have been to it on more than one occasion. A lake that my good friend from schooldays, Martyn Jones, and I had been to numerous times in our teens when we were both avid walkers. And we returned there decades later to renew our acquaintance with this glorious but isolated spot. Except that we couldn't find it! It was there alright – we have been back since and it hasn't changed one bit in many decades – but, even though it was midsummer, the hill mist had descended, it was raining and it was surprisingly cold. We had been walking due north from Drygarn Fawr and kept as close to that direction up and down one set of peaty hollows after another. Or so we thought.

We knew we must be near the lake; we had walked roughly the right distance. The grassy bank behind it was an obvious feature that stood out more than the lake itself and we were familiar with that bank from past visits. On more than one occasion, there it was, looming out of the mist. We recognised it. Only it wasn't the bank. Small peaty hummocks can seem surprisingly large when mist plays incredible tricks with your sense of perspective. Wandering off towards one supposed grassy bank after another, it was Martyn who checked his compass. We had walked ourselves in a complete circle, and we were heading back in precisely the direction from which we had set out. We were lost. It was time to stop, get out some food – in the cold and rain – and re-prime our drained energy levels. Colder and wetter still, though at least not hungry, we had to call it a day. We heard a stream, assumed it was the Afon Elan (in this, at least, we were right) that drains out of the lake but we were too tired to walk upstream to try and find it. Instead, we walked downstream to the Elan Valley, out of the mist and into distant habitation.

Getting lost in boggy moorland in mist is perhaps excusable; getting equally lost on waterways in a canoe in a national park and on a bright spring day hardly so.

I was in the Biesbosch National Park in South Holland, a delightful maze of creeks and river channels, many of them surrounded by tall willow and aspen woodland, located in the floodplain of the Rivers Rhine and Meuse. I'd come here to see European Beavers, reintroduced into this watery gem of a wilderness in one of the most densely populated countries in the world. It was background for a feature later published in *The Countryman* magazine.

Beavers were first reintroduced here from Germany's River Elbe, a programme that began in 1988, and they are thriving. Since then, many more have been reintroduced and, according to the national park's Hans Brunning, the Biesbosch now has around 250 beavers. They occupy about 90 lodges, accessible from underwater via a tunnel they dig themselves. Mainly nocturnal, they come out in the evening, often before the sun sets, and stay out all night.

I knew it wasn't going to be possible to spot a beaver until dusk; even then I realised that the odds were against it. But I wanted to explore some of the national park's myriad of narrow water channels by day. So I hired a canoe. Not being a swimmer, I made sure I had a life vest too. What I hadn't bargained on was how tiring the paddling is, especially when you haven't paddled a canoe for a decade or more! At first it was sublime. There was no one else on the water. I pootled along, avoiding overhead branches, stopping to admire bunches of canary-yellow Kingcups burgeoning along the sides of some of the tiny creeks. Stately herons flew up in front, disturbed from a morning's fishing; Mallard adults chaperoned their youngsters aside as I passed nearby; Reed Warblers sang from bulrush stands and thrushes from the trees above. Bluethroats, attractive little birds that come here in summer to breed, dived into cover from banksides and pouted their tumbling, fluted cacophony of a song.

By now, a few hours had gone past; I had turned this way and that at more water channel junctions than I could possibly recall, paddled along some that were hardly wider than my tiny vessel and others as wide as a large river. My map made little sense because I forgot to consult it most of the time. There was too much else to savour all around. Trouble was, I was completely lost.

Heading along a much wider waterway (the width I reckon of the Thames in London), I kept near one side to avoid the wakes of larger craft that all too easily sent my canoe heaving up and down disconcertingly. Until I spotted two ladies in a rowing boat heading towards me, I had not seen anyone to elicit naval directions from. So I canoed into the path of the oncoming Dutch ladies who stopped and told me that I was, indeed, paddling in the right direction to get back to the canoe centre. Mighty relief.

Except that, having paddled on along this huge waterway for maybe 200 m, I heard them calling behind me, 'Hello, hello!' What could they possibly want? I thought I must investigate so I turned my canoe and headed back to them. They had an apology and a correction to make. They had thought I wanted the town centre (this waterway headed into the centre of the nearest town and away from the National Park) and not the canoe centre. I was paddling in precisely the wrong direction.

I thanked them for the revised directions: 'You go back this way and take the next waterway on the left'. No naval 'port' or 'starboard' here. But by now my arms were aching. I paddled as far as the waterway junction, turned left into what was a much smaller canal and rested by the bank. After a while, a small boat came towards me, its four or five occupants rowing steadily along. Stopping to exchange a greeting, they asked if I had been looking for beavers. They knew that was almost impossible by day but mentioned an evening's beaver search led by experienced guides the following day.

Half an hour later I set off reinvigorated by tomorrow night's prospects. But I needed to get back to the canoe centre first. This didn't prove quite as easy – yet again – as the directions I was given. I was beginning to wonder how I would make out in the fading evening gloom the following night (even with a guide) if I was having this much trouble in broad daylight. The canal I was travelling along suddenly divided into two (the Dutch ladies in the rowing boat hadn't mentioned that); I gambled on the right arm and set off, encountered a moored boat and asked again for directions. Another couple of kilometres, weary and with arms that felt like lead, the canoe centre came into view. What a relief. I was over two hours longer than I had suggested I would be, they were getting worried for my safety, and they charged me another few Euros for the extended hire period! But all I was bothered about was getting some rest.

The following evening, with a group of six others and two guides, I set off again on the same set of waterways, each of us in an individual canoe. A rainstorm had passed over and the globe-like setting sun, low in the sky, had reappeared. Less than an hour later, we clustered our canoes together in a spot where two narrow waterways joined, the sunset lighting up the scatter of reeds fringing the muddy creeks a gorgeous orange-yellow. Our two knowledgeable Dutch guides, Frans Bax and Leen Fijnekam, were talking to us about beaver lodge construction, first in Dutch and then in English. They had already told us not to be over-optimistic about our chances of seeing a beaver. Most times on these evening canoe trips they didn't spot one; when they did it was usually swimming in the distance along a creek.

My optimism had sunk rather when, totally unexpectedly, a full-grown beaver swam right past us maybe 4 m away. For what seemed like several seconds those of us lucky enough to spot it were too awe-struck to speak. It swam slowly, nonchalantly right past us, almost within touching distance. Only after it had gone past did we blurt out 'beaver'. Frans and Leen were flabbergasted. Light fawn-brown, the metre-long mammal now swimming slowly ahead of us, it was hard to believe that it had come so close. We canoed quietly forward, following it along the backwater as it dived, then resurfaced several times ahead of us before we eventually lost sight of it, maybe because it swam underwater up a side-arm of the creek and out of sight.

Later that evening as darkness fell and grey puffs of mist started rising from the creeks around us, we heard a beaver dive from a bank and make a surprisingly loud splash in the muddy waters ahead. We had heard them and seen them, closer than we all had dared to imagine.

It had been a canoe trip worth remembering, in more ways than one.

A Hunter's Delight

Ron Nelsen was just packing up after a morning's turkey hunt in a forest near the tiny community of Providence Forge in eastern Virginia when we met him on a forest track. 'I had a Jake [a young male] that came pretty close early this morning but I didn't want to shoot him. Too young. It's important to have a strong population here. He walked away after a while and I just let him walk off. I love being out in the forest with nature. I've been hunting for 60 years and I'm 68 now. I just sit for hours, up against a tree maybe, using callers I've gotten to attract a Tom,' he commented dressed in full camouflage gear, shotgun in hand.

Ron, a Virginian by birth, was building a house on a piece of open land he'd bought within the forest we were walking in. It was to be his retirement home with his wife and he took us to see the construction. Made entirely out of wood, the living accommodation was built on the upper level so that he could look out into the trees he loved. It's this combination of a love for the land, the unquestionable right of people to have guns for hunting, a bit of the old frontiersman attitude that still prevails in the US countryside and all combined with good manners and friendliness that makes American rural culture so entrancing.

I was spending much of a day with Phil West of Virginia State's Department of Game and Inland Fisheries to learn about the recovery of the Wild Turkey here in the USA. It was to write a feature for *CNN Traveller* magazine but what I learnt there also contributed in much more detail to a chapter in my book *Back from the Brink* (Whittles, 2015). Phil and I were walking in a local area of forest, talking turkey, when we happened to meet Ron.

Ron Nelsen's turkey callers – all cleverly made to mimic some of a Tom Turkey's calls – were evidence of a craft in themselves. Little wooden boxes with sliding dowels to make rasping sounds; small wooden 'strikers' to click on a slate; and various other devices that yelp and cluck, some he had made himself and all to attract an enquiring turkey Tom who is likely to come close to see what competition he might have locally.

Turkeys, much like their close relatives and gamebirds in general, aren't blessed with much vocal talent; no songs or musical calls, just a range of what are rather euphemistically referred to as 'vocalisations'. To be realistic, these are better described as 'gobbles', 'clucks', 'putts', 'purrs', 'yelps', 'whines', 'cackles' and 'kee-kees' – take your pick – and Ron, and other hunters like him, can probably copy most or all of them using their turkey callers. In early spring, male turkeys gobble loudly to announce their presence to females and competing males. The gobble can carry long distances. Hens yelp to let gobblers know their location. Yet more confusingly, gobblers often yelp like females, and hens can gobble, though they rarely do so. Immature males – the jakes – often yelp too. So it's little wonder that hunters wanting to attract them towards their gun need a wide variety of callers producing an array of sounds.

Phil was incredibly helpful, filling me in on a series of attempts to supplement the very low numbers of turkeys that had existed in the state after the early white settlers almost wiped them out as they did across the whole of the USA. Turkey meat was seemingly just too tasty to be left with feathers attached in the American forests. Before the settlers arrived there might have been 10 million Wild Turkeys in the USA. By 1910 maybe 30,000 remained. Huge swathes of the country had none left.

Protection from hunters, breeding programmes and reintroductions into areas from which they had been extirpated did the trick, though it took several decades. Today there are an estimated 7 million Wild Turkeys in the USA with around 200,000 in Virginia alone, slightly fewer than the number of state-registered hunters!

'It's impossible to see them if you walk off-track into a forest,' Phil told me. 'They'll hear you coming way before you see anything. And even though they roost at night high up in a tree, they're real hard to spot in spite of their size. They're hard to hunt too. You have to get into an inhabited wood before first light. Then settle down and mimic the calls of the Hens to attract a Tom. It's a quiet yelp noise and he comes looking. You don't shoot until they are, say, 30 m away,' he said.

It was good advice. I found it impossible to spot one in any piece of forest even though every muddy track I walked along had a plethora of giveaway turkey footprints. On one such track it was easier to spot a green and brown camouflaged hide with a shotgun barrel pointing out of it. A quiet enquiry of the incumbent revealed that he hadn't seen a turkey either. He sounded a tad frustrated. But Wild Turkeys proved incredibly easy to spot in open fields where they often come out to search for and eat invertebrates and young plant shoots to supplement the berries, acorns and bark they eat in forests. Turkeys often walk about in groups searching the ground as they go, their bronze-sheened dark plumage and – on males – that bare-skinned blue and near-red head and neck a giveaway.

Unfortunately not all American hunters are as careful as Ron Nelsen. That fact came home to me on another US visit, this time to talk to experts about America's tallest bird, the elegant Whooping Crane and to see the birds on their wintering grounds along the balmy saline marshes of the Texas coast. It was the other American bird I was writing a chapter about for *Back from The Brink*.

Whooping Cranes – all-white beauties with red faces – were never as abundant as Wild Turkeys across the USA. Maybe there were 10,000 of them in total. Nevertheless, white settlers were once again the cause of their downfall, partly by shooting them for food, by taking their eggs to eat but also by draining the wetlands in which they nested and fed. By the 1950s only about twenty cranes survived. Extinction was looming fast.

Conservationists knew that they nested somewhere in the muskeg (part forest, part open marsh) of northern Canada but it wasn't until 1954 that their breeding site was found. The problem that Whoopers faced – and still do – is that they migrate south every autumn to Texas, a distance of at least 4,000 km ... and back again each spring. And that makes them vulnerable to exhaustion, to collisions with power cables and to the guns of hunters unwilling or unable to identify them as a protected species.

Even though their numbers have built up, very, very slowly to several hundred – with good prospects that this slow increase will continue – any unnecessary loss of birds is a setback. Nineteen were shot between 2001 and early 2014, losses the population can ill afford. In February 2014, two cranes were found shot in southwest Louisiana; they turned out to be the oldest pair among a newly reintroduced Louisiana population. The birds, which had been tagged and were monitored by Louisiana officials, were expected to produce a chick in a few years' time. That hope was extinguished by a hunter's gun.

'It's a devastating setback and such a senseless act,' said Robert Love, Louisiana Department of Wildlife and Fisheries administrator at the time. 'Don't shoot big white birds. It's that simple.' Officials said they could offer a $15,000 reward for information leading to an arrest. Since that incident, two more were shot in the state; one survived but might not fly again. Hunters often claim to confuse the much bigger and whiter Whoopers with the pale grey, and much more abundant Sandhill Cranes which can be legally shot in most states during certain months. Shooting a Whooper can lead to a $100,000 fine and a year in federal prison. In 2013, a 26-year-old South Dakota man pleaded guilty to killing a Whooping Crane and was sentenced to two years' probation and an $85,000 fine according to the US Attorney's office.

An abundance of easily purchased firearms combined with an incredibly strong hunting and shooting lobby representing their interests US-wide is something that most Europeans find hard to understand. If all US hunters were like Ron Nelsen there would be few if any problems. But Americans, especially those living in the more rural and the wilder locations on this vast continent, are but a few generations from the frontiersmen who 'conquered' this land and to whom the gun was an essential and everyday piece of equipment. And that inheritance and association is so firmly entrenched I can't believe that it will ever change.

While gun ownership is commonplace in the US and frequently commented upon, it is equally commonplace in several other countries, many of which have little concept of controlling their use for hunting. Malta, for instance, an EU country signed up to all the wildlife protection laws across its Member States, fails to implement them. And it's not alone. Cypriots, too, have a reputation for shooting almost anything that moves on legs or wings and is considered fair game. So it is that the Maltese and the Cypriots shoot and trap vast numbers of birds on migration south in springtime and north again in autumn. Not only what might be considered as game birds worthy of a decent meal – a duck or a pigeon perhaps – but also tiny birds like warblers and flycatchers; weighing hardly 15 g apiece they are trapped on twigs with sticky bird lime.

Britain, like most West European countries, has a well-regulated and largely very responsible wildfowl shooting fraternity, many of whom also carry out a good deal of positive conservation work such as habitat creation. But there is one shooting tradition that remains very controversial in the UK. It fires off from its starting blocks every year on 12 August, the so-called Glorious Twelfth – considered distinctly inglorious by its many critics – and it's almost totally confined to Scottish moors and a few in the North of England. It is, of course, grouse shooting.

Writing a book about inter-relationships between people and birds (*Life with Birds: A Story of Mutual Exploitation* (Whittles, 2011)) it was obviously a topic I needed to cover. Doing so without experiencing a grouse shoot myself (unlike, I guess, most of its critics) seemed wholly inappropriate. So I arranged, via an old friend and colleague – Dr Des Thompson at Scottish Natural Heritage (SNH), the Scottish Government's conservation advisers – to spend a morning on a grouse moor in southern Scotland. It proved to be extremely enlightening.

It was late August in the rolling Lammermuir Hills when I met up with Robbie Douglas Miller who owns 3,000 acres of moorland. It was a full day's grouse shooting and there were maybe ten 'guns', the grouse moor terminology for the number of men shooting, many of them friends of Douglas Miller. The day I was there, the moor all around was in flower, clothing the gentle slopes in an ethereal purple haze. There were areas of lush green too, rushy wet streamsides and grassy banks, all of it appearing slightly translucent in the light drizzly rain that was showing no sign of easing. An occasional Mountain Hare (the ones that have a white coat in winter) zoomed past, their extra-long ears almost flapping in the breeze as they ran.

Apart from the rain which, mercifully, kept the irritating biting midges away (but is most certainly not going to put the assembled gathering off a day's shooting), there was hardly a sound to be heard. Behind us the moor sloped down to a shallow, boggy valley where rushes, cotton grass and mosses took over from the heather. In front of us was a short up-slope of heather to the nearby heavily clouded skyline. Over this slope, though, it's all activity though nothing is yet visible. A line of maybe ten local men, all clad in full waterproofs and swishing noisy plastic flags low over the heather as they walk towards us, is getting closer.

I'm standing in a butt (a pit in the ground lined with boards) with Douglas Miller, trying to keep well back from what I know will soon be his shotgun's booming blasts. Other pairs of guns are standing in other butts nearby. Suddenly, the silence is broken as several shotguns punch the moist air, reverberating across the damp moor, only our heads – and shotguns – visible to the birds that are skimming low and incredibly fast in flight past and over us, mostly in small groups of between five and ten, their wings whirring like mechanical toys. They are Red Grouse and they are getting killed. Some of them anyway.

I'm holding my hands over my ears (there weren't enough earplugs to go round!) as his shotgun booms and a spent cartridge case leaps up and out of the gun as he fires, occasionally landing on me. The butt is quite small so I weave this way and that as he swings his gun about to fire at one grouse after another. And each time the beaters – the line of men employed for the day to disturb the grouse – do a drive of birds towards the shooting butts, somewhere around 30 or so grouse get killed. But the odds are stacked against the guns. Most of the grouse seem to get away, surviving for another day's shooting when they will take their chances yet again.

Red Grouse aren't large birds. Like small chickens in size, they are a rich brown with attractive white-feathered legs. They fly fast – at 80 km/h and more – it isn't predictable where they will suddenly appear in front of you very low over the vegetation, you might get a second or two to aim, and a shotgun is only effective over a range of about 30 m. To shoot Red Grouse you have to be a very good shot indeed. I wouldn't have been able to shoot an oncoming bull in those conditions (not that I would want to) but it seemed incredible to me that anyone could possibly hit a grouse at all.

I'd met Douglas Miller that morning near the rather oddly named Horseupcleugh, a remote farm in the eastern Lammermuir Hills. Here were gathered about 40 people, a motley collection turned out for a day's grouse shooting. Some were beaters. Several others were 'pickers-up' with their dogs – retrievers or springer spaniels – whose main task was to find the dead or dying grouse that had fallen into the heather and collect them up. The beaters and pickers-up, all local men or workers from adjacent estates, were paid just £35 for their day's work. By my calculations, for an eight-hour day, that was less than the minimum wage. OK, they did get a free lunch, maybe a warming drink or two in addition. But it seemed poorly paid to me.

'We shoot here probably four times a season,' Douglas Miller told me when we had time to chat walking from one set of moorland butts to another, each in different parts of his moor. 'We don't usually start on the 12th August because not all the year's young grouse are mature enough by then. And we don't normally shoot towards the season's end [10 December]. On a very good day I suppose we'll shoot about 200 grouse, but that's probably the tops'.

After each drive by the beaters, followed by the shooting spectacular which was over in a few minutes, the pickers-up were out with their sniffer dogs retrieving the dead or dying spoils. I couldn't estimate it but I guess that more grouse were dead than dying, any of the latter dispatched quickly by snapping their necks. The dogs, of course, were having a time of delight, hurtling through the wet heather, finding their quarry and taking them back to their pickers-up to be collected together in bags.

Then we were off on foot elsewhere on the moor, the beaters taking a different route to get into position for their next beating-up walk; the 'guns' dividing up into pairs in the scatter of butts. It's all very well organised. Then the long wait again when all was quiet before the storm, an eerie silence in the drizzle that was sweeping over the purple ground haze. The 'guns' got their shotguns loaded up, there was a little very polite banter. Then all hell broke loose once again as the small red-brown birds zoomed low around us.

'We charge the guns per brace shot [a brace is two birds] or we charge per day irrespective of how good the gun is. Say £150 per brace. So, if a gun shoots 50 brace in the day, it costs him £7,500,' Douglas Miller told me. Some moors charge well in excess of that. It isn't a sport for anyone short of the readies. The morning I was there, the 'guns' were all what might be considered 'well-to-do' or 'well connected' (one to the late Queen Mother); one was a banker from the south of England who had come with his shooting adviser no less! The contrast between them and the beaters/pickers-up, as you might expect, was enormous.

Grouse moors are expensive to buy, maybe £10 million for a small one, multiples of that for a large one. Most are owned by what is still regarded as the 'aristocracy' and may have been in the same family for generations – or they're owned by wealthy Middle Eastern Arabs or city bankers. They are not a paying proposition but they have prestige value. A day's shoot is as much a social event as a sporting one and the more traditional shoots will picnic in style at lunchtime before resuming in the afternoon.

But grouse moors do bring employment to very rural and often isolated places where jobs are usually few and far between, plus an income – albeit a very seasonal one – for local hotels, shops and garages. To the Scottish economy, grouse shooting is estimated to be worth £30 million a year and supports 940 full-time jobs according to a 2009 report from the Game & Wildlife Conservation Trust. Running a moor doesn't come cheap of course, and is the main reason why it's an expensive pursuit. Parts of the moor are burnt in the autumn, usually in small patches or strips in order to diversify the age of the heather, leaving some old and more mature heather while replenishing it with new growth where the land is burnt. That requires people to carefully control the burning so that it doesn't get out of hand. There are access tracks to repair, the shooting butts to maintain and many other tasks including, most controversially, predators to kill. It is all managed by the gamekeeper (more than one on most moors) who has to be paid for and provided with a home and an all-terrain vehicle so that he can get these jobs done.

'My keeper traps or shoots crows, foxes, stoats and weasels,' says Douglas Miller. 'If we didn't, then we'd hardly have a grouse population because they'd take most of the eggs and chicks.' That, of course, is the most controversial aspect of grouse moor management; many keepers have been prosecuted over the years for poisoning or shooting protected birds of prey such as Hen Harriers and Golden Eagles which sometimes take grouse for food. It's a practice that is never owned up to by the grouse shooting fraternity but research suggests strongly that illegal killing of birds of prey is the reason why these rare birds are almost entirely absent from keepered moorlands.

It is certainly true that numbers of Red Grouse are artificially high on these managed upland heather moors because the whole system is designed to benefit them. The habitat is manipulated to provide a range of heather ages. Young heather shoots provide food; mature heather provides shelter and nesting spots under cover; clearings provide places for the young birds to sun themselves in. Most of their natural predators are either eliminated or much reduced and are replaced with a new one: men with guns.

In total there are reckoned to be about 460 grouse moors in the UK covering between one and two million hectares of moorland, most of them in Scotland. As a result of killing off lots of the moor's natural predators, other birds that like this kind of habitat do well too. Birds such as Golden Plover and Curlew breed here and Mountain Hares usually prosper, something that grouse shooting apologists usually mention in support of their arguments. 'I come up here to the open moor on a spring day sometimes just to sit, to look and listen and it's simply wonderful,' Douglas Miller tells me. 'There are Skylarks in song, Golden Plover, Curlew and Lapwing calling. Plenty of Red Grouse of course. It's idyllic.'

Most shot grouse are sold to game dealers who sell on to restaurants and hotels. 'I sell most of mine to a local dealer and I'll probably get £5 a bird,' he says. 'Some of those we shoot today will be in London restaurants tomorrow night. They'll go by train or are flown south.' So restaurants that specialise in traditional British food, *Rules* in Covent Garden for instance, serve Red Grouse in season traditionally with game chips, redcurrant and bread sauce for £30 or so.

Organised grouse shoots like this – with beaters and pickers-up and the other adornments – are a fairly recent phenomenon. They began around the middle of the 19th century. In 1825 there are no records of Scottish grouse moors being let for shooting and, by 1837, just eight were available. The building of the railway north – by 1863 it had reached Inverness – combined with the invention of the breech-loading shotgun in 1847 (lighter and quicker to load) made organised grouse shoots on 'remote' moors a real possibility.

But the numbers of Red Grouse on these moors can go up and down like a yo-yo according to Dr David Baines of The Game and Wildlife Conservation Trust who I talked to after my visit. And not because they are being shot. 'Red grouse can suffer huge population crashes due to a parasitic gut threadworm they carry naturally. In order to maintain our grouse stocks, counter-intuitively, shooting older birds on the moor is a good way of controlling the disease as they often have very heavy worm burdens that will infect the younger birds. Climate warming has provided better conditions for the worm to flourish,' Baines told me.

While I am no promoter of grouse shooting, its critics have to think through what might happen to all this heather moorland if grouse shooting was not the main use of the land? That's something many of them often don't think about or tacitly assume that whatever replaced it would be better for wildlife. But would it? Des Thompson, Principal Adviser on Biodiversity at SNH and an expert on Scottish hills and mountains, is very clear. 'People need to realise that moors managed for grouse are unnatural because the way the land is grazed by sheep and burnt in patches stops scrub and woodland taking over as it would naturally. Grouse shooting generates substantial income, and it's unlikely that other uses of the moors could match that. In terms of wildlife, well managed grouse moors have a rich diversity of plants and animals, birds included, so long as birds of prey aren't persecuted and, ideally, if some areas are allowed to develop some scrub and trees,' he said.

There are, of course, many voices raised against grouse shooting because it is perceived by many as cruel. League Against Cruel Sports Chief Executive, Douglas Batchelor, is one of several critics. 'It is utterly ridiculous to label an industry which depends on the mass slaughter of wildlife for entertainment purposes as glorious. Barbaric and immoral would be far more appropriate under these circumstances,' he told me.

I felt that my day and grouse shoot had been a day well spent. I had seen how grouse shoots are conducted, realised how difficult it is to shoot such a bird and experienced the enormous dichotomy in culture, wealth and privilege that still exists between those doing the shooting and the men preparing everything for those participating in such an elitist experience. Whether pro or anti, one thing is for certain: the arguments about grouse shooting and the 'Glorious' or 'Inglorious 12th' will continue.

The Forest That's Fading Away

It was my first night in the tent and I had slept surprisingly well although that might have been the result of a two-day journey to get to this particularly isolated forest in central Kenya. It was early morning, still dark at around 5 a.m., when I woke up all too suddenly. Some incredibly loud, almost blood-curdling screaming quite close to our campsite had roused me, a noise I was soon to get to know each and every pre-dawn morning I was there. And it always sounded as if some animal or other was dying in utter agony, maybe in the jaws of a leopard.

I peered out of my tent. In the shards of distant light appearing through the trees I could see our Samburu campsite helpers moving about, completely unperturbed. Whatever the screaming was, no one paid any attention. Relax, I thought, it's got to be an everyday occurrence that needn't worry me, however horrific it sounded. Later that morning I asked Lentaaya, our Dorobo camp supervisor, what the early morning screams were.

'Oh that,' he said nonchalantly, 'That's the African Fish Eagles howling to each other in the trees by the river. They do it every morning at dawn.' The Ngeng River, a few metres down-slope from us here in the Mathews Forest, was hardly a river, more a series of small rivulets, so poor had the rainy season been. Nevertheless, the Fish Eagles were up and about early, keen on the first catch of the day no doubt. And I did see a surprisingly large number of fish of all sizes in those rivulets in which I washed over the next ten days of my stay.

I had joined Luca Borghesio, an Italian biologist researching changes in the biodiversity of this forest. With us we had two extremely pleasant young Kenyan research ornithologists from the Nairobi Museum – Lawrence Wagura and Samuel Bakari – plus four local Samburu as cooks and camp helpers. Two of the Samburu were employed as guards and were armed with ancient rifles that reminded me of the Lee-Enfields from the Boer War. Why did we need armed guards? Simply because it was possible that we might disturb some Wild Oxen or other large animals snoozing in some shade or encounter an elephant with young at close quarters. Firing a warning shot would deter a charge, though how rapidly our guards could load and fire I had no idea.

Getting out of the tent at night, unless it was a real emergency, was not something to be contemplated Luca had told me. His instructions had been very clear. 'Do not venture out of your tent at night, not for a call of nature or anything. Do what you have to do but inside your tent. So you will need a small receptacle,' he warned, his Italian accent inflecting his words. 'If you walk outside the tent at night you take a big risk; you would never hear the lion that comes up behind you in silence. They are huge animals, very powerful. The first thing you know – but not for very long – is that the lion is on your back with its jaw into your neck.' A tent-bound, night-time pee into a plastic bottle suddenly seemed a minor sacrifice.

He also mentioned daytime toilet habits and I recount them here merely for completion before I move on to other topics! 'Do not be at all surprised if, when you have finished what you do and you have yet to cover it with some soil,' he said, 'a couple of Samburu moran [their young 'warriors'] arrive to look at what you have produced. You will not hear them coming [rather like a night-time lion]; they are very silent. But do not be alarmed. They will be very serious. They are not being rude. They will discuss its colour and consistency; they might poke at it with a stick and decide if you are a healthy person or not. That is quite normal in Samburu society.' I couldn't help but think of those scenes in the film, *The Madness of King George* when George III's faeces were examined in minute detail by his physicians trying to grasp what was wrong with him and how he might be treated. Seemingly Kenya's Samburu were still at it. I'm not sure I found it reassuring.

Acting as a kind of camp overseer was Robert Lentaaya, a Dorobo who was also a knowledgeable naturalist (see Chapter 11); both he and Luca had helped me put together the story of honeyguides leading tribespeople to wild bee nests. That first morning in the forest, Lentaaya soon exhibited his remarkable animal identification skills. He was taking me (with accompanying rifle-holding guard) along the path that meandered above the Ngeng River. Within half an hour he had pointed out Bushpig, genet and elephant tracks, droppings from lion, porcupine and Olive Baboons plus a host of birds in the trees including vivid blue, green and chestnut-coloured Hartlaub's Turacos, black and white Tropical Boubous and delicate little chestnut and white Tambourine Doves. We heard Rock Hyraxes – correction, Lentaaya heard them, I didn't – calling from some cliffs a little further on. So we stopped and took a good look at the cliff ledges, some of them obscured by tree branches, to see if we could spot these rodent-like creatures. This time, though, we were out of luck.

A little later Lentaaya hears some distant grunts and, after a while, I hear them too. A group of Mantled Guerezas, a species of colobus monkey. They were on the far side of the Ngeng and quite a way up the forested slope in the trees. Strikingly beautiful but uncommon animals with black and white pelage, we strain to spot them. It's frustrating; we can see an occasional branch move quite suddenly, a glimpse of what might be part of a monkey, but no good view. Eventually the movements cease; we are not going to get a good look.

I am being shown so much that I struggle to get all the names written in my notebook. At times I have to ask Lentaaya if we can stay at the same spot for a couple of minutes to allow me to catch up with my scribbles. The wildlife riches we see on this short walk are incredible so it's easy to assume that the forest wildlife here is in very good shape. But Luca's research is telling him that not all is well in these remote and poorly explored forests of the Mathews Mountain Range. There are underlying problems potentially so severe that the very future of all this biological diversity is in doubt.

The forest occupies nearly 1,000 km^2 of land, most of it at least 1,500 m above sea level, the higher parts over 2,000 m, with a small proportion of scrub and grassland. Uninhabited, it is a critical natural resource for communities that live around its edges providing water, honey, medicinal plants, grazing and fodder for their livestock. Respected by local Samburu community elders, the forest helps sustain their pastoral lifestyle based on cattle farming in the dry savannah surrounding the forest. And therein lies part of the problem.

'When I first came here in 2004,' says Luca one evening, 'these forests were pristine. They were the best example of mountain forest I'd seen in East Africa. They were hardly disturbed and little was known about them. But with my team for the last four years I've been monitoring a sample of 600 trees – a range of species and sizes –and none of them are growing. The reason is almost certainly drought.'

The same dry conditions have prevailed in recent years across huge swathes of East Africa. In past decades, a bad drought might be expected every 10–15 years. But in the last 12 years there have been four. The finger of suspicion points to global climate change. It's making it difficult to eke out a livelihood for crop and pastoral farmers alike. Starvation is often very close. The August I was there, government-funded teams were driving from village to village slaughtering goats to reduce the burden of trying to feed them. Their owners were compensated and the meat divided up between the families in each community.

'There's another big problem in these forests, too, but that's also because of drought,' Luca told me. 'For a few years now the local Samburu [who, when the climate is normal, keep cattle outside the forest] have been bringing their animals into the forest where they cut down branches so the cattle can eat the leaves. Sometimes whole trees are felled, not large trees but many medium- and small-sized ones. It's a consequence of the droughts; they have little to graze outside the forest so they are forced to make use of the trees. And the cattle trample or eat any seedling trees starting to grow; consequently, large parts of the forest have no young trees to grow up for the future.'

While it is natural for large old trees to die and fall – thereby creating a gap in which young saplings start growing – and for elephants to push smaller trees over, it's the larger scale of the Samburu glade clearing that is worrying. It is a double whammy of drought and grazing that threatens the Mathews Forest, the two issues inextricably linked.

So Luca has started a long-term experiment within the forest. He has designed it to try and find out what biological damage this cattle feeding is causing. In 2007 his team felled all the trees in ten small experimental plots (where they then re-grow) and, over the years since, have been comparing the bird and insect species in these and in another ten similar plots left without any tree felling. It was these plots that the two Kenyan ornithologists, Lawrence and Samuel, were working in from dawn to dusk each day for a month. They had erected mist nets – fine mesh netting into which birds fly without harm but can't get away until released – which they examined every hour to record the birds.

What this study is showing is that the cut – and thereby sunnier – gaps harbour twice as many flying insects, partly because trees exposed to sunshine produce more fruit for them to feed off. Numbers of birds and the variety of bird species has also increased in the gaps because of more fruit, more plant seed and more insects to eat. Some birds that live mainly high in the tree canopy, many of them fruit eaters, have benefitted from this change – the huge, black and white Silvery-cheeked Hornbills, for example. But others inhabiting low trees and scrub, such as the little Blue-Mantled Flycatcher, have declined. The conclusion is that if the Samburu continue felling trees for fodder and their cattle prevent any new trees from growing a lot of the birds inhabiting scrub and smaller trees in the forest will decline. Luckily, so far most of the damage is confined to the lower-lying forest; the forest much higher up the steep hillsides here is in much better condition because the Samburu herders don't venture so high.

So what is the solution? Seemingly there's little action being taken to address global warming because governments around the world are too obsessed with economic growth to get to grips with serious alternatives to fossil fuels. So droughts might well be a regular and more frequent event here. Living with that prospect, the practical answer might be to plant large areas of additional trees outside the existing forest and for the Samburu to be responsible in times of drought for grazing their cattle in these areas rather than using the forest itself. But trees take decades or more to mature (assuming that the frequent droughts don't slow them to a standstill) so, in the meantime, it might be possible to identify areas of forest on its outer edges where grazing could be tolerated, keeping the forest core of the Mathews Range intact. And the Samburu could dig some ponds and build small dams on seasonal streams to hold water longer in the dry season, both for themselves and their cattle. That way, they would need to put their cattle into the forest even less.

When I was there, thunder clouds started gathering one day when we were a long way from our campsite visiting another part of these extensive forests. When the downpour started we were outside the forest in scrubby savannah with scattered trees. I have rarely seen rain like it. The whole land surface seemed awash with water under the gloomy, dark grey cloud. Even our 4WD was slithering in the conditions. Making our way back to the campsite, we approached what had been a dry riverbed when we had crossed it that morning. Not now. It had been transformed into a raging river 30 m wide or more; it's thundering, muddy waters carrying whole trees downstream. Far too dangerous to get close to, Luca turned the 4WD on a slope, it slid as some of the track gave way beneath us and we were almost on our side in mud and water. Luckily no one was hurt; we clambered out and, after at least an hour of work stabilising the ground, got the vehicle back on four wheels and into a safer spot.

That night we wild camped. We were wet and the ground was soaked. The rain had stopped before it went dark and our ever versatile Samburu helpers cooked a meal. We slept uncomfortably. It was several hours into the next day – and the river by then was no more than 10 cm deep – before we could chance the crossing and return to our campsite. None of that vast amount of water, as far as I could see, had been harvested or held in small pools. It had all soaked away into the arid, sandy soil. It might have stimulated a bit of plant growth to nurture a little more grazing for the Samburu livestock but the vast bulk of that enormous downpour had been squandered.

When I returned from Kenya I contacted both Oxfam and Save the Children, both of whom have programmes of work in Kenya. I explained the issues, not as an ecological problem but from the viewpoint of helping the pastoral Samburu to help themselves to secure a more reliable lifestyle. I suggested that excavating small ponds and building some low dams on seasonal streams would hold water for their cattle (maybe drinking water too) in periods of drought. It seemed a simple and relatively cheap idea to me. Maintenance would need no advanced equipment. The reaction from these two NGOs? The most generalised answers giving no sense of commitment to any such proposals. They didn't seem to want to discuss any ideas coming from someone with no experience of aid work ... though they do keep asking for donations!

One day in the forest I was walking along the Ngeng River, crossing little streams that run into it. Because of the otherwise dry conditions, these places held the most lush vegetation. What I wasn't prepared for were the clouds of butterflies rising up all around me. I don't think I have ever seen so many; confetti-like, they would temporarily occlude my view ahead. Most were white but in other shadier spots I spotted various combinations of scarlet, azure blue and yellow. There are well over 100 different butterfly species known from these forests, and probably several as yet undiscovered species too.

The extensive Mathews Range forests are not only isolated; their wealth of wildlife isn't fully explored. These are some of the more pristine forests remaining in East Africa and a place to be treasured. There is at least one plant species found here and nowhere else in the world; there might be others. A 2010 survey in parts of the forest by a team of biologists concluded that there are almost certainly a few invertebrates that are found nowhere else too.

The Mathews Cycad, the only known endemic plant here, is a kind of living fossil. With Lawrence Wagura I went off one day in search of the species and it wasn't long before we spotted what was very obviously a baby version of this age-old tree. Maybe 60 cm tall, it was clearly biding its growing time under a fairly dense evergreen tree canopy high above, blocking out a lot of the light it needed to grow. In appearance the cycad looks like a small fern growing out of the top of a palm tree trunk. But it is neither a fern nor a palm. It is, in fact, more closely related to the pines. Cycads are trees that evolved alongside the dinosaurs; look at many of the drawings of a reconstructed forest scene at the time the Coal Measures were laid down 300 million years ago and they are some of the main trees in the picture.

They can be found in many parts of the world and there are more than 300 different species. We walked further on and after a while we found a very much larger specimen in a clearing where it was obviously enjoying more light. In front of it, I get Lawrence to pose for a picture. This cycad is around 5 m high and verdant green with huge, arching, fern-like but immensely tough leaves. So tough, maybe, that nothing seems to eat them. Unless, that is, the leaves are known by forest-dwelling mammals and invertebrates to be toxic if nibbled. Slow growing, these cycads are known to reach venerable ages, reputedly as much as 1,000 years. Maybe this Mathews specimen was here in the Middle Ages? There are certainly plenty of Mathews Cycads scattered about in these forests, from tiny seedlings to venerable oldies. They are undoubtedly doing well.

From camera traps set up in the 2010 survey, we know that leopard, lion, hyena, elephant, genet, civet, bushbuck and porcupine are around most nights in the forest. Our Samburu helpers had identified the tracks or droppings of several of these and others besides. A few days of quiet walking here and I had seen Olive Baboons, elephant, bushbuck, waterbuck (much larger antelope than the more delicate, somewhat bambi-like bushbuck and the proud owners of an elegant pair of up-pointing horns) one or more of several species of mongoose and much else.

One day, I walked with Lentaaya and Lendiki – one of the armed Samburu – a few kilometres upriver, following a rough path meandering between the trees. Suddenly, I saw two moran – young Samburu 'warriors' – running towards us only a few metres away (I hadn't heard any sound of their approach), their pencil-thin but muscular legs carrying them fast between the great trees. Carrying their traditional steel spears, these young warriors are known by some of the other Kenyan tribes as the 'butterfly people' because of their garish colouring. These two – seemingly known to Lentaaya and Lendiki – were typically coloured and attired. I use the description 'attired' rather generously; their only clothing was a loose kind of wrap-around skirt/shorts reaching from waist to knee and a rubber sandal made from discarded car tyres.

Their faces covered in red ochre and their hair matted with it, groomed and braided into a distinctive pattern, they sported the usual huge necklaces of multi-coloured beads, bracelets on their wrists and large earrings. They were undoubtedly eye-catching. Theirs is a fashion statement that would steal any Paris haute couture show. And it is much admired by the Samburu girls – why bother otherwise? – many with whom the morans are allowed to have sexual relationships from a young age. It is these female admirers who make the enormous bead jewellery the morans wear.

All smiles when they got close, Lentaaya and Lendiki chatted to them, they said hello to me and we all sat down for a while under the trees. They had been upriver to check their cattle and were running back maybe 10 km or more to their village before returning to the cattle later that day, a bit like an office worker popping home for lunch. Fitness might be relative, but my mind wandered to thoughts of the great Kenyan and Ethiopian long-distance runners that seem to win no end of Olympic medals. Suddenly, their athleticism seemed less surprising.

As well as the ubiquitous, razor-sharp bladed spear each carried (and, I was told, could throw with incredible accuracy) every moran I saw in the forest carried a small leather bag. I asked Lentaaya what they carried therein. Apparently it was a small amount of rice. 'But what do they eat when they are in the forest for several days a long way from their village?' I asked. 'Oh, they eat well,' he said, 'They milk the cows and mix rice with that or maybe they bleed the cows a little and mix the blood with the milk to drink too. It's very good,' said Lentaaya.

Each moran carried another, smaller pouch too. This was seemingly just as vital to them, maybe more so. It was the pouch designed for their mobile phone. No self-respecting moran went anywhere without it … even though mobile phone signals penetrated almost nowhere in the forest. Like their beads – and, thankfully, their potentially lethal spears – the phone was yet another fashion statement. I felt positively under-dressed.

Further on during that same morning's long walk, Lentaaya suddenly signalled to stop and keep very quiet. I had heard nothing. Pointing upwards to the tree canopy maybe 40 m above, he had spotted a troop of Olive Baboons up in the branches gorging on tree fruits. If Lentaaya hadn't been with me I doubt I would have noticed them. Because the baboons were so high above I assumed that, if we walked on quietly, they would stay put. I didn't want to disturb their elevated feasting. But no! Loud, whooping 'wa-hoo' calls started high above, the calls were taken up in adjacent trees and within seconds they became a cacophony of sound. It was the Olive Baboon equivalent of 'let's get the hell out of here'.

That's exactly what they did. And at such a speed, it put any fireman's drop down the fire station pole into the beginner category. These baboons – all sizes from small youngsters to full-grown adults – were dropping down 40-m tree trunks in seconds, their hands grabbing the bark at intervals as they dropped. All around us, baboons were shimmying down; I assumed several must have injured themselves or even perhaps been killed. Each time one of the larger baboons hit the ground, I could feel the vibration under my feet.

But this was everyday life baboon-style. Continually whooping, once on the ground, they all made off in one direction from their scatter of fruit-laden trees, bounced along the ground and forded the stream-like Ngeng River, assembling together as a troop on a flat rock on its far bank. Not one appeared injured. There they gathered together; fathers, mothers and all the children – 30 or 40 of them including some very small youngsters – watching us closely and doing some mutual grooming as if nothing untoward had occurred. It was an amazing, surreal experience that lasted maybe twenty seconds. But what a great twenty seconds it had been.

Almost every night in the forest, similar 'wa-hoo' calls from Olive Baboons woke me. The call they make when stressed, a troop sleeping somewhere close to our tents was clearly responding to a predator on the prowl. And a few times I heard a leopard, apparently common in these forests. A kind of grunting bark, not loud, it was clearly enough to spook the baboons. Maybe the leopard wasn't even contemplating grabbing one – they might well be more interested in killing bushbucks here – but the baboons were agitated by its presence nevertheless. And I had soon become used to the endless, metronome-like calls of the abundant but tiny Yellow-spotted Tree Frogs that started up when darkness fell and ticked away all night long in a surprisingly loud chorus. It was somehow soothing, rather like the soporific effect a ticking clock has on some people.

So the only other sound that woke me a couple of times, apart from the pre-dawn cries of the Fish Eagles, was the almost nightly occurrence of a tree, presumably a small one, being pushed over by an elephant on its night-time wanderings. One particular night, this small-hours tree felling seemed particularly close to our tents; I unzipped the front flap of mine, peered out but could see little. No one else appeared to be moving so I assumed we were perfectly safe and not likely to get trampled on by an elephant or flattened by a large tree limb. I crawled back into my sleeping bag and off to sleep.

I knew there were dangerous predators about but most of the wildlife in these forests was a delight not a worry. I was particularly keen to keep a watch out for interesting birds and mammals every time I went across to the rivulets of the Ngeng River just below our camp to wash or to collect the drinking water I needed to purify before I could consume it. Here, Black Saw-Wings were always flying about, jet black swallow relatives that hunt aerial insects. And baboon droppings were a constant feature of the waterside rocks; presumably like us they came here to wash. They probably watched me a few times from the deep cover of the far riverbank but I could never see them.

The river, in spite of its low flow, was good for kingfishers too; black and white Pied Kingfishers hovering above the surface before plunging in to extract a fish and small, blue and orange Malachite Kingfishers darting past like fighter jets. But the crowning glory of the river was the crow-sized Giant Kingfisher, a speckled black, white and chestnut beauty of a bird I had seen before in South Africa, but then only a glimpse as it flew off. Here there were far better views to be had; perching on a river boulder or on a low slung branch of an overhanging tree to spot fish below. A magnificent sight but yet another creature utterly dependent on enough rain to keep the rivers flowing.

The World's Biggest Plumbing Job

On the dusty track of the Turner River Trail in Florida, the sauna-like, midsummer air is alive with the vibrant hum of squadrons of colourful dragonflies. Centuries-old Bald Cypress trees, their feet immersed in the turbid water, are draped with garlands of Spanish Moss. Flame-flowered bromeliads sprout from their damp, fissured bark. Star-shaped Swamp Lilies and a scatter of Cabbage Palms enliven brown expanses of tough sawgrass sedge. Butterflies the size of small birds do flypasts. In the plant-choked, water-filled shallows, huge, grey-as-slate, knobbly-skinned alligators rest uncannily motionless between Spatterdocks. Large turtles swim sluggishly or sun themselves on a protruding branch while tree frogs emit loud grunts. White-tailed Deer are common, even a few Black Bears and Florida Panthers still hunt in these marshes but are rarely seen amid the rampant vegetation. A Green-backed Heron, a miniature hunter, clings waxwork-still on the twisted shoots of a red-barked Gumbo Limbo tree while Turkey Vultures float languidly above. The day sky above the Florida Everglades no longer turns dark with birds as the American artist, John James Audubon, described in his visit here in 1832. But the wildlife in the primeval swamps of the Big Cypress National Preserve, part of the northern Everglades, is guaranteed to astound you still.

This huge, subtropical wetland is a wildlife paradise. Its sawgrass marshes; swampy forests; mangrove islands; shallow, coastal waters and sea-edge coral reefs support over 11,000 different seed-bearing plants as diverse as tree-hugging Strangler Figs and the blue spikes of Pickerelweed. It is hearth and home to over 300 bird species, from black and scarlet Pileated Woodpeckers to the peculiar Snakebird, so named because it swims underwater with only its reptile-like neck visible. The key to this vast animal richness is less obvious. The heavy rains of summer, combined with the shimmering heat of the Florida sun, send microscopic water-living plants and animals into a reproductive frenzy. Called periphyton, yellow-green mats of this mix float on the water. It feeds an array of insects – including the larvae of the Everglades' prolific mosquitoes – tadpoles of frogs and other amphibians, plus a myriad of tiny fish. In their turn, they fall prey to larger fish, birds and reptiles a rung further up the fast-food ladder.

In Florida Bay – into which Everglades water eventually seeps – the shallow, brackish waters are home to Red Mangroves that rise tiptoe on claw-like prop roots to form hundreds of tiny islands. Each is an impenetrable tangle of roots and shoots that shelter a wealth of creatures and protects the coast when storms hit. Fish-eating birds of prey such as Ospreys and a cornucopia of egrets and herons nest in the mangrove tops. Sea turtles; Spiny Lobsters; fish with peculiar names like Drum, Porgie and Sailfin Molly; and endangered species like the American Crocodile and the lumbering Florida Manatee swim in their shadows.

In 2001, I went to the Everglades because of a plan signed into law in the last days of the Clinton Presidency. This vast wetland occupying much of the bottom half of Florida State had been badly damaged and modified for over a century but, at last, there was hope that it was going to be restored to something approaching its former glory. Drainage, diversion of its lifeblood – water – building development and intensive sugarcane growing had all had an enormous impact. And *Saga Magazine* had commissioned me to write a feature about what the future might hold.

This story is not so much about the experiences that I can recall from a fortnight's visit to the south of the USA's 'Sunshine State'. There were experiences of course; memorable helicopter rides to get a bird's-eye view of the huge shallow wetlands constructed from sugarcane fields to provide pollution soak-ups; my first glorious views of a family of River Otters making their way casually along a waterside track; of hopelessly flamboyant Roseate Spoonbills feeding in watery shallows; and much more beside. I've included the story because it was the most complex issue I have ever had to grapple with in order to produce a well-rounded feature for a readership I had to assume would know little if anything of the wildlife impact of water pollution and the perils of too much water abstraction. And why should they. OK, I had 3,000 words in which to explain what had happened to severely damage one of the world's great wetlands, why that mattered and how the damage might be put right. And 3,000 words is a long feature. But it was probably the hardest writing job I have ever done. It was not made any easier when, as often happens, I discovered a far more complex set of issues – and less conformity on how to deal with them – than I imagined when I first suggested the idea to *Saga Magazine*!

You might recall the time that Clinton put his signature on the relevant piece of paper to start the long process of recovering the Everglades. Though, if you do, it will be for a very different reason. In December 2000, US media outlets were replete with seemingly arcane discussions about some other, very much smaller bits of paper. The implications of hanging, dimpled, and pregnant chads on Florida State's punch-card

voting slips used in the Presidential Election race between Al Gore and George W
Bush were getting more public attention than whoever invented the voting system
could possibly have imagined. Re-counts to determine which way Florida had voted
were relying on an interpretation of punch holes which had, or hadn't, been perfectly
formed. With legal challenges growing by the hour and Florida's Supreme Court and
the US Supreme Court jolted into action, Florida's critically close count determined
who would enter the White House and succeed Clinton. After days of wrangling,
Bush was declared the winner (though Gore had won the total count US-wide) and
the rest, as they say, is history. Upon some chads was the West's future involvement
in Iraq and much subsequent Middle East turmoil, death and suffering determined.

In the middle of all this debacle, it isn't surprising that virtually no one noticed
that President Clinton, carrying on business much as normal in the White House,
signed up to the costliest public works project in US history, almost certainly the
costliest the world has ever seen. It was all about water in the Everglades. It was to re-
plumb Southern Florida, an area at least half that of Scotland. And it was to cost more
than £9,000 million over the next 30 years.

First, I had to get some basic background. Until American soldiers pursued
Seminole Indians through this lush, subtropical wilderness in the mid-1800s, no
'Westerners' had set foot in it. For thousands of years, its waters flowed on a 500 km
journey south through vast Lake Okeechobee to the crystal-clear mangrove shallows
of Florida Bay.

Seldom more than two feet deep, this 'river of grass' – as Marjory Stoneman
Douglas, the US writer and environmentalist, dubbed it – was nearly 100 km wide.
Devoid of any currents or rapids, it mooched south across a virtually flat landscape.
Its waters took years to reach the sea. Not surprisingly, its vast sawgrass marshes and
wet Cypress woods churned with life.

One of the first people I interviewed was Johnny Jones, the ex-Executive Director
(and the first) of the Florida Wildlife Federation (FWF), a powerful environmental
campaign organisation in the state. Jones had been a plumber and was in love with the
Everglades from his early years. He recalled being out in the swamps as a young man:
'I'd hacked my way through half a mile of tall sawgrass to reach some open space,'
he recalled. 'Just before I broke out I heard a loud noise like a shot from a cannon. It
was the wings of ducks. It seemed like millions of ducks, Mallard and Pintail, herons
and egrets. They took off like a cyclone, only bigger. They blocked out the sky.' It was
the early 1950s. Jones led the FWF from 1971 to 1986, campaigning for much of the
legislation in place today protecting large parts of this vast wetland. He died in 2010.

But when Jones saw – and heard – his cyclone of ducks, the Everglades was already
changing fast. Wetlands were thought of as pestilential wastes. Selling land cheaply, the
developing Florida State had long been encouraging settlers to build canals and drain

the land, creating an agricultural Eden on fertile, peaty soils. Sugarcane has long since grown where a young Johnny Jones saw a sky-full of birds. When seasonal floods and hurricanes killed thousands of people in the 1920s, the state funded yet more canals and protective banks or levees. By the 1970s, the US Army Corps of Engineers had completed one of the most ambitious engineering projects ever. They had surrounded Lake Okeechobee at the northern end of the Everglades with a massive embankment that plugged the natural, sheet-like flow of water south across the marshes and down to Florida Bay. Meanwhile, well over 2000 km of levees and canals, and umpteen pumping stations, diverted water out of the marshes and into the sea. Three Water Conservation Areas covering nearly half a million hectares were created out of the northern Everglades swamps; these were flooded year-round as shallow, water supply reservoirs for the burgeoning urban population. No longer did their water levels alter with the seasons as they had for millennia; now their levels were determined by water use in the growing centres of Miami, Palm Beach, Fort Lauderdale and elsewhere. They remain rich habitats but much of their typical wildlife has long gone.

All this re-plumbing cost the Everglades dear; ever since, what was left of the once vast marshes has been on life support. Its original 4 million ha, an area twice the size of Wales, had shrunk by half, converted to urban high-rise, farm crops or water storage. Over 60 of its plant and animal species are endangered, including the Wood Stork, down from around 20,000 pairs in the 1930s to a few thousand when I was there, and the enigmatic Florida Panther, perhaps 70 of which remained then. Egrets and herons have plummeted by 90% since the 1960s.

The area has a plethora of wildlife tourism businesses, both near the Everglades and around Florida Bay at its southern end. I talked to one: Capt. Sterling's Everglades Tours operating out of Key Largo ('where reality ends and tranquillity begins') near the mainland end of that attractive chain of islands – the Florida Keys – that arc their way out into Florida Bay. 'I started here 20 years ago,' says Sterling Kennedy who runs the business. 'I used to take people in an evening to watch thousands of storks, herons, egrets and Roseate Spoonbills roosting on one particular mangrove island in Florida Bay. Now I don't bother. There's few birds there any longer.' Most other tourism operators told me the same; few places that are accessible in and around the Everglades are as rich in wildlife as they used to be. Most are a pale reflection of what was once here. I was finding it all pretty depressing.

The plan that Clinton signed off in December 2000 in order to deliver Federal US funding (in addition to Florida State funding) is the Comprehensive Everglades Restoration Plan, known as CERP. It had been hammered out over years by an unlikely alliance of Federal and Florida State engineering, water supply and conservation Agencies, native Indian Tribes who still have 'reservations' in the area and farming interests. It also had considerable political support from the then State Governor Jeb

Bush, George B's brother and now a contender for the Republican nomination to run for President in November 2016.

To get everyone on side, though, it had to guarantee water for a 250,000 ha of some of the most productive farmland in the world and supply drinking water to the 6 million people who live year-round in Southern Florida (the population of Greater London) and another 12 million that join them in winter, mostly other Americans getting away from the ferocious northern winter. The cash, half from Federal coffers and half from the state, is intended to build over 300 deep underground water storage wells, each costing up to £1 million, and a series of reservoirs.

From all this you might think that Florida is short of water. It isn't. What it's short of is the means and the determination to hold and manage what they do get so that the environment doesn't suffer. Florida receives 150 cm of rain a year, over twice that of southern England where the largest sector of Britain's population resides. But the Sunshine State wastes much of it, using drinking water to irrigate golf courses and gardens. Wastewater recycling plants are scheduled to help put that right as part of the plan to manage this precious resource more carefully.

I interviewed David Struhs, appointed in 1999 by the Governor as Secretary of Environmental Protection in Florida, and a Bush family friend. At the time, he was responsible for the state's implementation of CERP. 'This plan is our single highest environmental priority here in Florida. It makes good sense; it's not just nice to do, it's fundamental,' he told me. 'We must protect the Everglades and plan for the predicted doubling in our population over the next 50 years. I can't see any sensible alternatives. It could prove to be one of the largest examples of sustainable development anywhere,' he adds.

But others were critical. Shannon Estenoz was then the Everglades Programme Director for the Worldwide Fund for Nature (WWF) and I met her to get her views.

'With other campaigning groups we intend keeping up the political pressure to ensure that the urban lobby doesn't hijack the CERP. If Secretary Struhs believes that the urban population can grow for another 50 years because they can get enough water – and we can restore the Everglades at the same time – he's being unrealistic,' she adds. In 2014, US Secretary of the Interior in the Obama administration, Ken Salazar, announced the appointment of Estenoz as Director of Everglades Restoration Initiatives, his senior representative in South Florida for Everglades restoration.

According to the South Florida Water Management District, who are in the forefront of getting the work done, CERP will return most of the pre-drainage flows to the Everglades, mimicking the age-old pattern of summer wet seasons and drier winters. But water quality is as important as water quantity. Six wetlands (called Stormwater Treatment Areas, STAs) – over 20,000 ha dense with bulrush and willow or awash with floating plants like water lilies – are being built between the intensive sugarcane-growing farmland and the Everglades to absorb polluting phosphate from fertilisers before the water flows into the swamps.

Because all of this land is pancake flat, it's impossible to visualise these STAs by standing on a small embankment at their edge. So the Water Management District offered to fly me over some of them so that I could see them properly. It wasn't an offer I was going to refuse. Hovering just a couple of hundred metres above them, the waters were green with algae; stands of bulrush and willow grew at the edges and these vast shallows, sometimes covered in water lilies, seemed to stretch almost as far as we could see from the helicopter seats. The largest – at 6,500 ha, a huge wetland by UK standards – was costing £67 million to create, most of it spent on embankment building, levelling the land, building pumping stations and redirecting canals. A few years ago this had been wall-to-wall sugarcane. Laced copiously with fertiliser every year, much of the phosphate in the fertiliser would run off into the general southerly flow of water into the Everglades marshes, changing the composition of its natural vegetation and stimulating the growth of plants not naturally common here. Now the lush plant growth in the STAs would use up all the phosphate instead.

There were few birds visible in the STAs from up here and our pilot was more concerned about large birds in the sky around us. We had flown past a couple of Turkey Vultures earlier and he gave them a wide berth. 'They're our main hazard out here,' he said. 'We are often flying at a height where they soar and you don't want to hit one of them. A colleague of mine had one crash through the cockpit glass one day; he was injured but he managed to keep control and land the copter safely. He was very lucky.'

Because of phosphate getting in from the sugarcane crops in the past, 25,000 ha of sawgrass – the dominant, natural plant cover over much of the Everglades – has been ousted by cattail (bulrush), a toughie that does well where fertilisers pollute water. It grows so densely that any open water amongst the sawgrass, where most of the diversity of plants and fish exists, gets covered by it. Water Management District experts told me that it will take many decades for the sawgrass to return once phosphate is eliminated. So far, phosphate levels in the water entering the Everglades after travelling slowly through the STA wetlands have been reduced tenfold but the intention is to get it lower still.

For another angle on the same issue – a fundamental tenet of (hopefully) good journalism – I arranged to meet Rick Roth, the owner of Roth Farms and at that time Vice President of the Florida Farm Bureau. We walked over some of his vast sugarcane, vegetable and rice 'fields', part of his 2,000 ha estate near West Palm Beach. He argued that farmers have been using improved farm practices to reduce fertiliser runoff for years. Surprisingly, though, he was not set against the state buying up some farmland to flood the STAs. 'Phosphates aren't the problem they used to be,' he says. 'Our taxes go up if we don't keep phosphate levels down so it's in our interest to do so. But the STAs will bring it down more. The Plan is a good compromise because it lets us continue farming, restores the Everglades and improves water supply. Everyone wins,' he adds.

To help achieve more natural water flows through these vast marshes, 400 km of drainage canals are scheduled for infilling as part of CERP. Like many fishermen, Aaron Spicer isn't too happy about this; I had a chat with him as he fished from the grassy bank of a canal near Homestead in the very south of Florida. 'I come out here most weekends from Miami with my family. We fish these canals. They're good for Black Crappie and bass. We don't want them filled in,' he argues passionately as several other fishermen look on.

But fisheries experts point out that the loss of some canals will be nothing compared with the potentially huge gains in fish populations as a result of the changes to be made. In the Everglades, where inches are everything, areas of slightly deeper water will dry out much less frequently, boosting depleted populations of insects, amphibians and birds too. Reinstating natural water flows doesn't come cheap. Both Interstate 75 (known here as Alligator Alley) and US 41 (the Tamiami Trail), the two major roads cutting west/east across the Everglade swamps, will have culverts installed or embanked sections replaced by low bridges to allow natural north/south water flows once again.

The results of all this restoration won't be felt quickly. Typical was the reaction of Dr Bob Johnson, Director of the South Florida Natural Resources Centre at the Everglades National Park and a renowned Everglades expert. 'We'll have to wait and see how things recover. The Plan will supply about three quarters of the water we calculate we need but more could be necessary,' he told me. Nevertheless, Johnson was optimistic that improvements would occur.

The Seminoles, the largest Native American tribe in Florida with 2,800 members, are sharing the cost of a £33 million restoration of their huge reservation north of Big Cypress. They're optimistic too. 'We want to see the Everglades restored,' Jim Shore, General Counsel to the Tribe told me. 'Too much has been destroyed. The money will restore nearly 6,000 ha of swamp and forest but we will also be building some water storage areas to improve our citrus crops and cattle ranching.'

It didn't take long for me to realise that Everglades restoration was not all about water, even though it's easy to get that impression. There are huge problems with introduced plants that have literally gone wild, frequently at the expense of the locally native species. I arranged to meet Dr Mike Norland at the Everglades National Park's HQ; he's an expert on them. He told me that three quarters of a million hectares of the marshes are overrun with introduced plants like Brazilian Pepper (a South American evergreen tree reaching 10 m in height that thrives in swamps) and Paperbark trees (an Australian import that takes over from native sawgrass), ousting a host of native swamp species. CERP aims to speed up their removal but it's a costly and difficult business. When I was there in 2001, contractors were in the midst of clearing a dense, 2,000 ha forest of Brazilian Pepper within the national park; the land was being returned to wetland a bit at a time. 'We cut it with heavy machinery, chip it, and then scrape off the soil so it can't seed into it. All the typical wetland plants and animals are coming back slowly,' Mike told me as we looked out on yet another dense growth of the dreaded tree, a clump so dense that there seemed next to nothing growing amongst it.

As if the marshes here didn't have enough issues for me to try and write about, I soon found out that the end-point for all this water – Florida Bay at the southern tip of the state – had problems too. I hadn't bargained on that! Looking across the aquamarine glare of these subtropical waters from Key Largo towards Florida's southern tip, shallow discs of mangrove islets pepper the scene, some tiny, others much larger. Around them cumbersome Brown Pelicans lunge into the waters, piratical, red-throated Magnificent Frigatebirds duck and dive to harass other birds for a free feed and cormorants dive for fish. Idyllic is a description that comes readily to mind.

But I was learning fast that superficial impressions can easily deceive; idyllic this place seemingly isn't. Pouring more water into the sea sounds harmless enough. But in Florida Bay, the Everglades CERP doing just that is proving highly controversial. Florida Bay has been much altered by the water that flows into it, the water that filters its way through the great Everglades marshes. The Bay's once crystal clear waters now often resemble a pea soup, brimming with abnormal loads of mud and plankton, tiny plants and animals that have proliferated. Seagrasses that used to grow rampant and anchor its muddy sea bed – vital nurseries for invertebrates, young fish and shellfish – have died off, causing declines in Pink Shrimp, Spiny Lobsters and fish like Red Drum. Numbers of mangrove-breeding Wood Storks, scarlet-beaked White Ibis and gorgeous pink and carmine Roseate Spoonbills plummeted from around 300,000 in the 1930s to less than 30,000 in the 1990s. Ospreys, lumbering Florida Manatees and American Crocodiles have all declined; and the £39 million Pink Shrimp and £15 million Stone Crab fisheries have taken big knocks here too. Tourist brochures, of course, remain replete with dazzling pictures of birds, alligators and manatees. 'We see a lot of local publications with pretty pictures of spoonbills,' comments Dr Jerry Lorenz, a biologist with the National Audubon Society who has been studying these birds since 1989. 'But I'm down here watching the birds go all to hell,' he says ruefully.

Parts of the impressive coral reefs that stretch the length of the Florida Keys are dying off. In places up to 80% of the massive, branching Elkhorn and Staghorn Corals, and lattice-work Sea Fan corals that waft gently in the warm water, have been killed or are badly diseased. Nearly 600 species of fish depend on these corals; flamboyantly coloured species like the Rock Beauty, blue and yellow striped Grunts, and the aptly named Parrotfish live here alongside an array of sponges, shrimps, crabs and turtles. But expert opinion differs on the causes of these die-offs. Some put the seagrass kills down to the Bay's water becoming more salty because not enough freshwater has been getting into it from the Everglades for decades. Others, like Dr Brian Lapointe of the Harbor Branch Oceanographic Institution, pin the blame on nitrogen in fertilisers washing through the Everglades from farmland way to the north. He believes that restoring freshwater flows through the Everglades will kill more coral and seagrass, not less, because the STAs, while they reduce phosphates considerably, only cut fertiliser nitrogen by half.

The Environmental Protection Agency's Dr Bill Kruczynski is convinced it isn't that simple. 'I'd like to have an easy answer,' he says, 'But the data just doesn't support it. Some coral reefs well away from any pollution are dying too. There are other factors like fishing, climate warming and sewage discharges from thousands of cesspits and septic tanks in the Keys. It will cost £430 million for a proper sewage system here, money that's not in the CERP,' he says. Nevertheless, building permits are now harder to get on the Keys and there are proposals to modernise its sewage treatment.

The problems I heard about in Florida Bay are not just an ecological disaster; they're a potential economic disaster too. A multi-billion dollar tourist, fishing, diving and snorkelling industry depends on its good health. And, as you might expect, tourism operators have their own take on what's behind all the ecological change that threatens their livelihoods. Rarely has so much depended upon pouring some water into the sea. 'I've been diving these reefs for 35 years,' John Bell at Sharky's Reef Tours told me, one of many such businesses in Key Largo, 'and I've seen a huge die-off of corals. It's depressing. If the corals die, guess who dies off next!' Captain Dave Lee, who has been leading backcountry fishing trips in the Bay for nearly three decades, thinks some of these changes are natural. 'If they can mimic the old flow conditions down through the marshes, that'll boost fish numbers. It's either too salty or too fresh now; the flows are on and off. But I'm not sure they can achieve it,' he adds.

Thirty years is a long time to see this massive project through. It has the necessary legal backing but it relies on continuing state and federal political commitment to keep the cash flowing. There is a much bigger factor too. Any amount of cash and re-plumbing is impotent if climate warming produces the predicted sea level rise of up to 5 cm a decade. With the highest ground just 6 m above current sea levels, within a century the sea could inundate much of the southern Everglades.

The late Marjory Stoneman Douglas, who remains an inspiration for those who seek to protect the Everglades, had a simple answer: 'The Everglades is a test,' she once wrote. 'If we pass it, we get to keep the planet.'

POSTSCRIPT:

When I wrote the feature for *Saga Magazine* I posed the obvious questions: Will it work? Will it run out of political steam, unfinished as government cash gets diverted to more pressing and immediate priorities such as terrorism? Or will it turn into a water supply project for farmers and city dwellers, as some critics warn, relegating the desperate need to resuscitate the Everglades to a 'nice to do' extra that never quite gets done? Maybe you are wondering about the answers. So am I, but I don't intend spending weeks trying to evaluate what has – and what has not – been achieved so far, analysing the maelstrom of disparate information that's available in various reports. It is early days in the 30-year CERP plan which is trying to put right some of the damage caused by over half a century or more of land mismanagement.

What is clear is that, with George Bush as President from 2001 to 2009, the federal commitments promised by Clinton withered, and withered very substantially, as priorities switched to countering terrorism at home and to foreign invasions. Bush tried to cancel all federal investment against the wishes of Florida's Republicans and his brother, Florida Governor Jeb Bush, but he was overruled by Congress. What a contrast there would have been, it is safe to assume, had Al Gore – a fervent environmentalist – become the 43rd US President.

The State of Florida reports that it has spent more than £1,300 million on the various projects since CERP was signed. More than 15,000 ha of STAs have been built to filter phosphorus from Everglades waters. Fifty-five percent of the farmland necessary for restoration – 85,000 ha – has been purchased by the state, and environmental groups are pressing for more purchases. Some water storage reservoirs for urban supply have been built but environment groups claim that more effort and cash is going into securing water for the growing urban areas than into Everglades restoration. There are claims, too, that the whole plan is lost in a maze of bureaucracy, a victim of 'analysis paralysis' partly caused by the big sugar producers slowing down the process by influencing politicians. What a surprise.

Out of the Red and into the Black

Crashing through thorny acacia scrub and hurtling across the bleached savannah grassland, my driver – Jeff Gaisford of Ezemvelo KwaZulu-Natal Wildlife, the state Wildlife Authority in this part of South Africa – was doing his best to keep pace with the two leading Land Rovers as we all dodged the taller trees and swung wildly through head-high scrub. And after ten minutes of this adrenalin rush, the vehicles came to a stop one behind the other, doors were flung open and we all ran as fast as we could to the large, grey-skinned animal lying on the parched grassland amongst some scrub about 60 m away. A Black Rhino, a female about eight years old, had been darted from the helicopter; the tranquiliser had slowed her, gradually, but she had run perhaps the best part of 2 km before she collapsed on the ground, unharmed but sedated. Touching a rhino, not something it's possible to do every day, might be the nearest I will ever get to experiencing the outer covering of a dinosaur. It was an opportunity I had managed to arrange in the Hluhluwe-iMfolozi Game Reserve in KwaZulu-Natal some years back.

The first rhino ancestor evolved in the early Eocene around 50 million years ago when conditions on earth were hot and, maybe, humid. It was apparently a small hornless mammal that more resembled a tapir or small horse than a rhino. From this ancestor a number of different types of rhino-like mammal evolved; there were 'running rhinos', all adapted for speed and more like modern-day horses; others became aquatic and evolved more like hippos; while a third, much larger group ranging from dog-sized to large mammals – including the Woolly Rhinoceros – became well established over much of the world's land. It's from this last group that today's rhinos evolved several million years later. But they still retain that rather primitive appearance, maybe more so than any other living mammal.

Together with a group of vets, game reserve rangers and Zulu workers, I had been waiting around for a couple of hours for a helicopter to arrive, the one piece of 'equipment' so essential for the work we were about to participate in. Helicopters are expensive to hire so, when it did arrive, it was action stations with everyone racing into their 4WD vehicles. Except, that is, for the marksman, this afternoon a markswoman, armed with her special, sighted rifle and ammunition. She jumped into the two-seater helicopter and off it went.

By the time I had made it, breathless, to the first sedated Black Rhino of the afternoon, she was lying still on the ground surrounded by a team of vets and conservation workers, a cloth tied over her head and earplugs inserted in her ears. To minimize distress, they told me, it is better that the animal can't see and hear. Sedation causes extreme calm but the animal still retains its senses. The team's care was impressive. So here was a tonne or two of dark grey, leathery-skinned Black Rhino lying on her side, as still as ever she could possibly be. And that skin? It was leathery all right. Thick and protective, it has to prevent penetration by the vicious thorns of the savannah bushes and protect the animal against most skin-burrowing insects. It feels dry, somewhat reptilian; a flexible armour plating.

But capturing Black Rhino (they only differ from White Rhino by mouth shape) isn't done for the adrenalin-fuelled buzz of off-roading through the savannah, exciting though I have to admit it was. Thanks to strict protection and a good breeding record, in state-owned game reserves like Hluhluwe-iMfolozi – 960 km² of savannah, forest and scrub fenced off from surrounding land – Black Rhinos have done so well that there are now more of them than the land area can adequately accommodate. 'Each bull needs a territory of about 500 ha which it defends against other males,' Jeff Gaisford tells me. Jeff had set up the arrangement for me to participate because I was writing a feature for *CNN Traveller* magazine about their work. 'Because the game reserve is fenced, the Black Rhino population has reached the land's carrying capacity. We have viable young bulls that are failing to nail a territory here.'

'So we have put in place a plan whereby we are willing to offer spare Black Rhinos to private landowners who have sufficient land that they will guarantee for conservation purposes. Any land they provide has to be fenced and it needs to be around 20,000 ha to be viable,' he adds. These founder populations of Black Rhino remain the property of Ezemvelo KZN Wildlife (the governmental organisation responsible for maintaining wildlife conservation areas and biodiversity in KwaZulu-Natal Province) and are looked after on a custodianship basis by the landowners. Any drop in standards of management or care and the state body retains the right to move them elsewhere. And any such landowners taking Black Rhino have to provide assurance that they have sufficient protection in place to strongly deter any poachers trying to get rhino horn for illegal sale to Southeast Asian countries.

The team capturing Black Rhino here have clearly got the whole process down to a fine art. They're an impressive bunch; each team member knows his particular task and no time is lost in getting it done. The vets want the animal sedated for as short a time as practical but long enough to make sure that their capture after the sedative wears off – and the most dangerous part of the exercise by far – is done as safely as possible. And that is by no means guaranteed when a tonne or more of wild animal gets to its feet and is desperate to get away from these people.

Once a rhino has been darted from the air, the noise of the helicopter is used to try and make it run towards a track or other relatively easy access for the team of vets and operatives who have the difficult task of ensuring both that it stays sedated but suffers as little stress as possible. Accessibility is important, as I soon found out, so that the rhino can be pulled by rope, once the sedative wears off, into a huge metal crate carried on a lorry. To do this, the lorry has to get within a few metres of the sedated rhino, not a simple task if you don't know where the hapless animal is going to collapse.

'Black Rhino have a tendency to run into cover on low ground to hide once they've been darted,' Dave Cooper, the vet supervising this capture and a veteran of many more tells me when he has a few minutes break between one rhino capture and the next. 'Then we might not be able to get it out and into a crate so we have to administer the antidote to rouse it, then chase it out. That's a dangerous business for the men involved. One slip and you could be trampled.'

Bad-tempered rhinos weren't the only risk of the day. Flying the helicopter was most certainly another; it bucked and weaved, turned on a penny and generally jolted around in the air trying to enable the markswoman to shoot at the running rhino's muscle-bound rump. I would have been frightened for my life; San-Mari Ras, the markswoman in question, was air sick; I wasn't surprised. 'I had to get the pilot to land so that I could get out before I was ill,' an unusually rather pale-looking San-Mari told me when she joined us on the ground and a new marksman took over. San-Mari is the Section Ranger for this part of the Hluhluwe Umfolozi Game Reserve. As such she has a big role in selecting which rhinos should be captured and taken away to pastures new.

Where a rhino eventually keels over is not always best for his or her wellbeing. 'This one isn't in a very good position. We don't want her lying with her head facing downslope because it puts pressure on her stomach. We'll have to turn her round,' I heard Dave Cooper telling his team. But that didn't prove easy. With ship mooring-sized ropes – one around her head and horn, the other around a leg – a tug of war ensued with ten men hauling her around, at one point almost losing control as she rolled over and over down the slope until they got control again. It was an anxious time, not the least in case the sedative was wearing off and a particularly irascible, heavy animal might have broken loose. I overheard one of the older hands tell a male vet student participating in his first rhino capture to get up the nearest tree as quickly as possible if she breaks loose. It wasn't a reassuring comment. And there were very few climbable trees anyway.

I thought the best policy would be to hide behind the largest tree I could find and hope a charging rhino didn't come my way.

Much of the frenetic human activity around the sedated rhino is to find out more about the stress it suffers. 'We take blood samples from their ears to check on stress hormone levels and for a pregnancy test. We monitor their blood pressure and general condition and we take a sample of faeces,' Dr Jacques Flamand, the Project Leader for Ezemvelo KZN Wildlife and WWF told me later. Blood samples are taken from her ear, bloody skin lesions – caused by a parasite (they can somehow manage to penetrate even this armoured skin) – are treated with disinfectant, a vet monitors her blood pressure and general condition while someone with an arm-length plastic glove has the unenviable task of reaching high inside her rear end to extract a sample of poo to test.

This being a large animal, the poo sample is rather large too. A large handful to be accurate. But rhino poo isn't as bad as it sounds. Black Rhinos are vegetarian, devouring quantities of scrub, twigs and leaves. As a result, it's grassy green and not very smelly. I know because I smelt a handful. 'We measure stress hormones in the dung and these are related to levels in the blood. We also collect dung from sites where the animals are released later and test that for hormones too. By knowing more about their stress levels, the team can improve their understanding of what's going on and maybe improve techniques for future captures and reintroductions,' adds Flamand.

Then a small power saw starts whining; a surprising sound out here in the savannah but one that's become essential. The rhino is having its horn sawn off; equivalent to our having an extra-large toenail cut … and it's made out of the same material, keratin. Then a large hole is drilled into the horn's stump and a small tracker device fitted inside it with some powerful glue; that way the rhino's movement can be tracked when it's released in her new home.

Removing the horn is a wise precaution; poachers are killing rhino in every African country where they still occur, and although most victims that are killed are the more abundant White Rhino, it's totally indiscriminate and several Blacks have been killed too. While mumbo-jumbo medicinal uses for the horn in Southeast Asia have traditionally driven this horrendous trade, much of it today is used to satisfy the hedonistic nouveau riche in Vietnam and China with rhino horn bangles, necklaces and après party pick-me-ups. It's a devastating trade. Originally, there were thought to be hundreds of thousands of Black Rhino continent-wide. In 2014, South Africa had 2,044; that's 40% of the African population which currently stands at 5,055. Particularly in South Africa where safeguards are better, the numbers are increasing slowly.

Later that afternoon we chased after another rhino darted in a different part of the reserve. This was a male. The same thorough routine was carried out quietly and efficiently. But there was a rather different problem this time. He had collapsed on a slope with a number of trees between him and the nearest fairly flat ground the lorry could reverse safely on to. So it was chainsaw time again, though for trees not rhino horn this time. While the team was working on the rhino, two or three Zulu helpers were cutting down trees – and not small ones – to clear a route for the lorry. The heavy duty crate was lowered to the ground off the lorry and, with the hawser-like ropes attached to the sedated rhino, one of these linked through the crate to pull him in, and several Zulu workers on the end of each rope, he was injected with the antidote.

It took maybe 20 seconds to work. Then this tonne of animal staggered to his feet unaware that he was tethered. Floundering and presumably unaware of what was happening, he was tugged to the crate, given a couple of mild electric shocks with cattle prods on his rear end ... and in he went. The big iron doors were quickly closed and bolted, the crate was lifted on to the lorry and we all breathed a sigh of relief. Another Black Rhino was on his way to a new home, helping to secure a future for a magnificent animal.

The Hluhluwe-iMfolozi Game Reserve, a fairly traditional savannah-dominated habitat, a much smaller cousin of the famous Kruger, proved a good place to visit in other ways too, not the least of which is that it's easy to combine it with visiting the nearby coastal Greater St. Lucia Wetland Park. Now renamed the iSimangaliso (appropriately, it means 'miracle' in Zulu) Wetland Park, with nearly 3,000 km^2 of coast, lake, marshlands and woodland it adds a huge diversity of wildlife to whatever you can see out in the dry savannah. There are elephant, leopard, Black Rhino, White Rhino, African Buffalo, hippo and Nile Crocodiles and in the ocean, whales, dolphins, and marine turtles including breeding Leatherbacks and Loggerheads.

The birds around here are stunning. The safari lodge we stayed in was surrounded by woodland and scrub on the edge of these wetlands; we spotted at least nine different species of sunbirds in the week we were there. Mostly very small, they probe into flowers with down-curved beaks to extract nectar. While several are dark, most have bright bands of colour; the male Orange-breasted Sunbird, apart from the orange, has a green head and nape, yellow belly and long tail feathers. The female isn't dull either; she has an olive-brown back with yellow underparts. Watching them probe flowering shrubs while we ate breakfast on a nearby terrace is one of my favourite South African memories.

So, too, was walking on paths in the local woodland where Grey-headed and Brown-hooded Kingfishers hunted large insects. Two of the dryland kingfishers in the world, they are just as attractive and fast-flying as their sometimes better-known water-inhabiting cousins. There were also mousebirds; strange, long-tailed, scruffy looking individuals that creep about in dense scrub and low trees but, when they fly, almost always do so in follow-my-leader fashion from one bit of thicket to the next.

One of the most striking sights was to watch an assembly of herons and storks standing close together as if they were a school party or hiking group on a walking tour and had stopped en masse to listen to their guide. At first I didn't spot them. A group of us were walking across some damp grassland – much of it usually flooded in summer, but not when I was there – on the edge of the St Lucia wetlands. We were led by one of the managers at the safari camp and he was taking us to see some rather uncommon birds he had seen previously. Here we found three different species of longclaw, including the Cape Longclaw, found nowhere else but the very south of Africa. The male of this species, while brown on the back, has canary yellow underparts and a bright orange throat lined with black. It was a striking sight. Longclaws are like large pipits – to whom they are closely related – but much more colourful, larger and, yes, with surprisingly long claws.

It was when we turned to walk in a different direction that I noticed the bird 'tour group'. Perhaps 100–200 birds or more, standing several deep near the water's edge, huddled closely together. Presumably they had finished feeding, gorged maybe on a plethora of frogs and toads. Line-ups of Great White Egrets and smaller Little Egrets, rather angelic in appearance in their snow-white suits like choir boys on parade. Stately Greater Flamingos and their pinker Lesser Flamingo cousins. Some smaller, black-headed – and black beaked – African Sacred Ibises. There were taller, darker herons; Black-headed Herons maybe and a few giants of the heron tribe, head and shoulders above the rest, resplendent with their long chestnut necks. These were the aptly named Goliath Herons, not abundant birds here. But the stars of this avian line-up was a phalanx of Great White Pelicans, standing inshore I presume after a successful morning's fishing out on Lake Lucia. With their huge beaks and beak pouches, each looked self-satisfied and avuncular, rather like the conductor of a famous orchestra concentrating on the score before lifting the baton to start a well-known symphony.

It was one of those very special moments.

Some Gorgeous Places

They counted us in at the top and out again at the bottom to make sure that there were no casualties along the way or anyone left in there overnight. A ragged line of us; French, Greeks, Americans and Brits – maybe other nationalities too – all with characteristic puffy, red faces, hot and bothered, some extra exhausted by the searing heat of the last mile or so to Aghia Roumeli. In midsummer, walking the 20 km of the Samaria Gorge in the west of Crete, Europe's largest river gorge, is not just a test of stamina. It's a test of adequate footwear.

Trainers appeared to be de rigueur. Whether they are appropriate for a hard, albeit mainly downhill, walk on rough gravel and stone with occasional small boulders, depends, I suppose, on their quality. Gloating as my daughter and I were – me in my lightweight walking boots, she in walking shoes – at the number of walkers limping uncomfortably in their trainers, the gorge proved almost as amazing for its fabulous scenery as it did for inducing people to walk in the most impractical footwear. Canvas shoes, slingbacks, even believe it or not – one pair of beach flip-flops.

Eschewing the organised coach party trips to what has become, in the last few decades, a honey pot for tourists, we did Samaria the tough way. All public transport and delays. It would sound better, I thought, for the feature I would later write about our walk in *The Independent*'s Travel pages. After an Olympic-paced few kilometre walk, pre-dawn, from our hotel to Hania's bus station, we caught the first service to the top of the Gorge at 6.15 a.m. Hot, we dozed as it climbed up to the Omalos plateau set high in the Levka Ori (White Mountains), their limestone peaks rising to 2,000 m around us. An hour or so later, after a pastry and coffee in the large, neat cafeteria above the top of the Gorge, we were ready for the off.

Dawn had broken and temperatures were distinctly cool even though it was August. We paid our national park entrance fee and scanned the sunlit peaks before looking down into the pine-forested depths of the chasm below. There followed a 3,000-foot descent on an excellent hairpin path, this way and that in the dappled shade of Cretan Cypresses, pines, and the occasional Wild Fig, Almond or Cretan Maple tree. Anyone believing that this is the easy bit of the walk should contemplate that the descent is the height of Snowdon and that downhill walking takes its toll on knee joints and pelvis alike.

The analogy with Snowdon doesn't end there either. Samaria attracts hordes of people (over 300,000 a year) so we had little hope of sitting by a tranquil stream in an atmosphere of peace and serenity. Far from it. We spent the five hours the walk took us overtaking a steady stream of walkers (and limpers), many of them far from quiet and including one Greek man singing all the way. Minus bouzouki. Minus a decent voice come to that.

Along the route there are well signposted springs (apparently 22 of them), seemingly with an abundance of cool water at most of them. We knew this before we set off, but – belt and braces – we carried some water just in case. At the abandoned and isolated village of Samaria about 8 km down the gorge – inhabited by seven families until 1967 when the Samaria Gorge National Park was designated – it's hard to imagine how these people eked out a living, cut off in the winter months by the turbulent floodwaters which thunder down the gorge and nowadays closing it to walkers at such times.

The emblem of the park – and a major reason for its designation – is something which few people, we were told, now see. The goat-like Kri-kri or Agrimi, probably isn't native here. Brought to Crete (and probably to much of the rest of Greece) maybe at the time of the Minoan civilisation, it now only survives in these Cretan mountains and on a couple of tiny offshore islands. By 1960, the Kri-kri was under threat, with numbers below 200. It had been the only meat available to mountain guerillas during the German occupation in World War II. There are still only about 2,000 animals on the island and they are considered vulnerable: hunters still kill them (illegally) for their tender meat, grazing grounds have become scarcer and disease has affected them. Hybridisation with ordinary goats is another threat.

The Kri-kri used to be considered a distinct subspecies of wild goat but DNA analysis has since found that it is a feral domestic goat derived from the first stocks of goats domesticated in the Levant and other parts of the Eastern Mediterranean around 8000–7500 BC. So it is not considered truly wild though it is an ancient link to the earliest domestications. I really wanted to see some and the gorge is reputedly a good place to do so.

It wasn't looking too likely; more people here in the gorge means more disturbance. But, tipped off by a Park ranger, we were keeping a watch for the Kri-kri near Samaria village and, as we approached the few buildings, we spotted four or five nimble females crossing the dried up riverbed. On the edge of the village, where mules used for carrying provisions (and injured walkers) were feeding on some hay, a family group of Kri-kri were vying with them to devour it. More antelope than goat in appearance, altogether we counted about 12 females with their yellow-brown coats and black back stripe and eight khaki brown kids, a few of them no more than 60 cm tall. Another ranger told us that we wouldn't see the much longer horned males. 'The boys,' as he described them quaintly, 'stay high up in the mountains, away from all the people.'

Leaving Samaria village, with Chukar (a mountain partridge) croaking their guttural call on the steep slopes high above, we walked through the most photographed sections of the gorge. Here, with the river disappearing underground, then re-appearing again at intervals, the red-brown cliffs rise near-vertically like massive cathedrals reaching to the sky for hundreds of metres. The occasional Wild Fig tree, with its biblical connotations, somehow manages to grasp a foothold in a moist rock cleft. The path crossed the river from one side to the other where the gorge narrows to an incredible 3 m – at the so-called Iron Gates (no gates) – and you are left in awe, wondering at the turmoil of thunderous pounding these rock walls endure when the river is in flood.

Throughout the gorge, we were struck by the lack of litter, even though 2,000–3,000 people walk it on peak days. In spite of this human flow, the paths, by and large, are in good repair, helped, no doubt, by the entrance fee, something British walkers in our National Parks baulk at but which seemed universally accepted here. In fact the place remains very natural, except for the telephone wire on short wooden poles and the plastic water pipe both of which run from Samaria village to the bottom of the gorge. Most of the time we hardly noticed them but where the gorge narrows they can be an intrusion. No doubt they are a necessity for accident communications (heart attacks and broken limbs are apparently the most frequent) and for summer firefighting.

In midsummer when we walked it, birds like the impressive Lammergeier (Bearded Vulture) are hard to find but we did watch little Crag Martins riding delicately the updraughts of breeze alongside us as we neared the bottom of the gorge. Spotting birds of prey overhead – there are huge Griffon Vultures here too – is certain to be difficult; after all, the gorge is so narrow and its sides so high that there's not much overhead sky visible. That can be a blessing too. In midsummer, walking here would be extremely arduous if the sun penetrated these depths. We were hot and tired enough as it was.

For the botanist, the Samaria Gorge is a bit like paradise. With 400–500 different plant species, they range from a yellow-flowered flax and blue-flowering Cretan Rock Lettuce to cyclamens and bushes of the rare White Peony, the last one growing in profusion around the tiny, ruined church of Aghios Nikolaos, a few kilometres into our walk.

Quite suddenly, after the gorge constricts into its narrowest part, the valley broadens and we walked out of the national park at the ruins of what was the original Aghia Roumeli village, now a set of shaded drink stands and little tavernas. We couldn't walk past them without succumbing to a cool, freshly squeezed orange juice. It tasted heavenly. But the walk wasn't over. Not yet. The next part – about 4 km, albeit of flat walking – proved to be the hardest part. We were out in the full glare of the afternoon sun (we hit it early afternoon at 90°F in the shade) and it was an arduous trudge to the new Aghia Roumeli village, built by the sea where the inevitable knick-knack shops prevail. Then it was a case of waiting for the next ferry to Hora Sfakion, an hour's sailing time east along the coast – Aghia Roumeli has no road connections – followed by a service bus back to Hania. Falling asleep later in the bus was hard to avoid but the warm breeze on the ferry ride kept us awake. And as we sailed along the south coast of Crete I spotted a couple of Kri-kri grazing on the parched slopes of a rocky headland high above. One of them had horns; it was 'a boy' all right.

Later that week we tried a quieter gorge, one of about forty on Crete; it was a much easier walk too. The 8-km-long Imbros Gorge, well signposted from Imbros village around 24 km east of Samaria in the foothills of the White Mountains proved a far easier walk compared to the rigours of Samaria. We set off in an invigoratingly cool breeze wafting a heady aroma of Sage, Rosemary and other herbs. But it wasn't exactly tranquil. During the morning we got overtaken by pulses of German tourists, each pulse seemingly the contents of a coach tour. For some inexplicable reason we heard no other language. Come noon, all these groups had marched on and we suddenly had the gorge to ourselves. Here, we could sit and listen to silence, broken only by the breeze rustling some cypress or wild olive trees and an occasional mewing call from a couple of huge, young Bonelli's Eagles on the crest of the cliffs high above. It was hard to imagine a more romantic place on earth.

Half way down its rather genteel slopes, there was a small, stone-built Venetian water reservoir where a few people from Imbros village sell drinks and keep a donkey in case anyone has to be carried out. I presume the donkey does little business but who knows. Further on, the gorge narrows impressively and massive cliffs rise on either side, sometimes for 100 m or more. What is different from Samaria, apart from the smaller scale, is that Imbros only has water running down it after snow melt in spring. The rest of the year it is possible to walk it without fear of flash floods. At its end, where the steep sides fall away, a few tavernas by the main road from Hora Sfakion to Vrises (and on to Hania or Rethimnion) compete for your custom. To get back to Imbros village from here demands either a sauna-like walk up interminable hairpins on a public road climbing several hundred metres, a long wait for the infrequent public buses, or what was effectively a rip-off taxi fare. I tried bartering but the taxi drivers here are obviously wily enough to know from your knackered looks that a taxi at any price is a welcome relief.

Gorges are attractive places; they certainly attract me. I suppose it's because you can be pretty sure that their relative inaccessibility – steep sides, rocks and cliffs, stream liable to sudden spates of floodwater – has preserved much of what has always been there in terms of their vegetation and associated wildlife. Modern agriculture, thank heavens, can't get any purchase; grazing livestock are at least a little limited in where they can get to; and commercial foresters have limited scope for planting lines of trees that will be difficult and costly to harvest.

In complete contrast to the large scale and fame of the Samaria Gorge, a far, far smaller one marked on more detailed maps of western Cyprus intrigued me at a later date on holiday there. I decided to walk into it. The path to reach it was through a plantation of orange and grapefruit trees; pretty colours of course but it was the citrus aroma that was simply overwhelming. Combined with the incessant, bubbly songs of Olivaceous Warblers and the harsh chatters of black and grey Sardinian Warblers skulking in the glossed green leafy growth – we caught only glimpses of both though in reality, the Olivaceous's song is far more attractive than its rather dull brown appearance – this was a heady, and naturally slow start to a walk in a gorge.

Into the narrow cleft and we lost the warming sun; the citrus aroma was exchanged for the heavier scent of herbs: thyme, maybe Rosemary and Sage too. The cool, damp air hung like a veil above the turbulent little stream, the towering rock walls on each side sandpaper-smoothed over millennia by its waters. Fig tree roots dangled from high above like the tentacles of some giant octopus and dripped water on to vivid green maidenhair ferns eking a life from some narrow clefts in the shaded, greying limestone. After this, the path slowly became narrower and rockier. Burnished white limestone cliffs on either side closed in. Phoenician Junipers with their dark red berries left space for the occasional wild olive, leathery, long-leaved Oleander trees and a few Lentiscs with their fresh-looking leaves and bark with pungent resin (used to make mastic). On the stony ground, little yellow trumpets of Oxalis flowers were competing for attention with the paper-thin flowers of Crown Anemones, dazzling white with black-as-coal centres. The Avakus Gorge was turning out trumps; to say that it was a beautiful, tranquil spot underrates it.

But after 3 or 4 km of walking along the gorge, it was proving impossible to scramble further. The clear-running stream, confined by the sheer cliffs closing in on both sides, was too deep and its waters too cold. And there was no way on without wading through cold, thigh-high water. I would have liked to have gone further but turned back reluctantly … though there was the allure of the citrus grove on the return walk. And there were some ripe oranges on the ground just begging to be eaten. What a taste. Nearby in some heathy vegetation below the gorge where the Avakus stream turned towards the sea, Cyprus Warblers – found nowhere else in the world – black-headed on bush tops, vibrated with their powerful chattering songs like operatic divas at La Scala. And swallows did low-level strafing sorties over the bushes to catch airborne insects.

There are two Cypruses. Not the obvious Greek and Turkish sectors; rather the developed Cyprus frequented by most package holidays and – as yet, anyway – the undeveloped, off-the-beaten-track Cyprus. So here you have a choice. You can roast on a much contested square metre of sand at body-clogged Coral Bay. You can disco the night away in Agia Napa. And you can risk being mowed down by one of the numerous tourist coaches in Troodos, not a village but a line of tacky shops and ugly fast-food tavernas high up in the mountains. Or you can explore 'alternative' Cyprus. The Cyprus which hides away little places such as the Avakas Gorge and barely signposts its existence. Long may it be that way.

There are other gorges, too, that I have barely explored; the Nestos Gorge on the northern Greek mainland is carved out along the meandering course of the Nestos River then floods its way south from Bulgaria and out to the Aegean Sea near Thasos island. There is a small railway that runs the length of it but I walked a couple of kilometres or so (my time was unfortunately limited) from the bottom end on the footpath cut into its eastern side. At this lower end it's a wide river valley, part wooded but with steep, sometimes vertical cliffs. The occasional bubbling sound of European Bee-eaters drifted on the breeze but never drowned out the incessant fluting whistles – always reminiscent of the tropics to me – of Golden Orioles hiding in the trees near the side of the river. On the rocky slopes above were Blue Rock Thrushes, from where I heard a curious chacking noise similar to the alarm call of a Common Blackbird. Try as I might I couldn't find its source; it was later, having returned to Kavala for the night, that I realised that these were the rattling calls of Rock Partridges, shy doyens of very rocky ground in these parts. I wish I'd had more time in the Nestos Gorge; I'm sure that there was a lot more to see there, flowering plants included, but time didn't allow. One day I intend to go back and walk its whole length.

The gorges I have spent more time in – not surprisingly because they are in my home country, Wales – are the wooded river gorges of Snowdonia, some of the best places in Europe for mosses, ferns, lichens and liverworts. With around 200 days of rain per year, these plants that require moist conditions are in verdant heaven; in recent years these oak-wooded gorges have been described as our very own rainforests, albeit temperate rather than tropical ones. I think it's a fitting description. My favourite is in Ceunant Cynfal below the village of Ffestiniog in Snowdonia; it's reckoned to be one of the finest wooded river gorges in Britain.

In places the Cynfal stream (it's hardly a river) has carved a ravine up to 40 m deep providing an often sheer series of cliffs with ledges clothed in mosses and liverworts. A few flowering plants like Golden Saxifrage – a water lover – with their little mats of gold-green flowers add a splash of colour amongst the verdant greenery while the grey-green, hairy-leaved Wood Sage adds a faint fragrance to the damp air. Walking along the gorge, it's the noise of the waterfalls – a series of cataracts that gush and tumble over sandpapered boulders – that dominates. It's not always easy to pick out the mew of a Buzzard overhead or the metallic, shivering trills of tiny Wood Warblers visiting for the summer to breed amongst the gnarled oaks. They are joined by other migrants typical of these upland oakwoods; flashy-coloured Redstarts and elegant black and white Pied Flycatchers, both of which seek out tree holes to lay their eggs. But it's the profusion of non-flowering plants, the cushions of mosses, liverworts, the lichens on boulders and tree trunks, and the ferns that dominate this place. And they rely on its humidity. Over 150 different species of moss and liverwort are here. It's so humid that I always feel that if I stand still for long enough, mosses will start growing on me too.

The trees in Ceunant Cynfal aren't all Sessile Oaks, though most are; there are some white-barked Birch, Rowan with its bundles of autumn berries, Holly, Ash, Hazel and Wych Elm. Many of the ferns grow in damp, shaded spots between the boulders, on cliff ledges, in the clefts of tree limbs or just in shaded places on open ground; there's enough splashing from the waterfalls and general humidity to keep them happy. Both British species of tiny Filmy Fern, their fronds no more than a few centimetres long, grow here together with equally uncommon but larger Beech Fern, its lovely bright green fronds a delight to find.

In places the Cynfal stream – on its turbulent way downhill to the Dwyryd River which flows west and out to sea near Portmadog – has cut pillars out of the bedrock. The largest of these, maybe 10 m high, known as 'Huw Llwyd's Pulpit', is named after a well-known local character who was supposed to have been a magician. In the 17th century, Huw Llwyd used to stand on the top of the rock to recite poetry, preach sermons and converse with spirits. He claimed he was safe from evil while up there because the devil was afraid of water. I don't know about being safe from the devil but every time I look at the pulpit I wonder how on earth he was able to get up its vertical sides or stand on its slightly sloping top as curtains of moisture drift past on the breeze, just the right conditions for slippery algae and liverworts to blossom. And who came to listen to him down here with the thunder roar of the waterfalls just below and the wind sometimes howling madly through the aged, gnarled oaks.

But it's a good tale nevertheless. And, with myths and magic figuring prominently in Welsh folklore and tradition, what more mystical place to imagine the scene than in this – gorgeous – gorge.

Going Eco in Jordan

There are not many good hotels in the world where you park your car 8 km away and then, before you even see the place let alone have a look at the rooms, squeeze into an ancient pickup truck for a half hour bumpy journey with a driver who speaks nothing but Arabic. But then, not many hotels are as unusual as the Feynan Ecolodge, around 50 km north of Petra in, Jordan. For a start it's within the huge Dana Biosphere Reserve, a protected area of magnificent arid mountains, wind-roughed, pale sandstone cliffs, seasonal wadis brimming with red-flowered Oleander bushes, and some of the rarest plants and animals in the world. My wife and I had decided to stay there en route to Petra, that amazing rock-hewn city established possibly as early as 312 BC as the capital city of the Nabataeans.

We did as the hotel brochure suggested and found our way to the rendezvous carpark just off a metalled road where the hotel's carpark attendant called in a local Bedouin driver complete with his shambolic, battered pickup. Suitcases in the back, we scrambled into the cab and I spent the next 20 minutes with my right leg competing with his gear lever as we lurched about on the hotel's rough track.

It was a relief to see the place; a gorgeous sandy cream colour blending into its rock-scattered, mountainous desert surroundings. Designed by renowned architect Ammar Khammash in an arabesque style and built in 2005 it has no televisions, no phones (your mobile won't get a signal!) and candles instead of electric lights. It's a great switch-off kind of place. And if you are wondering if its sustainability ethic is rather like the pretence talked of by other hotels, get this: solar power generates electricity for the kitchens; food scraps are composted; candles are made locally and water is supplied from a nearby spring. The heating in the usually short winters, when these summertime bread oven-hot hills can get pretty cold, is provided by burning wastes from local olive processing.

We were there in spring and I think that's the best time to savour the place in equitable temperatures and to make the most of its isolated location together with the plants and birds around. Bright and sunny, warm but not hot – it's also ideal for a day's walking up Wadi Dana, the main wadi running past the ecolodge. The day we did it, the wadi was dry until we got maybe 5 km 'upstream'. Then, a growing trickle of water from the rugged slopes high above started to wet the gravel and sand between the gorgeous Oleanders and prickly acacias on the wadi riverbed.

We passed peat-coloured goat-hair tents of several Bedouin families, all of them living here so that they can graze their goats in this, the lower part of the 300 km^2 Dana Reserve. Friendly waves from gorgeous, dark-haired children spurred us along. Further on we passed a local shepherd tending a herd of goats and a couple of Bedouin women leading donkeys laden with water jugs from a nearby spring. Much further up what gradually becomes a wide valley with 1,000-m-high rocky slopes at its furthest point, we came across a scatter of Mediterranean Cypresses, slow-growing trees with their bottle-green leaves, maybe 20 m tall and some of them reputedly over a thousand years old. Here they are apparently growing at their southernmost location in the world. Widely planted elsewhere, here they are thought to be native.

Phoenician Junipers were around too, growing mostly in the rockiest places and either fairly prostrate on the ground or growing as large shrubs. I wondered whether farmed goats had been nibbling them so that they couldn't grow taller anyway. These arid mountains, not always as arid in the past, have apparently been inhabited from the Stone Age (there are remains of a 11,000-year-old Neolithic village) through to the Roman and Byzantine eras. So they have a long history of goat grazing and probably other uses too.

We kept scanning the high rocky slopes for a glimpse of a Nubian Ibex, a wild desert goat with long back-curved horns, now pretty rare. Pale brown in colour just like much of the rocky terrain they live in, it was a problem of small animal, vast mountains. Unfortunately, we didn't spot one. One animal we did see, and effortlessly, was the Sinai Agama, a 25-cm-long lizard, the males of which are bright blue in the breeding season, the females duller brown with red spots. We spotted males – they are the only bit of blue colour in this arid, generally pinky cream coloured environment – basking motionless in the warming sunshine on exposed rocks or scurrying into a crevice. They are a fantastic, almost surreal sight. Watching the males carefully through binoculars, I noticed them raising their heads and gaping, a threatening pose they adopt to frighten other males away. They also bob their heads, move their eyes from side to side and do push-ups with their front limbs. What a chap has to do these days to attract a mate. Considering that there are Short-toed Eagles – reptile-killing specialists – plus occasional Bonelli's and Golden Eagles hereabouts, it seemed particularly odd to me that the Sinai Agama males adopt such a standout colour in the spring. With an eagle's eyes they must be visible from at least a kilometre away. Presumably the speed of an Agama is their salvation. Or predators know that they are poisonous (which I don't think they are). Whatever, the need to be seen by a female agama must outweigh the risk of being seen by an eagle.

Equally easy to spot, because they occasionally ran across the dry wadi in front of us, were Sand Partridges. The colour of – you guessed it – sand, they couldn't be better camouflaged for where they live. Rotund little partridges, the females are very plain and best match their surroundings; the males, though, have lovely white and brown stripes on their flanks and a white eye-spot. Pretty birds, they are not found outside the Middle East. Equally intriguing were tiny but very noisy Palestine Sunbirds, no more than 10 cm long with little curved beaks, who busied themselves in flower-filled bushes extracting nectar out of the flowers, their dark blue and purple feathers glinting in the bright sunshine. They were common in the acacias around the hotel too.

Just as striking were the Sinai Rosefinches, the males mainly pink in colour, and found in the most inhospitable rocky dry places where you'd think it would be difficult for any living creature to survive. I must say, though, that they looked full of life, flitting about this way and that, examining what might be in the next rock crevice they liked the look of, a few seeds maybe from some dry-as-dust flower.

The bird I was really hoping to see was very much rarer but known to occur in the Dana Reserve; the Syrian Serin is a small finch related to the Canary, green and yellow in colour and slightly dishevelled in overall looks. Confined to arid mountainous country here in Jordan, Lebanon and parts of Syria and Israel, they are declining everywhere, likely the result of increasing drought (they need daily access to water) and – that perennial Middle East problem – overgrazing by goats. As seed eaters, these finches rely on flowering plants to set seed; if goats eat the plants before they set seed, the finches' food supply dwindles. There are maybe just a few thousand pairs of Syrian Serins left in the world, at least for now.

On our morning walk up the wadi from the eco hotel I thought I might have seen a pair but it was a distant view of two small, greenish birds flying off. They looked like finches and I tried, but failed to find them. It wasn't until well into the afternoon and we were on our way back that I heard a plaintive, Linnet-like call (there were Linnets around too!) from somewhere just ahead of us. Almost as suddenly, a male Syrian Serin landed literally a few metres away as if to show that he really was the bird I was hoping to see. Within a few seconds his mate joined him and we sat on a rock and watched entranced as they scurried about on the stony ground picking up seeds here and there. I stopped a couple of (I think) Dutch hikers walking past and pointed the delicate little pair out to them. They watched politely for a few seconds, smiled and hiked on.

With most of the day gone, we headed back down the valley passing a few more avid hikers who were doing the 14 km slog from the Dana Guesthouse at 1200 m above sea level to Feynan at 325 m. We spoke to a young American couple who had walked down from the guesthouse and were on their way back up, a climb up of nearly a 1,000 m. We envied their fitness. But such hikers, although they no doubt appreciate the wildness, the impressive landscapes and the relative solitude, almost certainly don't notice most of the wildlife around them. A Syrian Serin wouldn't register on their radar. And it seems to me that, in treating such hikes as something more akin to a gym routine, they miss an awful lot of what's to be seen.

Soon we were back to Feynan Lodge for a shower, the water hot thanks to the sun heating up the solar panels. The nightlife here consists of good vegetarian food cooked by local Bedouin employed at the hotel and eaten by candle-light, usually outside in the delicate evening warmth where it's as dark as pitch once the sun has set. It sounds, and is, rather romantic with the single proviso that eating near one small candle is not the best plan for knowing what you are putting into your mouth with each fork-full.

Along with a few others staying at the Lodge we followed the meal by lying back on pillows and floor mattresses on a nearby rooftop terrace to gaze up at astounding views of the Milky Way, shooting stars, and the planets. They even had a telescope and staff on hand who know their Cassiopeia from their Betelgeuse. The view of the night sky in this rocky desert with no city or highway lights to corrupt it is one of the delights of staying well off the beaten track; it's how to appreciate a pointillist, heavenly light spectacle that's awe inspiring. We were so relaxed after our day of walking and a hearty meal that we started to drift off to sleep as the rooftop talk turned to Mercury and Uranus …

A day later and we were in Petra, the fabled 'Rose City' hewn from the cliffs by the Nabateans as their capital. I had always wanted to see it and it lived up to every expectation I had. Visiting it, even at the equivalent of £45 per person per day (but little more for two or three days of visits) is an amazing experience; the sheer wonder at the first sight of the famous, iconic, pink-hued Treasury having walked a kilometre down the cliff-lined, narrow gorge – the Siq – to reach it is simply stunning. And there is very much more to see in Petra than the Treasury.

On the second day of our Petra visit I decided to get away from the crowds and climb up into the hills on its western side along some steep and narrow paths. Eventually I came to a plateau, arid and rocky with eroded stone pillars but with a scatter of juniper and wild olive trees. On the way up I'd seen the occasional group of Sinai Rosefinches, the males striking in crimson and pink; the females duller and plain brown. They were usually searching some clefts in the cliffs or hunting on the ground between boulders, picking up flower and grass seeds. Then, a wheezing, toy-trumpet type of call gave away a posse of aptly named little Trumpeter Finches. I saw several of them, the males with pink breasts (pink is the 'in' colour in Jordan) and orange-red, seed-cracking beaks. But the sound that took me off guard was some wolf whistling that echoed off the hard cliffs up here. I looked around, assuming someone else was walking nearby. But there was no one; in complete contrast to the tourists milling around the famous Petra archaeological sites way below me, I could see no-one. It was a magical experience.

It wasn't until I saw some blackbird-sized birds, all black with orange wing flashes that I realised what was making the whistling calls; they were Tristram's Grackles, a bird I had seen just once before in Saudi Arabia. There was a small party of them, flying from one set of berried bushes to another, wolf-whistling as they went. In this natural amphitheatre of rock, their calls echoed and amplified.

After they disappeared, off to find more berries to pluck perhaps, I could hear singing. And this really was a human voice. Again it echoed and I had no idea who the source was and where they were. After a while, a few goats came into view high above on a rocky ridge. Then a few more, bleating as they walked. And further behind a small figure dressed in long Bedouin clothes and a head scarf carrying a long stick and a bag. The singer waved; I waved back. The singing continued. I assumed that this shepherd and flock would simply walk past well above me. But no. They came my way; the goats dispersing to chew here and there on any manner of shrub they could get their teeth into; the shepherd, all smiles, came and sat next to me on a low rock. Only then did I realise. It was a Bedouin shepherd girl whose age I found it impossible to gauge. Maybe 12, maybe more. I felt uncomfortable. She showed me some of the things she was carrying but we could understand virtually nothing of each other. Her clothes were colourful, she wore soft shoes and herding the family's goats by day was probably going to be her life's work until she got married, maybe to one of her family's cousins as tradition here often demands. She wanted me to walk with her, to her Bedouin home I assumed, but I insisted on going in the opposite direction and we parted with yet more smiles and, before we lost sight of each other, more waving too.

A few days later we had driven much further north out into what's called the Eastern Jordanian desert, a vast stony dry-as-dust desert that occupies a large sector of this fascinating country. But here's an odd, almost surreal thing: in the middle of all this I'm looking out over a shallow, freshwater lake about twice the size of an average swimming pool. Behind me is another similar pool, both of them fringed in places with tall growths of reed and bulrush, typical plants of the water's edge. Some taller tamarisk bushes and other scrub nearby are alive with the calls of warblers like Chiffchaffs that have stopped off here on their arduous springtime journey from Sub-Saharan Africa north to their European breeding spots in woods and gardens. Barn Swallows on a similar trek are skimming low over the water, picking off tiny flying insects, their agile zooming and banking reminiscent of fighter jets, only very much quieter.

This is the Azraq wetland, the only area of water in this vast desert and a vital stopping-off place, a kind of transport café for the migrating bird world to take a break and stock up on food to fuel the journey ahead. Walking around these pools and the bits of marsh in between them, it's easy to forget where I am and how incongruous this wetland oasis actually is. Less than 40 km to the south of where I'm standing is the Saudi Arabian border; go 70 km north and you cross into Syria. Azraq is Jordan's only oasis and I particularly wanted to see it because its recent history arguably ranks among the most tragic cases of habitat degradation by humans anywhere in the world.

Until the 1980s it was considered one of the most spectacular areas of wetland anywhere, fed by two underground springs which resulted in the creation of a large, flat area of lush marshland supporting an abundance of diverse plant and animal life. It was reckoned to have covered an area of about 12,000 km^2, greater than that of Lebanon today. The soils were moist; small lakes and marsh covered much of the land surface. The remains of lion, cheetah, rhinoceros, hippopotamus, elephant, ostrich and other large mammals have been found here and the site was home to hundreds of thousands of migrating birds each year, huge flocks of ducks, herons, egrets and wading birds as well as countless thousands of smaller birds such as warblers on migration.

In the past, the huge areas of freshwater attracted camel caravans carrying spices and herbs traveling between Arabia, Mesopotamia (modern day Iraq) and Syria. It had been home to human communities as long as 200,000 years ago. The damage started in the 1960s. Water began to be pumped from the Azraq oasis to provide drinking water to the city of Amman, Jordan's growing capital and to Irbid, now the country's second largest city. The resulting drop in the water level wasn't really noticed at first. But, by 1967 when hundreds of thousands of Palestinian refugees flooded into Jordan after the Six Day War that all changed. They needed water urgently. Pumping increased enormously in the 1970s. And more and more people settled in that then fertile area to grow crops, sinking wells (illegally) deep underground to raise water to the soil surface to irrigate their crops, only a tiny fraction of which was ever paid back to the ground as rain.

Ironically, in 1977 as the wetland shrank and water disappeared from its surface, Azraq was added to the Ramsar list of Wetlands of International Importance, the tiny (12 km^2) Azraq Wetland Reserve was also established, managed today by the Jordanian Government's Royal Society for the Conservation of Nature (RSCN). According to RSCN information, 347,000 birds were at the wetland on 2 February 1967. A count on the same day in 2000 totalled just 1,200 birds. That's not surprising when you realise that the wetland at Azraq had shrunk to less than a thousandth of its original size.

As the wetland shrank, and pools of water dried up, an incredible discovery was made at the eleventh hour in 1983 by three German fish biologists: a fish whose existence at Azraq hadn't even been noticed. It was a species of killifish but one found nowhere else in the world. Named the Sirhani Fish after Wadi Al Sirhan at Azraq, it was surviving in what was left of the disappearing pools. Growing to no more than 6 cm in length – the more colourful males pale brown with dark brown vertical stripes – only a few could be found. The name 'killifish' is derived from the Dutch word *kilde*, meaning 'small creek' or 'puddle', the kind of place many of them live in. And because many of them prefer shallow lakes and ponds, the eggs of most killifish can survive periods of partial dehydration. That's pretty useful for Azraq, in summer especially. But here the prospects for the Sirhani Fish to survive were almost non-existent. Their lifeblood – the freshwater they depended upon – was literally drying up. What is more, species of fish alien to Azraq that made a meal of small fish like the Sirhani, were found in what pools remained. Someone had introduced them there.

By 1992, with more water being pumped out of Azraq for human use, more farming wells dug and the springs feeding the former oasis dried up, the Azraq Killifish was presumed extinct. But this little fish proved to be a real survivor. In 2000, after artificial pumping of water back into the Azraq wetland began as a consequence of international pressure on the Jordanian Government to reinstate at least part of it, a pair of Austrian scientists rediscovered killifish in one of the small surviving lakes. They collected 45 of them and a captive breeding programme was started in Jordan, the United Arab Emirates and the Vienna Zoo.

At Azraq I spoke to Ashraf Elhalah, a Jordanian ecologist working for RSCN on the fish's reintroduction. 'We built concrete lagoons within the reserve and started rearing the killifish in those where we could control the conditions,' he told me. 'Then we reintroduced them to the shallow ponds in the reserve. Sirhani Fish now constitute 70% of the fish living in the Azraq wetland. We have raised the number from a few scores to hundreds of thousands now.'

To help keep the pools as areas of open water for the fish and not naturally infilling with reeds and other water plants, the authorities have introduced Water Buffalo. They seem incongruous here; I encounter their huge black presence and intimidating horns as I wander along the short marsh trails. Changing direction to avoid a couple heading my way, they plunge into one of the main ponds, churning up the vegetation and the mud as they go. But in a Goliath helping David set-up, these lumbering buffalo are proving essential.

This once massive wetland in the desert will never again resemble more than a pale shadow of its former self. The 10 million m^3 of water per year provided by the Jordanian Ministry of Water to maintain Azraq is only sufficient to restore the wetland to 10% of its original size. Even this target is unlikely ever to be reached;

there are hundreds of illegal wells used to water crops by people who have long settled in the oasis, and furthermore the alternative pipeline carrying water from the south of Jordan to supply Amman will not be able to satisfy all of the city's needs. Add to that the obvious issue that the location of the wetland in the middle of a desert where shade summer temperatures can reach 40°C causes an enormous loss of water by evaporation from such shallow lakes.

Azraq will never again become a wildlife haven but the small population of Sirhani Fish surviving here might yet get further recognition. I'd heard that the Head of Nature Conservation at the Ministry of Environment, Hussein Shahin, commented that the Ministry is considering a proposal to make it Jordan's national fish. So I asked him, by email, for a comment. 'The Black Iris is our national flower and the pink Sinai Rosefinch is our national bird,' he told me. 'But we want the Sirhani Fish to be our national fish.' Japan has the Carp; South Africa the Galjoen; why shouldn't Jordan's Sirhani Fish be the third national fish in the world?

Finding the Unicorn

Sitting, cross-legged as always, on the patterned, carmine red rugs in the Bedu tent, I was listening to the Arabic banter. Abdulrahman and Mubarak, dressed in their traditional long white thobes with red and white check ghutras (headscarves), were having a lively exchange about the virtues, or otherwise, of having a wife. It was time, Abdulrahman said, that young Mubarak should start thinking of marriage. Their laughter was infectious.

Through the open, hearth-end of the tent a mesmerising, beacon-bright half-moon hung in the inky-black night sky. Walid, the camp's ever-smiling Pakistani cook, dressed for the long evenings in his brown-striped kaftan, came in with more dates and yet another silver-coloured, long-spouted pot of bitter, cardamom-rich Arabic coffee. He placed it carefully on the hearth, in reality just a scrape in the sand where burnt wood ash still retained enough heat to keep the refreshing brew warm. Very soon, wafts of wood smoke mixed with the heady aroma of cardamom began to scent the tent with an almost hypnotic air.

I was in a camp on the western fringes of the Empty Quarter, an uninhabited desert the size of France – the Rub'al-Khali made famous by the explorer, Wilfred Thesiger (1910–2003). It all seemed so reminiscent of a biblical scene, as if a robed itinerant preacher might come by any minute for a little food on his travels. Except that a couple of loaded AK47s lay casually on the carpeted floor of the tent, ready for use if they were needed, and a reminder that the Arab rangers had a potentially dangerous modern day job to do.

I got talking to Abu Ali, the Head Ranger whose home was at Sharurah, further south near the Yemen border. In stilted English he was able to tell me that his father, a local Bedu of the Sayari tribe who knew the Empty Quarter and how easy it was to die in its parched sands, had seen some Arabian Oryx and Sand Gazelles half a century ago. He knew that they were perched then precariously on the very cusp of extinction. Now Abu Ali was helping to return both animals to this magnificent sand desert where they belonged. He is one of the small Saudi team here whose work it is to help monitor the oryx and, if necessary, to use those AK47s to see off – or worse – any poachers that try to kill or capture them.

And it was these fabled animals, especially the oryx – thought to be the origin of the unicorn myth – that I had come to see. The reintroduction of the Arabian Oryx remains one of the world's most successful reintroductions of an animal once extinct in the wild and now breeding again in the core of its former range. Strikingly beautiful, salt-white oryx had roamed the Empty Quarter and a much larger area of the Middle East until the last one was killed five decades ago. Now, this enigmatic animal was back in one of the harshest, most unforgiving places on earth and seemingly doing very well. In exchange for writing a feature about their recovery for Kuwait Airways' in-flight magazine, *Al-Buraq*, a colleague and I were given free return tickets from London via Kuwait City to Jeddah in Saudi Arabia. It turned out to be a brilliant trip organised through Saudi Government channels.

We had arrived at the camp, a set of portacabins and tents in the Uruq Bani Ma'arid Reserve in the west of the Rub'al-Khali, in darkness, the kind of night-time darkness now hardly ever experienced in Britain and not even lit by a scatter of stars. The drive from Taif, inland from Jeddah, had been a long one, finished off by many kilometres of rough, stony track from the nearest metalled road up to the Uruq camp. The camp, like most Saudi installations such as roadside garages, oil production plants or roadside cafes, was brightly lit; it would have stood out as a beacon for huge distances all around in this enveloping darkness except that it was surrounded, I assumed, by mountain slopes. We didn't see it until we were maybe a kilometre away.

In the naturally bright light of the following morning, what I had assumed to be rocky mountainsides surrounding us turned out to be huge, sculpted, orange-pink sand dunes, the most fabulous I have ever seen, their slopes smoothed into perfect, voluptuous curves by the desert wind. For a while I did nothing but stare at their elemental beauty.

Later that first morning I was out in a 4WD heading east with Maartin Strauss, a South African mammal expert and Eric Bedin, a French biologist, who were monitoring oryx for the Saudi Wildlife Commission which has reintroduced the animals here in the Empty Quarter. We were driving along heat-hazed, almost white gravel plains, folded pink-orange sand dunes, some of them huge, on either side. In the searing heat, by mid-afternoon I had begun to wonder how any animal could possibly exist in such an inhospitable place, let alone thrive, give birth and raise young. There were no animals in sight.

Then quite suddenly, scanning ahead with binoculars, Maartin Strauss spotted them. Some distant, fuzzy white shapes and a flurry of orange-ochre sand were all that was obvious to me as I searched the vast, heat-shimmering plain. Could these distant, hazy objects possibly be the legendary Arabian Oryx? 'Seven oryx. All adults I think. They're grazing on some bushes. They look pretty settled; I don't think they're going to move on for a while anyway. We'll try and get closer,' commented Maartin, as we drove further into the sands to get a better, and clearer, view of the distant white spots.

Eventually we got within a kilometre of them, seven oryx watching our every move. The size of large deer, their gorgeous deep, black eyes contrasted with their bleached-white coats and their enormous pairs of horns caught the bright sun like skyward-pointing rapiers. When these animals stand sideways, it can seem as if they have only one horn, the probable origin of the unicorn myth. They were even more magnificent than I had contemplated.

'Four of them are tagged with collars,' whispered Maartin as we sat huddled in the Jeep, binoculars held handcuff-tight, the sweltering heat building by the minute. 'The numbers printed on their tags means that these four are released animals. I can date the releases from the tag numbers when we're back at camp tonight. The other three must have been born out here in the wild,' he added with obvious pleasure. We left them on the sun-baked, bleached white gravel, eloquent testimony to their ability to live out their lives in one of the most arid places imaginable. Here, in the scorching heat of summer where temperatures in the sun can easily reach 50°C, a human can barely survive for eight hours without water.

The smallest of the four species of oryx in the world, Arabian Oryx stand about 1 m high at the shoulder, females weigh up to 80 kg; males, up to 100 kg. Apart from this difference in weight, and the fact that females usually have longer horns than males, the sexes are very similar and it's very difficult to distinguish them in the field. I certainly couldn't. Their coats are an almost luminous white to help with camouflage and to reflect away the sun's heat, their undersides and legs dark brown, and they have black stripes where the head meets the neck, on the forehead, on the nose and going from the horns down the face to the mouth. Because they have hooves that are splayed and shovel-like, oryx can walk effortlessly on sand dunes. Fast runners, their newborn calves are able to trot with the herd almost immediately after birth.

I hadn't realised how visually impressive their horns really are; long, straight or slightly back-curved, they have a kind of barley-twist pattern along their length and can be up to 75 cm long. Viewed sideways or from a distance, an oryx looks something like a horse with a single horn (although, in the oryx's case, the 'horn' projects backwards not forwards as in the classic unicorn). Nevertheless, early travellers in Arabia could quite easily have derived and embellished the tale of the unicorn from these animals.

And it was these exquisite horns that made them too tempting as a prized game trophy. The demise of the Arabian Oryx became a virtual certainty when Arabian princes and newly oil-rich Arabs in Jeeps and big American cars fitted with sand tyres started making incursions into the Rub'al-Khali in the 1930s and 1940s. Armed with more powerful rifles, even machine guns, oryx hunts grew in size, many of them employing animal-exhausting chases from 4WDs, even helicopters, and some were reported to use as many as 300 vehicles. It rapidly became a slaughter on an epic scale; many of these people didn't even want the horns, they simply wanted to chase and kill wild animals. Their carcasses were left to rot where they were shot.

The desert-living, nomadic Bedu had always hunted oryx. After all, they would provide a much more bountiful supply of meat than a desert hare and add variety to an otherwise torrid diet. Their leather hides were important too. But, armed only with primitive rifles until perhaps the 1920s, they would probably have been able to kill very few. By the 1960s, fewer than 100 oryx were thought to survive in the wild, almost all of them here in the Rub'al-Khali. A couple more raiding parties and there would have been none. And that's when the forward-looking Fauna and Flora Preservation Society, FFPS (now Fauna and Flora International, FFI), with World Wildlife Fund cash, decided that the only way to guarantee their survival was to capture some animals and set up a captive breeding population before the last wild oryx were hunted down. Time was not on their side.

And FFPS were proved right. The last wild oryx had been spotted in 1972 and they were either killed or captured a few weeks later. Bred in captivity at the Phoenix Zoo in Arizona and some other centres, the first oryx were reintroduced into the Omani sector of the Rub'al-Khali in 1982. And they were initially successful. By 1995, they numbered around 280. The scheme was looking really positive. Then problems surfaced once more. Poaching resumed and some oryx were illegally captured for sale to be kept as live animals outside the country. A downward spiral started yet again. By 1999 there were 85 oryx left and a decision was taken to capture them and move them into a large fenced enclosure (at 27,000 km² still a vast area by European standards) where they could be protected. Even protecting them in that so-called 'Arabian Oryx Sanctuary' proved difficult. Personal greed apparently knew no bounds when it came to capturing these magnificent animals to decorate the grounds of some rich Middle Eastern or overseas estate.

Thankfully, here in the Saudi Arabian part of the Rub'al-Khali, oryx reintroduction has been much more successful. Between 1995 and 2002, a total of 174 animals, in a large number of social groups, had been released into the Uruq Bani Ma'arid Reserve, in reality a large section of the western side of the Empty Quarter. Now there are at least 200 oryx here and their breeding is increasingly successful. There are other reintroduced populations; in the UAE, Jordan and in Israel, giving a total in 2011 of about 1,000 wild oryx. Others are kept in 'captivity', in practice mainly in large areas of suitable desert habitat where they roam freely.

Here in the Uruq Bani Ma'arid Reserve there is no surrounding fence so it's open to the bewildering expanses of the arid Rub'al-Khali to the east. It's difficult to comprehend its magnitude; peering eastwards in the strong sunlight, the dunes, folded one into another, seem to go on forever. And that's not too much of an exaggeration; the Empty Quarter measures about 1,000 km west to east, the same distance as London to Prague. Uruq was selected for the reintroduction because it contains greater biological diversity than any other part of the Empty Quarter with vegetated wadis, gravel plains, and inter-dune corridors. And oryx had historically been present here.

Eric Bedin told me that most reintroductions have been in winter when temperatures are lower and there is more chance of some rain reinvigorating the few thorny shrubs, providing young growth for the grazing oryx. Where we were, though, no rain had been recorded for two years. When it does rain, bleached and tinder-dry shrubs quickly green up, and plants spring up from hidden underground bulbs and rhizomes, quickly flower and set seed again until the next shower passes that way, maybe a couple of years later. It was not a phenomenon that I saw any trace of. All the plants I spotted – and there were precious few of them – were shrivelled up remnants of coarse grasses or viciously thorny shrubs with so few healthy leaves, most gardeners would have dug them out well before. Most of these arid plants eke out a harsh existence on the gravelly plains but some, too, grow on the lower slopes of dunes or in the hollows between them, their long penetrating roots anchored way below in the deep damp sand often tens of metres below its fiery surface.

Arabian Oryx, like their oryx cousins elsewhere in the world, can survive by browsing any of these and by rooting in the ground for juicy rhizomes. They get all the water they need from these dried-up plants and by licking up any early morning dew. It is why the Bedu of Arabia call the Arabian Oryx *jawazi* – 'he who drinks not'. 'They rest during the hottest part of the day; they often dig shallow depressions in the sand under a shrub or small tree, particularly in summer when they spend more time seeking shade from bushes,' Maartin Strauss told me.

Although no one lives permanently out here nowadays (though nomadic Bedu certainly used to), there are some semi-nomadic Bedu who keep herds of goats. Today, they usually sit out the obscene heat of summer in a distant village home. But goat grazing, though less than it was in previous times, is still in competition with the oryx's needs. In years when rains encourage plant growth, this competition for grazing isn't usually a problem I was told but in droughts – and especially if climate warming gathers more pace – it certainly might become a significant issue.

The majestic natural beauty of this massive, arid sand desert, a place seemingly without end when you are alone in a tiny part of it, is overwhelming; its striking orange-ochre dunes brighten to an oxide red in the setting sun, sculptured by the wind into huge, sensually smooth mounds, one folded into the next and stretching as far as the eye can see to the horizon. Here in the west of the Rub'al-Khali these dunes aren't higher than perhaps 40 m. In the east, though, they are on an epic scale, some of them huge, wind-smoothed ridges five times higher, more akin to small mountains and formidable indeed if you need to cross them.

Oryx aren't the only animals that have, or continue to live their lives here. Although most others such as the Striped Hyena, Arabian Ostrich and Honey Badger have long ago been hunted to extinction and their habitat degraded, both Arabian Sand Gazelles and Mountain Gazelles have been bolstered in number by reintroductions. I accompanied Maartin Strauss one day to track Sand Gazelles, some of which had been fitted with small radio collars around their necks. For a long time his receiver was silent, but after a couple of hours driving along one long gravel plain after another, it suddenly picked up a signal. The blips were intermittent at first but got stronger and more regular once we turned off the gravel and into the dunes. A more arid place you would be hard pressed to find. A withered bunch of dried up grass was even a rare sight here and I found it hard to believe that we could possibly find a little Sand Gazelle somewhere amongst all this dry sand. I thought that I might have the answer; the gazelle had died of starvation but its radio collar had continued transmitting. Maartin quickly dismissed that notion.

And he was right. A few minutes later, as the receiver's blips were at their strongest and most regular, we lurched to a halt. About 30 m in front of us stood a gorgeous, sandy-coloured, bambi-lookalike Sand Gazelle, an adult female around 50 cm in height at the shoulder and with a pair of tiny horns. And what's more, she was having a pee. Not just a few drops as you might expect out here where there is not the faintest sign of any water, but a good long pee that took maybe ten seconds or more. I was amazed. It almost defied belief that in these arid conditions with nothing but dehydrated plants and shrubs to consume – and maybe a few moist rhizomes – an animal could possibly produce so much urine. But few mammals are so well adapted to these incredible conditions as a Sand Gazelle. Finishing her toilet, she watched us closely then turned and walked slowly away, out of sight behind a small fold in a dune.

One dark, cool desert evening when we returned to camp in Uruq after a day of searching for oryx, a visitor was already drinking the typical green, aromatic, cardamom-laced coffee. Mohammed, a man in his eighties, was a Bedu of the Dawasir tribe who had driven his ancient pickup to our camp from his distant home. With a ranger acting as interpreter, Mohammed recalled with fondness seeing oryx in the Rub'al-Khali half a century ago. His eyes became noticeably brighter in his leathered, weatherworn face, and he tapped his stick excitedly on the floor as he told us how the oryx would move deeper into the sands in the cooler, winter months and return to the edges in the fierce heat of summer. Once again, he said, oryx are rediscovering their old ways. He looked genuinely pleased.

The next day, my last, we spotted oryx in the cool of the early morning as we scanned with binoculars along some gravel plains. In the distance we could see two adults running like well-trained horses, clipping the stony, white gravel with their hooves and sending up tiny dust clouds in their wake. It was Maartin Strauss again, his eyes well trained, who noticed something different. There was a young oryx too.

'It's a calf!' he shouted. It still had its fawn-coloured infant coat and it couldn't have been more than a few weeks old. And here it was, little more than 30 cm high, keeping metronome-like pace with its parents, hardly visible above the broken, stony gravel as all three of them cantered elegantly along the edge of the plain. A tiny Arabian Oryx calf providing the greatest symbol of hope for the survival of these impressive animals.

In 2011 the IUCN downgraded its threat category for the Arabian Oryx from 'extinct in the wild' to 'vulnerable', the first species in the world to have come back from being described as officially extinct and given a less threatened status. It's a considerable achievement by a large number of committed people in several countries, some of whom I had the privilege to meet. And I feel even more privileged to have seen these magnificent and unforgettable animals in their incredibly harsh habitat.

Gardens in the Sky

You get a hint of what delights you might see long before you reach Schynige Platte on the little cog wheel railway that takes you up there from the village of Wilderswil, a suburb of Interlaken down in the valley way below. Opened in 1893, this little railway was electrified in 1914 and it takes just under an hour to get its passengers from 600 m at Wilderswil to nearly 2,000 m at the Schynige Platte station where the views are framed by a trio of famous Alpine peaks – the Jungfrau, Monch and Eiger, snow and ice-covered monoliths towering nearby. It is a typical piece of Swiss mountain engineering in which getting to some almost inaccessible spot is simply a minor problem waiting to be overcome.

Today, the Schynige Platte railway is of historic interest in itself; it still operates one of its original steam locomotives, together with the four electric locomotives built for the line's electrification. Parts of the climb are at a 1 in 4 pitch and there's a passing place half way up where the down trains sneak past the up trains. From the windows in the two coaches on our train with the square-set, cream and red painted electric engine named *Flühbluhme* pushing from behind, we jogged and rattled along the narrow gauge through shaded spruce forest before we encountered the first alpine meadows above.

And *Flühbluhme* turned out to be a rather prescient engine; dotted about in some of the shadier spots between small rocks on the route up were its namesake: the remains of what had been vibrant yellow flowers on tall stems above somewhat fleshy blue-green leaves; these were the remains of Mountain Cowslip, or *flühbluhme*. They would have been in full flower maybe a month earlier because this is a spring-flowering beauty. Spring here means June; at this altitude the snow hasn't melted fully until then.

Just metres away from the platforms of the Schynige Platte station, the alpine garden of the same name, founded in 1927, would blow the mind of any alpine gardener I have ever met. It is loaded with nearly 700 different alpines; from tiny saxifrages to alpine ferns and large shrubs, all of them native to the Swiss Alps and growing in natural locations. And the labelling would put even the best of Britain's National Trust gardens to the test. Here, at over 2,000 m with a four-month growing season – June to maybe mid-October – and the rest of the year snow and ice-covered, is one of the highest botanical gardens in the world set in scenery that would be the envy of many a picture postcard.

You can walk up here if you wish – with typical Swiss organisational efficiency the paths through the spruce forests are clearly waymarked but it is hard going and once you get here you are likely to be too exhausted to be looking at flowers. With that old British Rail motto 'let the train take the strain', I was glad not to have attempted it. My biggest difficulty after a splendid train journey was where to look first. Surrounded by every colour imaginable dripping over patches of rock and gravel, it proved best to follow the well-marked gravel paths from one re-creation of a botanical habitat to another.

That way I was able to get a picture of the alpine plants typical of snowbeds; plants of calcareous rocks like the little, delicately white-flowered Dangling Cinqufoil; dwarf shrub heaths dominated by the black-berried Crowberry and similar; plants such as the tall, purple/blue-flowered Alpine Sow Thistle found in wet Green Alder scrub and many more besides. But it proved difficult not to get attracted to the most colourful: the little buttercup-yellow, rather oddly named Orange Poppy lighting up the rock crevices and gravel they thrive in; the foot-high clumps of fragrant, white St Bernard's Lily like miniature trumpets springing from grey-green grass-like leaves; or the elegant, tall and intensely blue spikes of Alpine Larkspur. I tried not to fall into the trap of overlooking some tiny gems by getting too entranced with the more showy species but it wasn't easy. The delicate and tiny fronds of the Moonwort fern for example, no more than maybe 7 cm tall, a single frond with pairs of fan-shaped leaflets accompanying a second stem bearing grape-like clusters of spore bodies. It peeped out from amongst a dense cover of grasses, not an obvious plant but a beauty nevertheless and one that I had once found very rarely in one or two damp Welsh meadows back home.

June – as the last snows melt – is the best time for blue and purple Soldanella, its flowers like downward hanging bells and for Crocus, and yellow-centred, white-petalled Pasqueflower. July is maybe the peak time overall at Schynige Platte (depending on season) and I saw an array of colours: grey-white Edelweiss, that symbol of the rugged purity of the High Alps and said to be Hitler's favourite; Alpenrose, the dwarf, pink/red-flowered azalea that grows like a carpet; the Alpine Poppy, white-flowered with yellow hearts growing here amongst boulders and scree; and the lavender-petalled Alpine Aster, each flower with a vibrant yellow centre. August signals the end of the summer, but it certainly goes out with a bang. Tall, dark pink-purple Martagon

Lilies compete for height with clumps of Yellow Gentian and their layers of showy flowers. More subtle is the small Alpine Toadflax, having bright purple flowers with orange centres, while the tall single white flowers of St Bruno's Lily are elegant in their simplicity.

But I didn't want to spend the day in the alpine garden; I headed out amongst the surrounding natural meadows on a waymarked loop towards the moderate peak of the Loucherhorn. This route gave me amazing views north and northwest (way down below) of the twin Thun and Brienz lakes, both shimmering blue, and of the appropriately-named town of Interlaken between them. I made slow progress; out here many of the meadows, the slopes, rock outcrops and screes all around were burgeoning with a profusion of wild plants including very many that I had seen labelled in the garden. At times it seemed as if there was little distinction between the cultivated alpine garden and the natural alpine meadows. The whole place is one of the finest in Western Europe in which to search for alpine plants.

It wasn't only the plants that proved to be an attraction up here in the mountains. Later that day, walking along the top of a steep slope, I heard an occasional whistle-like scream from somewhere below. Scanning with my binoculars, it took me a while to find its source: an Alpine Marmot sitting on a low rock presumably acting sentinel to warn his companions of trouble (me) nearby. I didn't spot the rest of his – or her – colony so I assume they had dived for cover when the sentinel gave his first whistle. I'd seen colonies of marmots elsewhere in the Alps and the Pyrenees over the years, usually feeding just outside their burrows and I had sometimes watched from a distance as family groups played in the sun or simply lay down and seemed to sunbathe on some nearby warm rock. After at least seven months of underground hibernation to see them through the long cold winter, maybe they just love basking in a bit of summer sun. But most of the time after coming out of hibernation they spend feeding; they will have lost half their body weight through the long winter months so need to put weight back on to face the following winter.

Equipped with strong claws, marmots can burrow into soil so hard a pickaxe would find it difficult to penetrate. They even remove stones with their teeth, not something most dentists would recommend! Alpine Marmots are actually squirrel relatives but much larger; they grow to about 50 cm in length. This one had mid-grey coloured fur though it can vary from blonde through to rusty-brown and dark grey.

There were alpine birds here too of course. Predictably, there were the usual noisy, yellow-beaked Alpine Choughs, flying about in small posses but concentrating more around the Schynige Platte railway station and associated hotel/restaurant where a few scattered crumbs (not that such a thing is permitted in Switzerland) might enrich their normal diet usually obtained exclusively by probing the short alpine turf for invertebrates.

All day, small birds dotted about the extensive pasture here were flying up into the air, singing all the while and then parachuting down to the ground on open wings and spread-out tail. Very obviously advertising their breeding territories to the other males around, these were Water Pipits, birds of these high alpine meadows and somewhat similar to the Meadow Pipit of British moorlands. Their incessant tinkling songs were an auditory complement to the visual impact of this majestic landscape with the ice-covered Jungfrau and Eiger looming in the near distance. Tiny green Citril Finches with their steely grey heads were another feature; they didn't do song flights but flitted from shrub to shrub, calling as they went and constantly on the move, searching for seeds in every bush.

My love of these alpine landscapes, the magnificent vistas they provide and the wildlife they nurture was fired, believe it or not, by a school trip. Aged about 15, I was one of thirty or more from our school to travel by train one summer via Ostend and Basel to a – probably quite basic – Swiss pension somewhere above the historic town of Thun in the Bernese Oberland. We were accompanied by three teachers who seemingly kept a fairly loose rein on us. These were, of course, a time-warp before the concept of health and safety loomed as large as it does nowadays.

One day four or five of us lads decided to hike from somewhere near Grindelwald in the Lauterbrunnen Valley – famous for the peaks Jungfrau, Eiger and Monsch – up into the high mountains. I don't know if we had maps. I don't know if we had planned where we were heading to. And I certainly don't recall how it was that our 'supervising' teachers had seemingly made themselves scarce or whether we had told them what we were up to. All I recall is that we hiked all day; we had arrived in Grindelwald by train (it was our only means of transport) and I presume we intended to meet up there with the other pupils and our teachers at the end of the day.

And what a day it turned out to be. Coming from Mid Wales – from where all of us hailed – I was used to hill walking but my walking experience was confined to traversing mere pimples in the landscape compared with the alpine slopes we set about now. Up and up we scrambled, all of it on well-marked paths but quite frequently climbing vertically on fixed wooden ladders up short rock faces too. Presumably we had taken some food with us. Eventually, I recall spotting the alpine town of Grindelwald way down below and found it difficult to assimilate how tiny it now looked.

How far we climbed I have no idea. But we ended up clambering over bare rock outcrops and snow patches (this was July or August) devoid of any other human presence. We had climbed above virtually all of the alpine vegetation. Then I remember vividly that we started walking out between rock outcrops and on to a mass of frozen, blue-grey ice in a narrow, cliff-lined valley, the whole of the surface scattered with small boulders and stones. It took us several minutes before any of us realised that we were walking across a glacier! None of us had ever seen anything remotely like it though we had been taught about glaciers in geography lessons. Here we were, standing on one, its bright, sun-reflecting surface under our feet. We were walking across a valley filled with ice, a huge mass of ice capable of carving out its own valley profile in the rock around it.

But what glacier was it? The obvious one in the area is the mighty Aletsch Glacier, up to a kilometre thick and the largest in Europe. But we probably hadn't made it that far; it was perhaps a much smaller, lower one, the Lower Grindelwald Glacier maybe. Whichever it was, we had reached a height of at least 2000 m, a height that seems highly unlikely to me now and a climb of well over 1,000 m from Grindelwald. But there is no glacier that's any lower thereabouts. And we were most definitely walking on one.

We must have retraced our steps back down to the Lauterbrunnen later that day to meet up with our teachers. Whether we told them where we had been I have no idea. All I can say is that thank goodness they had given a few 15-year-old lads a free rein. Otherwise we would never have had such an experience. The repercussions if one of us had fallen at that elevation are best left unwritten.

Several times through the day on the Schynige Platte I couldn't help contrasting its profusion of flowering plants with that of the mountains I know best, those in North Wales. It's an unfair comparison in many ways. The underlying geology is different for a start. Most of the Welsh mountain rocks are acid, hence its soils; and acid soils support a far less rich flora than more alkaline soils such as those here (Schynige Platte is on limestone). Rainfall is very much higher in our Welsh mountains all year round, hence the development of waterlogged peaty soils, also poor in terms of plant variety. At least half of the precipitation in the Alps falls as snow and the ground never gets particularly waterlogged. And Britain, isolated from the European continent for much of its comparatively recent life, has a generally poorer flora because many continental plants never got across the sea after the last Ice Age and the severing of the land bridge joining Britain to the European continent.

Then there's the way the land has been managed; mis-managed in the hills and uplands of much of Britain. While dairy cattle and sometimes a few sheep grazing on alpine pastures are usually kept in low numbers, Britain's mountains and moors have often been burned regularly by farmers and overgrazed with livestock. The result has been a loss of plant diversity and a damaged landscape. A former Professor of Forestry at Bangor University used to comment at the wonderful view of the Carneddau – the string of mountains north of Snowdon adored by many mountain walkers – from his office window, and tell anyone who would listen that it was the most degraded landscape in Europe. Most hill walkers would disagree but they maybe don't realise how much more rewarding a hill walk could be if the footpaths meandered through some occasional scrub and woodland, especially on their lower slopes.

I walk on the Carneddau and some of the other Snowdonia mountains now and again but I sometimes wonder why I bother….apart from the views! Most of the vegetation is monotonous; large areas are dominated by tough grasses, bits of heather and little else. There is precious little variety of birds; mostly Meadow Pipits with a scatter of Wheatears where the ground is more broken by boulders. And some crows. Maybe a raven or a Peregrine will show up on a good day.

Only where less acidic rocks outcrop – places like the famous corrie of Cwm Idwal and the huge wet cliffs of Ysgolion Duon, the Black Ladders – do alpines begin to burgeon, places that the plant-nibbling sheep can't get access to. Then things improve dramatically. There are saxifrages, Mossy and Starry Saxifrage, both with their delicate white flowers, though the Starry's petals are spotted. There are usually some cushions of earlier flowering Purple Saxifrage too, clinging to steep rock faces and covered with a striking shock of bright pink-purple flowers. In a few spots, usually crevices in cliffs, the tiny Snowdon Lily grows, its white flowers a contrast to its few thin, grass-like stems. Out of season it's a plant that's virtually impossible to find. There are sedums too, Roseroot in particular growing in great bunches of glaucous, fleshy leaves topped with a flurry of yellow flowers at its tip.

Exploring such spots takes me back to the Alps, if only briefly. The pity is that these riches are confined to comparatively small areas, gems of places among the expanse of Snowdonia. They don't compare with the Schynige Plattes of this world … but I admire their less blousy beauty all the same.

On the Rocks

The phone message came through to me in Peterborough, that rather nondescript eastern England town where English Nature (now Natural England) then had its headquarters. The date: Friday 16 February 1996. The news: a supertanker had run aground on rocks just outside the entrance to Milford Haven near St Ann's Head in Pembrokeshire at 8 p.m. the night before. The information hadn't travelled very rapidly, seemingly due to over optimism on the part of some of the agencies involved in the emergency that the vessel might be re-floated very quickly. *Sea Empress* was carrying 130,000 tonnes of crude oil from the North Sea to the then Texaco oil refinery in the Haven, one of the busiest oil ports in Europe. Its spill of crude oil was to be one of the worst in British waters.

At that time I was the Countryside Council for Wales' (today, Natural Resources Wales) Chief Scientist so the worrying news was sent to me as soon as my HQ was told about it. It was the news that I, and my organisation, had always dreaded and had hoped we would never receive. Pembrokeshire has some of the most impressive cliff coast in Britain and some of the finest – and cleanest – bathing beaches and coves too. Many of them are immensely popular with holidaymakers and this part of Wales depends on summer tourism to survive. Its importance for wildlife, both in its coastal waters and on its shores, was immeasurable.

Pembrokeshire's offshore islands such as Skomer and Grassholm support internationally rated populations of seabirds. Skomer has around 150,000 breeding pairs of Manx Shearwaters and nearby Skokholm has 45,000 pairs; small black and white seabirds that breed in burrows in the ground, many of them vacated by rabbits. Skomer's is the largest British colony and it represents well over a third of the world's population of this enigmatic bird. Grassholm Island, further out to sea, holds about 35,000 pairs of breeding Gannets, much larger, mostly white seabirds that dive like arrows into the water to catch fish. It's one of the largest breeding colonies in the world where the birds nest so hugger-mugger that, from a distance, the island seems as if it has been painted white.

The superlatives continue. Around 5,000 Atlantic Grey Seals breed in coves and sea caves around this coast in autumn, a considerable proportion of the British breeding population. Bottle-nosed Dolphins and Harbour Porpoises are seen from shore too, sometimes extremely close in. And all this very visible animal life is utterly reliant on a welter of less visible creatures; myriads of rock-clinging limpets and barnacles; seaweeds of all colours and shapes; crabs and prawns; sea urchins and corals; horse mussels and mud-burrowing worms; and a plethora of fish from tiny to large. Little wonder, then, that large sections of the coast, islands and sea areas are protected by EU designations; they are internationally valued.

Amid all this sea and intertidal wildlife, the bathing beaches and the tourist industry that much of the county depends upon, there's another industry that sits far less comfortably. Milford Haven, a natural, deep water channel, is located on the west coast of the county just east of some of the most wildlife-rich islands and close to many of the best bathing beaches. So oil tankers, most of them huge vessels constantly bringing in their viscous cargoes from the Middle East and elsewhere, are routed through some of the most sensitive sea areas in Britain.

Little wonder, then, that my colleagues and I had always contemplated the possibility of an oil spill; one that could cause enormous damage to wildlife and to the tourist industry. And here it was.

Initially, the reports I received gave us considerable hope that the damage might be minimal. Sailing against the outgoing tide and in calm conditions with a Milford Haven pilot on board, *Sea Empress* had been pushed off course by the current and became grounded after hitting rocks in the channel. The inquiry later blamed pilot error due to his inexperience and inadequate training in piloting large tankers. But it also found that relations between the Milford Haven Port Authority and the pilots left a lot to be desired. The collision punctured the tanker's starboard hull causing oil to leak into the sea. We learnt after the event that 2,500 tonnes leaked as a result of the initial grounding, a small spill in a large sea area and not too alarming.

But the situation quickly deteriorated over the next few days. Tugs from Milford Haven Port Authority attempted to pull the vessel free and re-float her. During the initial rescue attempts, by now in quite rough sea conditions and high winds, she detached several times from the tugs and grounded repeatedly – each time slicing open new sections of her hull and releasing more oil. By the time *Sea Empress* was successfully floated off the rocks and got under control by tugs to be taken into Milford Haven, she had leaked a total of 73,000 tonnes of crude oil plus another 480 tonnes of fuel oil. It had caused an ecological disaster.

Some years before and because of my organisation's increasing responsibilities for the wildlife of the marine environment, I had set up a large team of marine biologists with a variety of specialisms. Now, they certainly came into their own. Locating some of this team, plus our bird and mammal experts, near Milford Haven, the operational headquarters for dealing with the incident but keeping some at our North Wales HQ in Bangor, we were constantly feeding in advice alongside the emergency services as well as funding contractors to gather information on the extent of the ecological damage at sea and on shore. Our initial advice to the consortium of Agencies led by the Maritime and Coastguard Agency was to pump out as much of the Sea Empress's oil cargo while she was still grounded, transferring the oil to small tankers. But with the weather getting rougher, this option had to be rejected as technically too difficult because of the ship's location and the state of the sea. Another accident to a smaller tanker receiving the oil was too much of a risk.

The *Sea Empress* spill was by no means the largest oil spill in the world – that 'honour' goes to the *Atlantic Empress* off Tobago which spilled 280,000 tonnes in 1979 – but it was the 12th largest in the world and Britain's third largest ever. It was horrendous enough. Viscous, black crude oil clothed pristine sandy beaches; it coated tonnes of shingle in numerous inaccessible coves, some of them used by breeding Grey Seals; and it replaced the seawater in animal-rich rock pools with lethal, coal-black oil that killed everything it came into contact with. In all, over 100 km of shoreline was oiled.

My first view looking out from St Ann's Head at the listing *Sea Empress* stuck firm on rocks below was a surreal experience. DC3 twin propeller planes were doing flypasts low over the sea to spray dispersants on the leaking oil. And the smell of fuel pervaded the clifftops and everywhere around. I went to Tenby, a popular local resort heaving with holidaymakers in summer, to find its main bathing beach covered in a thick black sludge of oil. The strong odour of diesel hung like a polluted curtain in the streets and a few locals cried as they looked out on their once lovely beach, shaking their heads in despair.

We kept receiving reports of oiled seabirds being washed ashore, some dead, some badly oiled but still alive. Within a week there were thousands of them: Common Scoter; Guillemots, Razorbills and Kittiwakes; waders, like Curlews; and a scatter of gulls and others. Survivors were taken to a cleaning centre set up hurriedly – and manned largely by volunteers – to try and save as many of these pathetically oiled birds as possible for future release. I walked near Saundersfoot to some rock pools on the shore, places that delight small children in summer as they try to catch tiny crabs or touch the waving tentacles of wine-red sea anemones. But there was no life left; the pools were shining in the dim sunlight with stinking black tar and all the creatures were dead. This, I thought, is the price we pay for our oil-fired lifestyles.

It was depressing, but I was too busy – getting advice from my expert staff, putting out daily bulletins to our Council Members and fielding questions from civil servants in government and the EU – to spend much time dwelling. There were, of course, rather irritating moments. One such was a senior Welsh Office civil servant several days into the spill asking me not to use the word 'disaster' in our press releases! He wanted us to use 'impending disaster' because the scale of it wasn't then clear. It was one of the few occasions when I almost lost my temper; I asked him how he defined a disaster if 72,000 tonnes of crude oil spilt in one of the richest sea areas in Britain and slopping on to over 100 km of shore wasn't one. We continued to use 'disaster' in our press releases.

I put a temporary ban on much of our normal, planned research and survey programme, and supplanted it with a huge amount of data gathering and survey work so that CCW could assess the damage and monitor the recovery of key habitats and species affected by the spill. William Hague, then Secretary of State for Wales (this was pre-devolution days) who had – thankfully – taken over from the less-than-helpful John Redwood, was quickly on the phone to our Chairman releasing £500,000 to us for additional monitoring and survey costs. It was a helpful gesture.

All commercial and recreational fishing around much of the Pembrokeshire coast was banned for months and the impact on that summer's holiday season was, we all thought having seen the amount of oil ashore, bound to be virtually terminal. In fact, local services faired quite well; large numbers of people needed accommodation and feeding in many of the areas hardest hit by oil: marine experts, journalists, researchers, bird people, tourism advisors, fisheries experts and large numbers of clean-up personnel. Many B&Bs were full.

Horrendous though it was, it gradually dawned on me and my colleagues that, in spite of the enormous damage, we had been very lucky. The Atlantic Grey Seals were well away out at sea and there were no reports of casualties. It was too early in the year for most of the seabirds – around 200,000 of them – to arrive from their winter ocean wandering and start setting up shop to breed on the cliffs and islands around. A few early birds, so to speak, had been oiled but a similar disaster in May would have been horrendous.

The weather, too, had been somewhat in our favour. It hampered a speedy recovery of the vessel but the rougher the seas are the quicker the oil gets dispersed into tiny globules in the seawater and the quicker the bacteria in the water can decompose it. A big oil spill in calm water would have been much more of a problem. Out at sea, this turbulence combined with early spraying of 'dispersants' (detergents) on slicks of the stuff floating on the water, helped get it broken down quickly. Such dispersants are far less toxic that those used in earlier spills such as the *Torrey Canyon* off Cornwall in 1967 where the detergent is thought to have caused more ecological damage than the spilled oil.

Nevertheless, following our advice and most modern practice, no such dispersants were sprayed on shore nor at sea within a kilometre of the shore. The clean-up of bathing beaches had begun immediately, all of it done mechanically with suction, pressure washers, with diggers and by hand with spades. It was filthy work. Amazingly, most of the tourist beaches were clean by the summer though remnants of the tar-like oil could still be found in sheltered spots where physical clean-up was impossible and in rock pools three years after the spill. On shingle beaches and coves, on rocky stretches of coast and in many other places, although some oil could be removed physically, most could not – and some coves are inaccessible anyway – so here nature was left to its own devices, an open air laboratory to study the sequence and rate at which different creatures made a comeback.

Results from a study to see how effective the oiled bird clean-up had been, something never before examined, proved particularly depressing. In spite of huge efforts made by an army of volunteers and experts from the RSPCA and other agencies, 70% of the Guillemots cleaned and released died within 14 days of release and only 3% of them survived for three months. This was not what anyone wanted to hear but it did suggest that it would have been kinder to humanely kill the worst oiled birds wherever they are picked up rather than subject them to the clean-up trauma in an environment that was completely unnatural to them, stressing the birds even more. It was a lesson for any future disaster like this: trying to do good can result in more harm.

When I looked at some of the bathing beaches and the least accessible foreshores polluted with oil, like many others at the time I assumed it would be several years before everything became normal again. How wrong we were. The £60 million clean-up had brought the tourists back in good numbers by the following year, the contamination levels in fish and shellfish had reduced so that fisheries were re-opened, and by 2001 – five years after the spill – it was difficult to find a location in which the marine life was not back to normal. Fish populations were healthy once again. Breeding seabirds are all doing well. The Grey Seal population continues to grow. And all of these depend on a healthy food chain from limpets and barnacles and much else that can't even be seen.

Sea Empress also recovered unbelievably well! Following the spill, she was repaired and renamed five times. In 2004, she was sold and moved to Chittagong as a floating production and storage ship. In September 2009, she was acquired by Singapore-based Oriental Ocean Shipping Holding PTE Ltd, renamed *MV Welwind* and converted from an oil tanker to a bulk carrier. In 2012, she was renamed for a fifth time and is currently known as *Wind 3*. She remains prohibited from entering Milford Haven and has not visited Pembrokeshire since she was towed out later in 1996.

Long term, the *Sea Empress* incident gave increased impetus to international regulations for all oil tankers to be double-hulled. All passenger ships have long been double-hulled – two steel hulls separated by a distance of up to 60 cm – in order to reduce the chances of oil spills from more minor collisions or groundings on rocks (being less likely to penetrate through two hulls than one). It was a requirement we at CCW had long considered should have been mandatory. In practice it has taken many years to take effect because single-hulled oil tankers were allowed to operate legally until they were taken out of service.

But *Sea Empress* had another, I think more important, consequence too. At the time of the incident there was a proposal to import orimulsion into Milford Haven to use it as a liquid fuel for the Pembroke Power Station. This station was located on the haven but not operating because of the high cost of oil that had been used there in the past for generating electricity.

Orimulsion is bitumen-based fuel that was developed for industrial use in Venezuela in collaboration with Britain's BP. Like coal and oil, bitumen occurs naturally and is obtained from the world's largest deposit in the Orinoco Belt in Venezuela. There are massive deposits there. It's cheap and can be transported by tanker where it has to be kept liquid by heating it. But orimulsion, being heavy, sinks in water and a spill at sea would result in it coating the seabed and killing off any living creatures it was in contact with. The risk of that happening, combined then with many single-hulled tankers in common use and the huge ecological and tourist value of the southwest coast and seas of Wales was, in my view, a risk that should not be taken. My position was supported by CCW's Council and I had advised BP accordingly that we would be very strongly opposed to orimulsion ever being used and transported into Milford Haven.

The *Sea Empress* incident sealed its fate. With huge public concern and our opposition, BP dropped its plans. The Pembroke Power Station, unfortunately for its employees, was closed. But it was the right decision for the environment and for Wales and I remain proud of it.

A Monk's Harsh Life

Out fixer hadn't turned up. Here we were, my wife and I, standing on the quay at the little harbour on Alonissos, the most easterly inhabited Greek island in the Northern Sporades. A sublime spot; the little town of Patitiri – the main town on the island – tumbling down the hillside in front of us framed with a scatter of pines and with the gentle splashes of the all-azure sea behind us.

Trouble was, we were the only passengers left standing there; everyone else had dispersed on foot, by taxi or with local relatives. We waited for Jimmy to turn up. And waited! 'I will meet you from the Dolphin [the Aegean Flying Dolphins are the inter-island fast ferries] at the harbour in Patitiri,' he had emailed just before we left the UK.

I was here to talk to experts and islanders on Alonissos about one of the rarest sea mammals in the world, the Mediterranean Monk Seal. The US-based *Zoogoer* magazine wanted a feature about how it was faring and the measures being taken to try and bolster its flagging numbers. We were to be on Alonissos for a week. I needed local contacts and, back in the UK weeks before we left, I had help initially from Dimitris Skianis, a kind of one-man fixer who seemed to have the contacts on the island that I needed. He was arranging meetings with key local people for me. More recently, Jimmy had taken over his role (or so I thought). His not turning up on the quay made me wonder if anything else might unravel too.

So, after a long and isolated wait, we got a taxi and headed to the hotel his mother ran where we were staying. Jimmy had arranged that too. We could see the hotel name emblazoned across the building high above the harbour. It took a while before we raised anyone in the little hotel but relief was at hand. Jimmy's mother knew about us, our room (rather basic and old fashioned but comfortable enough) was ready but Jimmy 'must have got the day wrong'. Not an inspiring start.

The following day he turned up, full of apologies. My meetings had been arranged. All was good. I thanked him and asked about Dimitris, his predecessor. 'Would we meet him too?' I asked. 'That's me,' he replied. 'I am Dimitris Skianis but it's easier for you, maybe, that I call myself Jimmy.' Whatever.

The next day we were out in the Aegean with Vassilis Kouroutos, the Scientific Officer in charge of the National Marine Park of Alonissos, and some of his team, on the marine park's boat. The park, designated primarily to protect the seals but including internationally important breeding birds too, covers a sea area of well over 2,000 km² and includes seven islands – only the largest of which, Alonissos itself, is inhabited – plus a further 22 islets and rock outcrops.

It was a gorgeous, late summer day and we headed past the steep-sided, rocky islands of Peristera, then further out Panagia before turning east to the destination Vassilis was particularly keen to show me ... the steep-sided island of Piperi around 40 km east of Alonissos – also uninhabited – its near-white limestone cliffs scattered with tall pines, some of them maybe a couple of hundred years old. A lot of the rest of the island is covered in evergreen shrubs. It was an idyllic place to anchor.

At around 4 km long and 1 km wide, Piperi is one of the smaller islands in the Aegean and its combination of limestone and seawater has been good for the Monk Seals. That's because limestone is more easily eroded than some rocks, resulting in a plethora of deeply incised small coves and caves at sea level in which many of the seals give birth to their pups. Vassilis pulled the boat in close to the cliff base by a small sea cave. Far inside was a gently shelving shingle beach where, last autumn, two seal pups had been born. Many of the Monk Seals give birth in such places; others do so on remote shingle beaches in coves surrounded by inaccessible cliffs, not dissimilar to the breeding sites of Grey Seals in the UK (Chapter 9).

The Mediterranean Monk Seal – once abundant across a 6,000 km swathe of sea from the western North African coast, through the Mediterranean and into the Black Sea to the east – is now extremely difficult to find. Little wonder. There may be just 500 or so left, scattered over isolated stretches of coast and offshore islands. More than half of them survive here in Greek waters. 'At this time of year, the seals are scattered well out to sea. They rarely come close to the islands so it's difficult to find any,' Vassilis tells me as our boat bobs gently in the shallow water close to another of Piperi's caves. 'There may be no more than 20 seals in the whole of the park's sea area at any one time and they often travel huge distances to feed.'

Piperi has arguably the best protected remaining Monk Seal breeding colony in the world. In recent years about eight pups have been reared here. A decade ago, an average of three were reared annually on Piperi. Because, he says, the seals are very sensitive to disturbance when they are breeding, Vassilis is convinced that the 5 km boat exclusion zone around the island has boosted their breeding success. We didn't spot any Monk Seals that day; there were none around Piperi and none seemingly en route from Alonissos either. This was rapidly becoming one of those all too common needle-in-a-haystack searches.

We did, though, catch glimpses of Eleonora's Falcons, their dark silhouettes against the bright sun-filled sky, as they scythed through the air above some of the islands we passed on our return trip back to Alonissos. We also noticed a solitary Audouin's Gull, a large, smart gull with a black-tipped scarlet beak standing on a rock at the very edge of one of the uninhabited islands. Confined mainly to Mediterranean coasts, it's an uncommon gull that rarely scavenges and relies on catching fish mostly at night. So its future is tied indissolubly to the future of fisheries in this very sea and the hope that the whole of the Mediterranean doesn't become as over-exploited as many areas of it are at present.

If you're lucky enough to spot one, Monk Seals look like big-eyed torpedoes. Males can reach 2.5 m in length and 300 kg in weight, making them one of the largest species of seal worldwide. Females are only slightly smaller. Adult males are black with a distinctive white belly patch; females are browner or greyer with a lighter belly patch. They can live for 20–30 years, sometimes longer. Clumsy and sluggish on shingle beaches, once in the water they are impressive swimmers that can easily out-dodge a shark. Pups, when they are born in the autumn, measure no more than1 m long and have dark woolly coats with a white belly patch. By the time they are two weeks old they are masterly swimmers but stormy seas before this can leave them extremely vulnerable to drowning in their caves. They are suckled for around six weeks, although the pup might stay close to its mother for as long as three years.

Monk Seals reproduce very slowly, an important factor slowing their recovery here. Adult females don't have pups until they are over four years old; even then they might give birth to one pup in alternate years. Feeding mainly at night, they feast on spiny lobsters, eels, octopus and reef fishes and they can easily dive to 70 m, sometimes more. Not often seen, except by fishermen, they generally keep away from any human presence although in winter when there is less boat traffic, one sometimes turns up close to shore or even in an island harbour.

It wasn't until a few days later, when we were out at sea again – this time closer to Alonissos near the uninhabited island of Panagia – that we spotted our quarry. At first, it wasn't very obvious at all, an occasional rounded blob poking out of the water maybe 50 m from the island's shore. But the blob was a head and, as we got our boatman to drift a little closer, the torpedo-like shape became obvious. A Monk Seal swimming nonchalantly in the shallows, diving now and again – sometimes for what seemed a minute or two – then bobbing up somewhere else in these waters brimming with fish and other sea life. A Monk Seal that could have no intimation that a whole marine park had been designated for it and its mates; a Monk Seal for whose future a huge number of marine and mammal experts, plus a load of concerned volunteers, were working in earnest. And a Monk Seal for which much of this care and concern was stirring up a great deal of angst in the community of fishermen in this part of the Mediterranean and probably much further afield too.

The marine park here was designated in 1992 though discussions about its need began in the 1970s and, in good Greek fashion, it was several years again before the government allocated any funding to give it some staff to implement any practical protection. It is divided into two zones. Zone B, a third of its area – including the main island Alonissos with 3,000 residents and about 10,000 tourists each year – has few restrictions. Oil tankers and hazardous cargo boats are banned and all boats have to keep under ten knots near parts of the coast so that they don't disturb any breeding seals. Zone A, which includes Piperi, is more restrictive and larger in area. No scuba diving is allowed nor any spear-gun fishing. And fishing boats have restrictions on how close they may fish around islands. Pleasure and passenger boats are restricted to a few marked anchorages.

Drawing these lines on a map is the easy bit. Formulating the safeguards and measures needed to put the protection into practice is more challenging. Winning the hearts and minds of local people – particularly those that have fished these seas for generations – is very much more difficult to achieve. And on Alonissos, suspicions abound.

Jimmy arranged for me to meet Theodoros Malamatenias who represents the Fishermen's Union of Alonissos. We talked over a drink at an outdoor café looking out over Alonissos from old Patitiri, the island's original main village high above the sea, hit by an earthquake in 1965 but rebuilt. The incessant calls of cicadas from the café's shade-bearing trees reverberated, metronome-like on the village's stone walls as Jimmy doubled up as interpreter.

'The Greek Government has imposed this designation on us, restricts our fishing but gives us no compensation', argues Malamatenias, a pleasant, middle-aged man with a typically large, black moustache and hands roughened by ropes and fish catches. 'We have 60 boats on Alonissos, all family owned. We have fished the seas around these islands for many years, generations before us. This is our livelihood. Piperi used to be good fishing. They've stopped us going there but the marine park doesn't give us any information to show if fish numbers have increased there. The marine park people don't seem to want to work with us so we're suspicious', he tells me.

These concerns are mirrored by Dimitris Christou, a younger man and another contact Jimmy has lined up for me to interview. Christou runs the Nautical Union of Alonissos in his spare time, a voluntary organisation promoting opportunities for sailing, canoeing, fishing and diving in an environmentally responsible way. 'The marine park staff are new here. They're not as friendly as people expected. There's no joint working with them. I think they've got off to a bad start', he tells me in broken English. 'I don't agree that the seals are so easily disturbed; they come close to fishermen to take fish. People here want to visit Piperi but we are banned. We are local people and we would not cause any damage. We could go when the seals aren't breeding. I've never been there in my life,' he adds, frustrated.

It's a concern I hear echoed by other tour boat operators. Ikos Travel, whose owner Pakis Athanassiou was involved in getting the marine park designated, and whose boat trips concentrate on wildlife and culture, thinks that some of the regulations are unnecessary. 'It's a big advantage having the marine park and it attracts a lot of people to Alonissos,' he says. 'But there are some silly restrictions such as no snorkelling or swimming except in two small bays around one of the islands where there are no seals breeding. Why so much restriction?'

Hearing this, I begin to wonder if these aren't vested interests that would very much prefer to have no restrictions at all but yet they want the kudos value of the marine park because it attracts more wildlife tourists. So I ask Jimmy if he can fix up a meeting with the island's mayor.

So one evening I met Panagiotis Vlaikos, the Mayor of Alonissos, a courteous man who was formerly a physics teacher at the island's high school. We meet at a taverna on the harbour front – where else on a Greek island on a balmy summer's evening? Mr Vlaikos, it turns out, has a more balanced attitude. Through Jimmy he explains that tourism is by far the most important component of the island's economy. 'The marine park is a benefit for the island. There is no point having such an area designated for conservation unless there are some restrictions. It wouldn't make sense. And we have an international responsibility to protect our wildlife including the Monk Seal,' he says over a drink or two. His views turn out to be as refreshing as the cold beers.

The answer to bridging the gaps between conservation and fishing, maybe tourism too, may lie in a project being run here partly with EU money by an NGO. They seem to be acting as an honest broker between all the parties with sectoral interests who clearly distrust each other. The Hellenic Society for the Study and Protection of the Monk Seal, happily abbreviated to Mom, has 7,500 members and was set up in 1988. It was instrumental in getting this marine park designated. But it also does seal monitoring, research and conservation education.

To talk about their work I arrange to meet Eleni Tounta who runs Mom on Alonissos. 'Our project is trying to bring together fishermen and conservationists to reduce problems such as seals taking fish from nets. We are concentrating on seven hotspots across Greece including here at Alonissos, working with fishermen to look at the value of fish lost to seals and seeing if we can use deterrent devices on the nets so that they keep away. Seals sometimes get injured or killed by getting tangled in nets so this can benefit them too,' she tells me.

'We have good relations with most fishermen. There's no evidence of seals being killed here although there are reports every year of some being killed in other Greek waters. We want to see this marine park extended to include part of Skopelos [the island immediately west of Alonissos] and other sea areas protected, particularly Kimolos Island in the Cyclades and Karpathos in the Dodecanese,' Eleni says.

Fishermen and Monk Seals (seals of all species anywhere perhaps) have not always been in such competition. In Ancient Greece, Monk Seals were venerated because they showed a great love for both the sea and sun, ironically two of the main reasons tourists flock to the Mediterranean today. To fishermen and seafarers they were an omen of good fortune. Ancient drinking vessels like water jugs sometimes bore their images and the seals were immortalised in the writings of Homer, Plutarch and Aristotle.

The Romans changed all that and by the Middle Ages many populations had probably already died out. Naturally confiding, Monk Seals were easy to kill using clubs, spears and nets for their meat, fur for warmth, skins for shoes and clothing, and their fat for making candles. But the human population at the time was small so it's probable that seal numbers held up reasonably well until the last century or two. Pollution, two world wars, increasing industrialisation of fishing and, since the 1970s, the enormous boom in tourism, have all depleted their numbers further. Today, a whole host of threats are arraigned against these exquisite mammals: coastal developments, especially for tourism, have destroyed their habitat and breeding sites; increased pleasure boating causes disturbance; deliberate killing by fishermen and entanglement in their nets has had a direct impact; a decline of fish and shellfish caused by pollution and over-fishing; and occasional disease outbreaks are the main offenders.

About 140 million people now live along the Mediterranean's 45,000 km of coast, a population that is more than doubled by summer tourists. And the numbers of both continue to grow, especially in some of the North African countries along its south coast. Raw sewage; oil from tankers, other ships and from leaks onshore; plus runoff of agricultural fertilisers constantly pollute this almost entirely landlocked sea which, as a result, has very restricted mixing of its waters. There has long been plenty of talk about clean-ups but little happens. Covering only 1% of our planet's sea area, the Mediterranean is home to 6% of all our marine species. But many fish and shellfish are in decline, maybe other wildlife too, though as yet there is no evidence of any food shortages for Monk Seals.

Something that became obvious from this visit is that, if Monk Seals are to prosper, this marine park needs to generate a continuous dialogue with local interests to try and eliminate their fears and garner their support. And other sea areas need to be designated and managed appropriately by other Mediterranean countries in cooperation with local fishermen to provide it with more comprehensive protection. I consulted an international expert on Monk Seals to get an overview of how the future looks for Monk Seals; Dr Giuseppe Notarbartolo di Sciara, a Sicilian international sea mammal expert, was non-committal about this fabulous mammal's chances of survival long term. 'Greece hosts the world's largest amount of Monk Seal habitat and the greatest number of animals. Its survival will largely depend on the capability of Greece to protect the Monk Seal in its waters,' he tells me.

Leaving Alonissos was a wrench because it is such an attractive island, much of it unused and left wild, its tourism fairly low key, at least at present. But there was one thing I had forgotten to try and find out: how did the Mediterranean Monk Seal get its name? Is it because many of the islands in the Aegean had monasteries? Even today, one of the islands next to Alonissos still has a single monk as its only inhabitant. Or is it because the smooth, dark brown coat of an adult seal is said to resemble the robe of a Franciscan friar? Or maybe the explanation lies in the fact that Monk Seals never live in groups, leading what is, for seals, a pretty solitary existence. Maybe that's why we saw just one of their number fishing on its own.

Up Close and Personal

A scatter of soil thrown in the air from a patch of bracken, a quiet wheezy grunt, and out on to the Bluebell-spangled turf emerges Britain's most endearing bird a couple of metres from where I'm sitting. An adult Puffin, its multi-coloured, outsize beak glowing in the sunshine, takes a few glances at me then waddles its way like a diminutive penguin to the cliff edge where Irish Sea breakers thud into the rocks below.

It's spring on Skomer Island, a National Nature Reserve off the west Pembrokeshire coast, and on the edge of one of its Puffin colonies the birds are cleaning out their breeding burrows. Here they don't need major excavation; most are expropriated rabbit holes, the sort that led Alice into Wonderland. And what animal could be more suited to the tale of *Alice's Adventures in Wonderland* than this waddling, grunting, penguin-like bird with such an outrageous beak? Around 6,000 pairs of Puffin breed here on Skomer and they are an absolute delight to watch.

More Puffins are lined up nearby on the cliff edge, bowing and bobbing to each other like a line of miniature (less than 30 cm tall) up-market restaurant waiters receiving instruction from their maitre d'. Now and again, one takes flight over the waves, its short wings whirring fast like some wind-up child's toy. At six wingbeats a second, it will use its wings to zoom underwater too, with its red-webbed feet acting as rudders, as it dashes this way and that to catch a beak-load of silvery sprats or sand eels.

Later in April, at the back of the burrow, each pair – Puffins mate for life – build a nest lined with grasses, seaweed and feathers. After the female lays a single egg, both parents take turns incubating it for about 40 days. And that's a great time again to sit out here, the Bluebells over and Red Campion starting to dot the turf. Sit still and within a few minutes an adult Puffin will clatter to its landing spot on the clifftop, its beak loaded with ten or so small fish (apparently the world record is 80!), shake itself down to dry off, then waddle up-slope to its burrow where the growing youngster will devour the catch. It's an experience I recalled for a feature in *Country Life* magazine.

It's an experience that reminds me unfailingly of wading birds on coastal shorelines in the USA. I haven't been to Canada so I have no idea what happens there but on US seashores it's quite possible to sit on the sand and have wading birds such as sandpipers, tiny near-white Sanderlings and larger waders such as brown-specked Willets walk right past you within a metre or two. They seem to take no notice. Try doing that in the UK or elsewhere in Europe where seashore-feeding waders are easily spooked. You can't get within 30 m of a Sanderling and that's if you are very lucky. But why? I've heard some explanations: because there are fewer people on US beaches (not always true) or because American waders spend half the year breeding up in the Arctic where there are no people (but much the same applies to European waders). And yet hunting is a way of life for many people in the US, more so than in the UK anyway; 14 million people hunt something or other in the US, whereas it's about 1 million in the UK. So neither of these explanations ring true.

The only way to be sure of getting up close and personal with wild animals is, of course, when they are in cages or held in captivity some other way. Well-run zoos excepted, I usually find wild animals kept like this a very depressing business and I don't go out of my way to find them. But I had taken advice from Richard Thomas, Communications Coordinator at TRAFFIC International (the British-based wildlife trade monitoring network), because I needed to experience a market where illegal trade in birds was rife, part of a key chapter for my book, *Life with Birds: A Story of Mutual Exploitation* (Whittles, 2011). He had suggested Chatuchak Market in central Bangkok (we were in Thailand on holiday). It wasn't an experience I was looking forward to. And it turned out to be even more depressing than I had assumed.

It was a typical blazing hot Saturday afternoon in Bangkok so it was initially quite a relief to get into the (albeit airless) shade provided by the vast rows of stalls at what is reputedly one of the largest outdoor markets in the world. With over 8,000 stalls that set up here every weekend, Chatuchak Market has a reputation for selling almost everything you could ever wish to buy. Certainly there seemed to be anything and everything on sale; furniture, books, jewellery, CDs, any size of Buddha statue you might care to have, aquarium fish, puppies and much else. For some time, we had no idea where the 'bird market' part of this great tented town might be; it wasn't marked on our market map (yes, a map!). Maybe that was because what goes on there is illegal. But, after an hour or so of wandering, we heard some faint bird calls and songs echoing between the stalls in the near distance.

Then we found them; row after row of stallholders selling caged birds. Not just the very familiar budgies and Zebra Finches almost always bred in captivity or even aviary-reared cockatoos. But bamboo cages of illegally trapped birds taken from the Thai countryside or from much further afield. Many of these cages contained the Red-whiskered Bulbul, gorgeous brown and white birds with scarlet face-patches and a black crest. They are popular not only for their looks but also for their lively song, a double whammy that confines all too many of these common countryside birds to a life of captivity. In theory, though, they are protected by Thai law; they shouldn't be captured and caged at all. Nevertheless, even some Thai Government officials have one in their office and point to them proudly.

There were far more exotic captives here too and many of the stallholders, knowing that what they're doing is illegal, are keen to ban any photography. 'No take photo,' they kept saying to me as I politely ignored their pleas. One stallholder took more direct action. Unimpressed by my determination to carry on, she quickly picked up a metal pole and deftly pulled down a canopy holding the last rain shower that had past that way. Doused in water – actually not at all unpleasant in these hot temperatures – I wiped my camera and carried on. Thai people are too polite to become aggressive, except in political street demos anyway.

Here were all manner of illegally trapped birds for sale: tiny owls looking abject and scared in bamboo cages so small they could hardly move; exquisite golden yellow and black orioles; a Hill Myna, glossy black with yellow ear patches and an orange beak; even a young Black-shouldered Kite, a small grey bird of prey of open savannah country, tethered to a perch. And all of them supposedly protected in Thai law against capture. There were plenty of others, many from other continents even: African hornbills, toucans and macaws, and cages full of small finches. Whether any of these had been obtained legally is questionable. From the attitude of the stallholders who didn't want any attention, that's pretty doubtful. What made it worse was the absence of any police or other law enforcement presence even though it's well known that Chatuchak Market in Bangkok is *the* place to go if you want to buy illegal cagebirds. Passing laws to protect wild birds is easy; implementing them seemingly less so. Especially in Thailand.

It is an amazing privilege to get close to an animal in the wild. You can argue that you can get very close to a lion or a leopard if you are particularly lucky on an African safari but you would want to be seated in your Jeep, not lolling about on the savannah grassland when a great cat comes by within nudging distance. But, it is feasible to get extremely close to animals larger than the African cats, and a lot more safely. Take for instance, the Florida Manatee.

I was with Wayne Hartley – a Florida Manatee expert with the NGO, *Save the Manatee Club* – canoeing the 600 m of the Blue Spring stream in Florida. I had arranged the day with the club to get first-hand experience of these endearing creatures for my book, *Back from the Brink* (Whittles, 2015). It was the sound of frequent nose blowing on the water's surface that made the experience particularly surreal. It wasn't a sound that I had expected to hear. But these loud exhalations and intakes of air were a reminder that the aquatic creatures lying on the bed of this naturally warm, spring-fed waterway were mammals – and they needed occasional gulps of air to keep body and soul together. The stream, no more than a metre or two deep, was full of grey-brown, leathery skinned Florida Manatees, the adults 3 m long, their youngsters, some of them suckling, distinctly smaller. They look a little like a (very lazy) chubby dolphin but with a flattened tail and a face a bit like a cow's. I assume that's why they are often called Sea Cows.

In this short stretch of water Wayne counted no less than 102 manatees basking in its warmth; sometimes he counts over 300. The manatees idle away the winter months here, requiring warmth because, unlike seals, they don't have a layer of insulating blubber under their skin. Come springtime, they swim the 240 km back along the St John's River to the coast where they spend the summer in Florida's warm coastal waters.

Gentle vegetarian giants though manatees undoubtedly are, our concern was that a 600 kg adult might come up for air right underneath our canoe, tipping us into the Blue Spring. It was, at least, reassuring to know that the water wasn't cold and that you can't get eaten by a manatee. Wayne and I were joking about such an incident (thankfully it never transpired) when a full grown American Alligator slinked past the side of the canoe and hauled out on a part-submerged tree stem.

Its banks shaded by thickets of spiky-leafed Saw Palmetto under a canopy of Southern Live Oaks draped with hangings of Spanish Moss (not a moss and certainly not Spanish but a plant that grows attached to tree bark), Blue Spring is one of Florida's manatee public viewing sites. It attracts tens of thousands of people each winter who come to admire these remarkable and endearing animals. Stand on one of the riverside viewing platforms constructed for the purpose and these lumbering giants are very close to you in the water below. But from the canoe their closeness was simply magical. We glided slowly over them as they lay on the riverbed or sat alongside them as they meandered up to the water's surface, exhaled air and took a deep breath before effortlessly drifting back down to rest once again. It seemed like a very relaxed lifestyle.

When animals are resting – or hibernating through the cold winter – it is possible to get very close to them. The important precaution is not to touch them or disturb such deep sleep. It was to see some hibernating mammals that I found myself being taken one day into a maternity wing as dark as a mole, shuffling uncomfortably along its dusty, uneven, stone-flagged floor. To make sure we caused the minimum of disturbance, we spoke in low whispers, and only then if it was essential. In the faint, yellow glimmer of our dim torches I could make out rough brick walls, an occasional pile of coal and some rusting, long-disused boilers. Creepy, certainly, but at least the place was dry and warm. Outside it was cool and a persistent drizzle had set in.

'Through that gap,' whispered Jean Mathews, a mammal expert who then worked with me at the Countryside Council for Wales and who was leading me in this subterranean place of birth. 'Look up there, you'll see them when your eyes get accustomed to the dark,' she said, pointing to a hole in a brick wall. This grime-covered maternity department wasn't, of course, part of some NHS hospital from hell. This was bat nirvana. Lesser Horseshoe Bat nirvana to be precise. Here, in the cellars of Glynllifon Hall, a former stately home near Caernarfon in North Wales, is Europe's largest known breeding colony of these tiny mammals. In recognition of its importance, the colony – and the building – are both protected by the EU's Habitats Directive.

Peering up through the gloom, as my eyes slowly get accustomed to the dim light, I could eventually see what Jean is pointing at. Hundreds of bats, each no bigger than a large plum, hanging like little parcels on thread-legs from the blackened ceiling. Sleeping the day away in darkness. No wonder they look so small with their wings folded in; an adult weighs no more than 8 g.

The Glynllifon site is unusual because the cellars serve as both a hibernating site and a maternity roost. A small amount of heating has been installed in the maternity roost whilst the colder reaches of the cellars provide the cool but stable temperatures and high humidity that these bats need for hibernation in winter. Jean tells me that these aren't true hibernators but instead they enter a state of torpor where their temperature drops and their metabolism slows to save energy. So whenever the winter weather warms enough for insects to be on the wing, these Lesser Horseshoes will wake to fly outside and hunt at night. Moths, lacewings, small wasps and dung flies are high on the Lesser Horseshoe menu, snapped up in their thousands each summer's night.

'There's only one entrance, high up on the cellar wall, so they stream out of there at dusk and back at dawn when they're breeding. We know there are several hundred of them because we have an automated counter at the entrance,' Jean tells me as we crouch down and whisper, determined to cause no disturbance. By mid-winter when we were there, only 100 or so bats remain in the cellars, hibernating in characteristic hanging parcel fashion from the ceilings in the unheated part. The rest disperse to other cool winter roosts including some long-disused copper mines several kilometres away, also a protected site.

Incredibly, at least seven other species of bat are known to hunt by night in the pastures, woodland, gardens and streamside around the old mansion, a reflection of the rich insect pickings that abound here. None of them, though, mix with the Lesser Horseshoes to breed in the cosy cellars.

With flying bats hunting down their minute insect prey in the dark by echo-location – giving out tiny sounds and assessing the echoes that return – an insect that gives off tiny pulses of light in the dark is presumably no more vulnerable to getting eaten. And given that the insects in question are located on the stems of grasses or flowers near the ground, maybe bats can't so easily make a meal of them anyway.

Glow Worms are found in meadows, woodland edges, in gardens, on heaths, along hedgerows and railway embankments, though we rarely notice them because so many of our country roads and green spaces are bathed under street lights at night. In Britain they might be more common than entomologists have assumed; we just don't go out at night in dark places.

Although I had seen a few of their pinprick green, night-time flashes over the years, the best 'colony' I'd ever seen was while I was walking with my wife and our two youngest daughters one evening in Italy. We were walking along a dimly lit road on the outskirts of Pisa heading back to our hotel. There was nothing special about the roadside pasture; it looked full of flowering grasses and nothing much else. But it was alive with Glow Worms. First we spotted one point of green, winking light. Then another switched on for a split second; and off again. Then we realised that the whole meadow was alive with minute green flashes. It was as if someone had set out an array of tiny LEDs in the grass.

Then we noticed a few 'LEDs' on grass stems at the road's edge, winking away incessantly. Courtesy of a mobile phone light, we found the flightless female, pressed hard against the grass stem. Small beetles maybe 1–2 cm long, by switching our phone light off we could see that the occasional green flash came from the end of her abdomen. What she, and all the other little flashers were doing, was trying to attract the male beetles that fly around until they choose a partner, then come down and mate. They'll keep flashing for maybe two hours and, if no male flies in, retreat down into the vegetation until the next night when they'll try a bit more flashing again. Flashy they might be, but a female Glow Worm's life is a brief one. Once a male is attracted and they mate, she lays up to 100 eggs in the vegetation and dies.

Like bumblebees homing in on their underground nests or a wasp grinding wood fibres off a tree branch, Glow Worms are attractive insects to watch. Intrigued by them I wrote a feature for *Country Life* magazine with a request that readers send any observations to Britain's sole (amateur) Glow Worm recorder, Robin Scagell. He's found that they occur in all counties of England and Wales and several in Scotland too. But all might not be well for Glow Worms. Street lights might well be causing them a problem, the flying males attracted by brighter lights than the flashing females can muster. Until someone does sufficient research to find out, we'll be in the dark about what's happening to them.

Entomologists are lucky: they can get up close and personal with their subjects. The only downside is that there are so very many species to identify. With birds and mammals the difficulties are reversed; fewer of them but almost impossible to get close to in the wild. And many mammals are nocturnal into the bargain. Only rarely have I suddenly happened upon an animal close up that I have previously had only the most distant views of. It happened to me with otters. I had seen them below some sea cliffs on Shetland paddling about in the surf shallows, presumably hunting out various crustaceans and molluscs they could get at to eat. Playful animals, they are always wonderful to watch (but are often nocturnal). I had seen glimpses of them on holiday in the small, shallow rivers of Extremadura in spring but only at a distance. And in Florida we had watched a whole family of the closely related North American River Otter walk nonchalantly along the gravel surface of the Turner River Trail in the Everglades as we followed behind them (at a distance) in a car. Finding their sprints – faeces that usually smell disgustingly of putrefying fish – on riverbanks, on boulders or under bridges is not unusual, particularly now that these attractive creatures are once again back on virtually every river and large stream in Britain.

So imagine my surprise – shock actually – when I was talking to an engineer working at a flood barrier construction site near the village of Cowbridge in South Wales, and an otter ran past us. For a second or two, I could do nothing but point; no words would come out. We followed him as he ran quite slowly over piles of stone until he got to a nearby stream. There we watched as he casually worked his way upstream, pausing frequently to examine some stone or other, presumably in case it hid a tasty small fish. It was several minutes before he disappeared from sight. It was the closest sighting of an otter I have ever had. And in broad daylight.

An even closer view of a very different animal, another chance encounter, could have turned out rather badly. Very badly indeed. Not long after we had seen the River Otter family on the Turner River Trail I had noticed a large snake crossing the track some distance in front of us. As we got close, it stopped and coiled up, feigning death. A photo opportunity not to be missed. So, without thinking I grabbed my camera and dashed out of the car. It was close-up time. At least 80–90 cm in length, it was dark grey in colour with black cross-banding; a very attractive reptile. I could only see glimpses of its much lighter underside. Assuming it was lying doggo, I took a series of pictures, all within spitting distance. It was a while before I acknowledged that this could be a ploy before suddenly striking out with its fangs, or that it could even be a deadly species. I retreated and after we had driven off I watched the snake uncoil and slink away into the nearest trackside water-filled ditch. It was only that evening that I remembered to identify it from the pictures I had taken. It was a Florida Cottonmouth, a common snake in the Everglades … and a venomous one with a potentially fatal bite. When provoked, they hold their ground by coiling their bodies and displaying their fangs. While their aggression has been exaggerated, territorial males sometimes approach intruders in an antagonistic manner. Clearly not all Florida Cottontails are aggressive; I'd come across a softie.

Birds don't come less aggressive than a tiny Willow Warbler, a rather inconspicuous olive green/brown bird that migrates in huge numbers every year between sub-Saharan Africa where it winters and northern Europe where it breeds in scrub, gardens and woodland. I had probably heard thousands of them over the years singing their languorous, rather melancholy little song, a descending ripple of clear notes, but I had never seen one at close range.

So I was astonished to have one land behind me on the back of my camel as we trekked in the Moroccan sector of the northern Sahara. It was hot and the wind was blowing sand in our faces (something a camel's eyes can cope with better than a human's because they have evolved naturally long eyelashes to protect them). This being late February I assumed that the warbler was making his northward crossing of the mighty Sahara and that the poor creature was likely worn out, with no access to water and little available insect food. It sat there for a while and eventually flew off, probably to die – as many do – of exhaustion. Migration was in full swing, confirmed that evening when we made camp. A squadron of Barn Swallows kept performing flypasts just as if we were on the edge of an English village, and nearby a Yellow Wagtail – a bird of wet meadows across Europe – searched for insects on some arid sand dunes. It all seemed a bit bizarre. It was a reminder of the enormous distances that some tiny migrant birds – a few butterflies too – fly twice a year, across some of the most inhospitable terrain on earth.

978-184995-028-2 £18.99

... Malcolm Smith's intriguing narrative is both informative and constantly engaging. **Birding World**

... his book is a terrific read. **Cage & Aviary Birds**

... A refreshingly balanced look at the relationships between us and the birds around us. **BTO News**